Understanding Autistic Adults

Understanding Autistic Adults

Supporting Personal and Professional Pathways and Overcoming Challenges

Sagit Blumrosen-Sela

ROWMAN & LITTLEFIELD
Lanham • Boulder • New York • London

Published by Rowman & Littlefield
An imprint of The Rowman & Littlefield Publishing Group, Inc.
4501 Forbes Boulevard, Suite 200, Lanham, Maryland 20706
www.rowman.com

86-90 Paul Street, London EC2A 4NE

British Library Cataloguing in Publication Information Available

Library of Congress Cataloging-in-Publication Data

Names: Blumrosen, Sagit, author.
Title: Understanding autistic adults : supporting personal and professional pathways and overcoming challenges / Sagit Blumrosen-Sela.
Description: Lanham : Rowman & Littlefield, [2025] | Includes bibliographical references and index.
Identifiers: LCCN 2024034245 (print) | LCCN 2024034246 (ebook) | ISBN 9781538197165 (cloth) | ISBN 9781538197172 (paperback) | ISBN 9781538197189 (ebook)
Subjects: LCSH: Autistic people. | Autistic people—Employment. | Autistic people—Psychology. | Autistic people—Social conditions.
Classification: LCC HV1570.23 .B58 2025 (print) | LCC HV1570.23 (ebook) | DDC 616.85/882—dc23/eng/20240829
LC record available at https://lccn.loc.gov/2024034245
LC ebook record available at https://lccn.loc.gov/2024034246

Contents

Acknowledgments

Many years ago, as a young psychology student, while reading Patrick Casement's book *Learning from the Patient*, I experienced a tinge of envy, wishing for the opportunity to engage with patients who could enrich my understanding and expand my knowledge. Fortunately, in recent years, I have been fortunate enough to continuously learn from my patients in the realm of autism, meeting hundreds of individuals on the spectrum, each offering their own distinctive insights and enriching my understanding in profound ways.

I find the exploration of diverse perspectives on the world truly captivating, as it allows for a deeper understanding of the remarkable variety within the human mind. I find working with autistics particularly rewarding, because many of them exhibit extraordinary gifts, such as candidness, insight, self-observation, and imagination. In addition, witnessing their positive emotions flourish when they feel genuinely understood and validated by a professional, often for the first time, is incredibly moving. I sincerely hope that as our comprehension of autism continues to grow, such affirming experiences become more commonplace. I am profoundly grateful to all the autistic individuals who opened their souls to me, sharing their profound experiences and teaching me valuable lessons about subjects such as ableism, inclusion, and autistic pride. In particular, I express my gratitude to those who have generously shared their personal stories in this book, enriching it with their descriptions and insights. I extend my appreciation to Amit, Galit, Gili, Gitit, Gonen, Julie, Hagar, Hillel, Lena, Moshe, Natasha, Nicole, Nir, Reut, Ron, Rona, Rotem, Ruth, Shai, Sharon, Shira, and Sivan (all pseudonyms). I have chosen to use pseudonyms and conceal personal information to protect their privacy, as it is still not easy in our society to openly identify as autistic.

My heartfelt thanks to the wonderful team of Rowman & Littlefield Publishing—Lilith Dorko, Jonathan Joyce, Sarah Rinehart, Tricia Currie-Knight, and Felicity Tucker, for their most professional and dedicated work throughout all phases of the publishing process. Special thanks to the book's copyeditor, Joanne Foster, for ameliorating the text, and to many others not mentioned here. I am deeply grateful to Resling Publishing for publishing the Hebrew version of this book (2023), including the chief editors, Itzhak Beniamini and Idan Zivoni, along with Ronit Rosenthal and Maayan Eitan, whose invaluable assistance greatly enhanced the refinement of the text.

My deep thanks to my dear friends Orna Gilboa-Shavit and Tamar Avron-Aharoni, whose unwavering interest, support, and invaluable feedback on the manuscript have greatly contributed to its improvement.

My gratitude also extends to Michal Berkowitz-Bar, Adi Krief-Navon, and Tal Alon-Man, who assisted in revising the summarizing chapter of this book and served as a source of inspiration and consultation throughout various stages of the book's development.

I extend profound gratitude to my beloved parents—my dear mother, the late Rivka Blumrosen, who unfortunately passed away during the writing of this book; and my dear father, Avraham Blumrosen, who I hope will enjoy a long and distinguished life—for all the goodness they have bestowed upon me throughout my life.

Lastly, I express my deepest love and gratitude to my beloved family: to Zlil, who has been my steadfast companion throughout my journey in the field of autism, offering wise advice and unwavering faith; to my beloved children, Meitar, Tahel, and Clil, with whom I have shared my thoughts and enthusiasm for the subject of autism in recent years and who learned to recognize and respect the diverse experiences of many autistics around them.

Introduction

For many of us, the term "autistic" conjures images of individuals with a distant gaze, limited speech, and characteristic behaviors like hand waving or head banging, sometimes accompanied by extraordinary abilities, as portrayed in the movie *Rain Man*. Even seasoned therapists may not readily assume that some of their patients, who may exhibit high eloquence, self-awareness, interest in others, or meaningful friendships, and who may pursue distinguished professions such as doctors, lawyers, researchers, teachers, or even therapists, could also fall within the autistic spectrum.

Unfortunately, many autistic adults often go undiagnosed for various reasons, earning them the designation "the lost generation of autism" (a term coined by Baron-Cohen and Lai in 2015). First, a specific diagnostic category for them did not exist until the late 20th century: Hans Asperger identified the phenomenon in children in 1944, but it was not published in English until 1981 by Lorna Wing and was officially recognized as a diagnostic category only in 1994, under the title "Asperger's Syndrome" (in the *DSM-4*). Moreover, the majority of references in theoretical and clinical literature focused on children rather than adults. In addition, autistic adults often remain undiagnosed because they adeptly conceal their difficulties using high intelligence and learned imitation of social behaviors. Further complicating matters, many features of autism overlap with those found in other disorders such as depression, anxiety, attention and concentration problems, personality disorders, psychosis, and others, often resulting in partial or incorrect diagnoses. Nevertheless, the primary reason for the underdiagnosis of autism today is the lack of sufficient familiarity of most mental health professionals with the profile of autistic adults.

Underdiagnosis is notably more prevalent in regard to women, as they are more inclined to mask their challenges, form close relationships with single friends, and show less interest in pursuits typically associated with autism, such as science, computers, or transportation, and often gravitate toward more common interests such as psychology, books, TV, or animals, albeit with the heightened intensity typical of autism. Therefore, despite exhibiting characteristics of autism, women are less likely to be referred for an autism diagnosis (see Marshall, 2015; Yurkievicz, 2009; Baker, 2004; Bargiela et al., 2016).

The ramifications of underdiagnosis are profound, as many autistic people struggle with significant social and professional challenges, often accompanied by feelings of inferiority and low self-esteem, particularly when the sources of these challenges are not clearly understood. Such struggles often lead to depression, anxiety, frustration, self-harming behaviors, and elevated suicide rates (Wylie, 2014, p. 49; Cassidy et al., 2021). In contrast, an autism diagnosis can empower these individuals by fostering increased self-awareness, self-acceptance, and facilitating access to appropriate psychological and social support. Numerous studies and reports from autistics attest to the positive impact of such a diagnosis on their quality of life (see Attwood, 2007; Baker, 2004; Baron-Cohen & Lai, 2015; Bargiela et al., 2016; Robison, 2007).

Hence, the purpose of this book is to deepen the understanding of autistic adults and their pathways in life. Autistics may discover within these pages insights into their virtues and challenges. Mental health professionals may acquire a more profound understanding of such patients, enabling them to offer them a more informed and supportive care.

The book explores various areas in which autistics may navigate throughout adulthood. On one hand, it presents how autistics can harness their exceptional abilities in fields such as medicine, music, teaching, and therapy. Such areas of fulfillment have been underrepresented in autism research, which has primarily focused on pathological aspects. On the other hand, the book delves into challenges that autistics may face, including gender identity issues, eating disorders, dissociative disorders, and more. The book offers insights into the causes of these challenges and suggests potential coping strategies on personal and societal levels. Due to space constraints, the focus remains primarily on these selected areas, however with the belief that they can shed light on other realms in which autistics encounter similar experiences.

In exploring the world of autistics, I have relied predominantly on their own insights and accounts, striving to distill broader meanings from their narratives. This approach aligns with the current flourishing paradigm in autism research known as the emancipatory paradigm, which emphasizes the need to include autistics' perspectives and experiences rather than look at them solely from an external standpoint. The call to incorporate autistics' experiences in research and decision making is gaining prominence in autistic communities today, as epitomized by the slogan "nothing about us without us" (Charlton, 1998), a widely embraced mantra in contemporary discussions on disabilities. For instance, historically, most professional conferences on autism primarily involved professionals and family members of autistics, with few to no autistic representatives present. As Ari Ne'eman writes, "we who are the targets of this discussion have not been consulted . . . this situation has to change" (Ne'eman, 2012, pp. 88–90). Davidson and Orsini (2013) similarly stress that "what we know about autism needs to be informed by a deep appreciation for what individuals living on the spectrum have to say about what it means to be autistic." The autistic population holds an outstanding potential for enriching the discourse surrounding them, as they possess the most intimate knowledge of autism, often combined with exceptional intelligence and remarkable abilities for self-observation, insight, and truth seeking. In my encounters with autistic individuals, I am consistently amazed by their ability to accurately describe their inner experiences, often with illuminating examples and imagery, sometimes on the very first attempt, as evidenced by the accounts in this book.

The book draws heavily from my experiences with autistic individuals during diagnostic or psychotherapy sessions, and I am grateful to those of them who graciously agreed to further share their experiences for this book. In addition, insights from autobiographical writings by autistics such as Gunilla Gerland, Donna Williams, Liara Roux, Temple Grandin, and others, as well as personal accounts from internet blogs and sites, have been incorporated. These personal narratives are integrated into a broader context of academic research on the discussed topics. Nonetheless, it was disheartening to note the scarcity of studies exploring the connections between autism and the other topics discussed in this book, such as medicine, teaching, psychotherapy, eating disorders, sex work, homelessness, dissociative disorders, and gender diversity. Moreover, only a few numerical estimates examine the prevalence of autistics in each of these domains. Nonetheless, obtaining such estimates is challenging due to the underdiagnosis of autism and the lack of validated diagnostic tools today. An expansion of research, data, and tools related to autism is hoped for in the near future to address this gap.

Several crucial clarifications regarding the approach to autism and its associated terminology in this book warrant attention:

First, the book focuses mostly on autistics who have normal or above normal intelligence and language abilities. Previously, they may have been referred to as "high-functioning autistics" or as having "Asperger's syndrome." However, since the publication of the *DSM-5* in 2014, all autistic spectrum disorders are included under the umbrella term "Autism Spectrum Disorder" (ASD).

The book aligns with the pivotal conceptual adjustments advocated by autistic activists today, steering away from the outdated medical model that regards autism as a disorder or disease and autistics as impaired. Instead, it embraces a more respectful and empowering perspective toward autism, adopting terminology that potentially supports and empowers autistics and enhances awareness within the broader community about their rights and struggles (see Monk et al., 2022). In light of this positive awareness, the book employs corrected terminology in the following aspects:

- Autism is not regarded as a "disorder" but as a part of the natural spectrum of human diversity. In line with this, Baron-Cohen suggested replacing the term Autism Spectrum Disorder (ASD) with the term Autism Spectrum Condition (ASC) (see Baron-Cohen, 2017), which is considered more respectful and is sometimes used in contemporary discussions on autism. However, ASD may simply be replaced with the word "autism," as often done in this book.
- Instead of autism "symptoms" or "impairments," the book will refer to "autistic characteristics."
- Instead of using "comorbidity" to describe the co-occurrence of autism with other disorders, the term "co-occurring" will be used.
- Instead of person-first language (e.g., "person with autism"), which may be associated with a disorder or illness, identity-first language will be used (e.g., "autistic person" or even just "autistics," as many of them prefer).
- Many autistics reject the terms "high-functioning" versus "low-functioning" autism, arguing that all autistics exhibit a range of strengths, challenges, and support needs that fluctuate over time and across different contexts. Therefore, they advocate for recognizing autism as a multidimensional spectrum, suggesting the use of levels of support rather than levels of functioning.

Further, the book deliberately underscores both the strengths and challenges of autistics, aligning with the shift in autism research toward acknowledging and valuing both regards (see Silberman, 2015; Armstrong, 2012). By highlighting the strengths of autistics and their substantial contributions to human culture, this book aims to counterbalance the predominant focus on weaknesses in the older medical model. For instance, notable figures such as Albert Einstein, Isaac Newton, W. A. Mozart, and others, presumed to have been autistic, serve as compelling examples of the profound positive impact autistic individuals can make.

Another crucial concern addressed in this book is the danger of ableism, which refers to the expectation that autistics (or other disabled individuals) should conform to societal norms and adapt accordingly. Within autistic communities, resistance to ableism is mounting, advocating for the recognition of autistics' unique strengths and challenges and for the respect of their rights. This discussion is not purely theoretical but translates into practical implications, particularly regarding the extent to which autistics should endeavor to adapt to societal norms and how much society should accommodate their challenges in terms of budgets, laws, attitudes, and knowledge. Such questions will be explored in relation to the specific subjects discussed in the book.

The book is organized into three main parts: Part I is dedicated to exploring areas where autistic adults can find fulfillment, with chapters that shine a light on autistic professionals such as medical doctors, therapists, musicians, and teachers. Each chapter delves into the unique strengths and challenges that autistics may face within these professions, with the final chapter briefly touching on other potential careers for autistics. Part II delves into various challenges that autistics may encounter, covering topics such as eating disorders, gender diversity (or gender dysphoria), Klinefelter syndrome, employment in the sex industry, dissociative disorders, and issues related to professional and social stagnation, including experiences of homelessness. Part III presents a range of border theoretical subjects, with a concluding chapter offering recommendations for autistics, mental health professionals, governmental organizations, and researchers.

More specifically, the book includes the following chapters:

Chapter 1 delves into the notable presence of autistics within the medical profession, a concept popularized through TV series such as *The Good Doctor*, *House*, or *Grey's Anatomy*. This chapter offers insights into the advantages and challenges autistics encounter in this field, illustrated by the personal journey and insights of a successful autistic Israeli doctor.

Chapter 2 explores the involvement of autistics in therapeutic professions, shedding light on their remarkable empathy, self-awareness, and understanding, which defy common stigmas, as well as the challenges they may face. The narratives of several successful autistic therapists enrich this discussion.

Chapter 3 investigates the prevalent phenomenon of autistics engaging professionally with music and explores their experiences and creative processes. This investigation is informed by an insightful discussion with three accomplished Israeli musicians, who generously shared their reflections and perspectives on this topic.

Chapter 4 delves into the realm of autistics working as educators and caregivers in schools and kindergartens. It examines their attraction to this field, highlighting their typical strengths, challenges, and recommended coping strategies through various illustrative examples.

Chapter 5 provides a brief overview of alternative career paths available to autistics. These include technology, research, linguistics, writing, art, design, photography, cinema, acting, stand-up comedy, animal care, nature exploration, fantasy pursuits, culinary arts, technical professions, social and legal advocacy, investigative work, sports, chess, telemarketing, modeling, and more.

Chapter 6 sheds light on the often-overlooked co-occurrence of autism and eating disorders, with estimates suggesting that 20–30% of individuals with eating disorders are autistic. The chapter offers an explanatory model specific to autistics with eating disorders and proposes treatment guidelines. All these are illustrated by a poignant personal narrative.

Chapter 7 delves into the common occurrence of gender diversity or gender dysphoria among autistics. Drawing from research data and firsthand accounts, the chapter offers explanations and explores suggestions for psychotherapy tailored to the unique experiences of autistics in these realms.

Chapter 8 uncovers the connection between autism and "Klinefelter syndrome," a condition distinguished by an extra sex chromosome (XXY). This underexplored correlation may shed light on a deeper linkage between autism and the sex chromosomes.

Chapter 9 addresses the involvement of autistics in the sex industry, an often-overlooked phenomenon. Through a collection of personal narratives, the chapter delves into the attitudes, challenges, and intricacies faced by autistics engaged in this field. It sparks thought-provoking questions about issues such as victimhood, psychological integration, and alternative value systems.

Chapter 10 delves into the relatively underexplored connection between autism and dissociative disorders. Through three compelling case studies, the chapter offers valuable insights into the intersection of ASD and DID (Dissociative Identity Disorder), outlining the various factors contributing to autistics' heightened susceptibility to dissociative disorders, their unique characteristics, and recommended therapeutic considerations. Further, the chapter sheds light on the link between autism and depersonalization/derealization disorders, which are also common within the autistic population.

Chapter 11 addresses the challenges faced by autistics who feel "stuck" and struggle to fulfill their professional and social potentials, offering insights into coping strategies for navigating these difficulties. The chapter also discusses the danger of homelessness among autistics and ways to prevent it.

Chapter 12 highlights the frequent misdiagnosis of autistics with major psychiatric disorders such as affective disorders, schizophrenia, or personality disorders. Clear distinctions between these conditions and autism are emphasized to facilitate accurate diagnoses and appropriate treatment.

Chapter 13 discusses the characteristics of autistic thinking in terms of the key psychoanalytic concepts of primary and secondary processes, formulated by Freud and his followers. Autistic thinking is described as characterized by the dominance of primary processes, while also noting the presence of secondary processes, with a disrupted integration and alterations between these two kinds of processes in autistic thinking.

Chapter 14 offers a matrix for mapping the various manifestations of autism by placing them at the opposing ends of axes that represent different traits, thereby creating various typical clusters of characteristics.

The book's endnote offers suggestions for supporting individuals on the autism spectrum, with implications for autistics themselves, mental health professionals, government systems, and future research endeavors in the field.

Part I

PROFESSIONAL PATHWAYS FOR AUTISTIC ADULTS

Chapter 1

Autistic Doctors

> Practicing medicine is advantageous to me as it allows me to channel my constant inner noise into purposeful action . . . being an autistic doctor provides me with a sense of professionalism, grounded in my knowledge, curiosity, intuition, patient care, and playfulness. (Julie, an autistic doctor, cited below)

In recent years, awareness has been growing of the existence of autistic doctors, largely propelled by their portrayal in popular TV series such as *The Good Doctor*, *Grey's Anatomy*, and *House*. However, beyond the realm of television, there exists a wide and fascinating range of autistic doctors, most of whom have probably not been diagnosed as such due to the problem of underdiagnosis of autism among adults. This chapter explores the distinctive strengths and challenges that autistic doctors encounter during their admission, training, and professional work. It also suggests ways to support them in overcoming these difficulties and to benefit from their exceptional skills. The discussion also raises important questions about society's attitude toward neurological diversity.

To provide further insight into the experiences of autistic doctors, the personal narrative of Dr. Julie Kenan (a pseudonym) is shared, as she kindly agreed to offer her firsthand experiences and insights on this topic, providing valuable perspectives for understanding the challenges and triumphs that autistic individuals may face in the medical profession.

AUTISTICS IN THE MEDICAL WORLD

Many autistics are drawn to careers in medicine due to qualities that align well with this profession, including excellent memory, attention to detail, pattern recognition, high focus, curiosity, independent thinking, creativity, empathy, and strong ethics (as will be shown in more detail below). A study by Doherty et al. (2021) found that approximately 1% of 304 doctors identified as autistic, similar to their rate in the general population.

Although it hasn't been formally researched, it would be interesting to explore which areas of medicine autistic doctors are more likely to pursue. It is possible that autistic doctors gravitate toward fields that require high levels of data processing, such as oncology, neurology, or radiology, given their strengths in logical thinking, attention to detail, good memory, and pattern recognition. One may assume that because of their typical challenges in communication autistic doctors would prefer areas with limited patient interaction, such as research, pathology, radiology, or anesthesia; however, in contrast with this belief, many autistics doctors do seek contact with other people and may display emotional empathy, understanding, curiosity about people, and a strong desire to help others (e.g., see Baker & Shelly, 2015), and therefore many of them are rather drawn to areas where interactions with patients are needed such as psychiatry or GP. For example, according to Doherty et al. (2021), in a Facebook group of autistic doctors that includes several hundred members, most of the group members work as general practitioners or psychiatrists, both requiring substantial patient interaction. Of course, this is not a controlled study; however, these findings challenge the notion that autistic doctors are inclined to avoid contact with people. Another hypothesis may be that autistic doctors might be inclined toward specialties such as psychiatry or neurology to gain a deeper understanding of the human psyche, perhaps as a means of navigating their own psychological and social challenges. To explore these hypotheses and other intriguing questions emerging in the dynamic field of autism research, further dedicated investigations are required.

It is important to note that autistics have diverse inclinations and skills. Temple Grandin has identified three primary thinking styles among autistics: visual thinking, logical and linguistic thinking, and thinking in patterns (Grandin, 2013b). Consequently, autistic doctors may gravitate toward different medical specialties based on their particular cognitive style. For instance, those with visual skills may pursue radiology; and those with verbal skills may find psychiatry appealing. It is also important to acknowledge that autism is a continuum, and individuals may exhibit varying degrees of difficulties, with some individuals appearing less autistic overtly due to their ability to mask their challenges.

Common Assets of Autistic Doctors

Autistic doctors possess various assets that can contribute to their work:

High Intelligence—Many autistics exhibit a high IQ, fueled by deep curiosity, attention to detail, excellent memory, pattern recognition, and creativity.

High Curiosity—Autistics are often drawn to specific areas of knowledge, diving deep into them to attain proficiency and expertise, aligning well with the complex demands of the medical field.

Attention to Detail—Autistic doctors typically excel in paying meticulous attention to details. Coupled with exceptional long-term memory and keen visual or auditory memory, they can notice patterns and nuances that might elude others, such as small fluctuations in their patients' indexes or medical status. This ability to notice details and patterns, stemming from their need to find order in the world, may help them both in daily interactions with patients and in promoting valuable insights in medical research.

High Focus and Perfectionism—Autistics tend to work meticulously and with a strong focus. Their adherence to routines can be advantageous in terms of ethics, safety, hygiene, and patient care, though it may also foster rigidity and inflexibility.

Independent Thinking—Autistics tend to rely on their own perceptions and intuitions, often disregarding conventional ways of seeing things. This can be beneficial in advocating for just causes, but it may also lead to rigidity or overlooking mistakes.

Creativity and Inventiveness—Autistic doctors may find innovative approaches to aid their patients, leveraging their strong intuition, vast knowledge, and ability to think outside conventional boundaries. Some autistics have considerable expertise in diverse fields beyond medicine, such as psychology, science, languages, or spiritual pursuits. These additional skills can enable them to break new grounds and establish meaningful connections with patients. However, these unconventional approaches may at times be perceived as inappropriate, unusual, or even risky.

Logical Approach—Autistics tend to remain calm and make sound decisions even in stressful situations. Studies show that autistics tend to function well under stress, due to their logical thinking, creativity, resourcefulness, and intuition (see Attwood, 2007, p. 301). However, this can sometimes be perceived as inappropriate or even offensive in situations where a more emotional response is expected, though it should be stressed that they may also be very caring and affectionate on occasions.

High Ethics—Autistics typically possess high ethical standards, honesty, loyalty, and a strong commitment to their patients. They also tend to respect diversity and actively work toward empowering vulnerable populations.

Identifying Malfunctions—Autistics, driven by their moral compass, easily spot malfunctions within their work environment and may openly criticize faults or corruptions. This can lead to conflicts with the system but may also play a vital role in promoting the system's ethical standards.

Lack of Manipulation—Autistics are typically devoid of manipulation, power struggles, flattery, or intrigue, as they prioritize professional and humanitarian objectives. Although their tendency to rectify others' mistakes may sometimes be interpreted as condescending or arrogant, it stems primarily from a sincere desire to set things right, often without full awareness of the emotional impact it may have on others.

High Level of Emotional Empathy—Although autistics may encounter challenges in grasping the intentions or emotions of others (known as "cognitive empathy"), they frequently demonstrate a heightened level of "emotional empathy." This means that they can empathize deeply with others, particularly when directly witnessing their distress. Hence, autistic doctors are often exceptionally devoted to their patients, sometimes to the point of sacrificing their own well-being, which may render them vulnerable to exploitation or burnout.

Typical Difficulties That Autistic Doctors Face

Alongside the positive qualities that autistics bring to the field of medicine, they also struggle with many challenges stemming from their autism at various stages of their professional path:

Challenges in the Admissions Process—Despite possessing advantageous skills required for medical school admission, as outlined above, autistics must overcome significant obstacles related to autism during the admission process. These challenges include difficulties in adhering to social etiquette, such as maintaining eye contact or conversing appropriately (e.g., they may talk too much or keep too silent), being overly candid (e.g., they may too openly point out their shortcomings or criticize others), and presenting too much self-doubt or too much self-confidence, which may be perceived as arrogance. It's essential to note that these difficulties revolve around adapting to neurotypical norms rather than indicating severe internal limitations.

Difficulties during Medical Studies and Training—Autistics may encounter challenges in navigating behavioral norms, deciphering ambiguous instructions, managing sensory sensitivities, or grappling with challenges in executive functions (such as planning, organizing, prioritizing, and meeting deadlines). They may also face hurdles in social situations, such as being too naive or too honest; or experiencing difficulties in seeking help or in participating in teamwork. Attention and concentration challenges, a slower work pace, struggles in emotional regulation, depression, and anxiety further contribute to the array of challenges they confront during their medical studies and training.

Specifically, autistics have typical challenges in writing tests or assignments, such as difficulties in discerning the intentions behind questions, discerning subtle differences between multiple-choice answers, comprehending intricate instructions, and adhering to deadlines, as well as a tendency to either write too excessively or too sparingly. Moreover, they typically have more learning disabilities such as dyslexia, dyscalculia, or graphomotor difficulties, which can further complicate their academic performance.

Difficulties in the Working Environment

Challenges in Social Situations—Doctors on the autism spectrum typically face challenges in navigating social situations, potentially causing them to be perceived as distant, indifferent, condescending, tactless, or overly serious. The endeavor to conceal these difficulties through imitation may give rise to feelings of depression and a heightened sense of artificiality. Staff meetings may be challenging due to uncertainty about appropriate behavior, resulting in being too quiet or too critical and receiving negative responses.

Autistic doctors may also find it difficult to collaborate with others as they often lack the required openness and patience, though they sometimes have a genuine desire to either help or receive help. These gaps may be confounding for them and for those around them.

Autistic doctors may have considerable difficulties in dealing with their superiors or with the system because they are drawn to criticize the system's shortcomings, often in a blunt or tactless manner, and may therefore be perceived as rude, rigid, or too critical.

Toward people subordinated to them autistics may also be too rigid, matter of fact, blunt, or lacking consideration for their feelings. However, when directly exposed to the emotions of others, they may demonstrate a heightened sense of empathy and consideration.

In their interactions with patients, autistic doctors may skip social niceties or encounter difficulties in understanding patients, particularly if they are unclear or manipulative. They may also prefer patients who present complex and thought-provoking medical issues over mild cases that may call for sheer sympathy. However, over time, many autistic doctors learn how to communicate successfully and exhibit genuine care and empathy for their patients. Consequently, they are often appreciated for their sincerity, professionalism, dedication, and compassionate approach and derive satisfaction and meaning from these interactions.

Difficulties in Understanding Intentions, Thoughts, and Emotions of Others—Autistics may struggle with implicit communication, which can lead to misunderstandings and potential dangers, especially in critical medical situations. However, autistics often possess sharp intuition and may perceive things more than others intuitively.

Over-devotion—Over-devotion is a common trait among many autistic doctors, leading them to take on more work than necessary, resulting in feelings of being exploited or exhausted. They may also lack awareness of their rights or encounter challenges in asserting them, resulting in disadvantageous work conditions or salaries.

Difficulties with Executive Functions—Autistics often experience challenges in executive functions, encompassing issues such as planning, organizing, initiating tasks, mental flexibility, and prioritization. These challenges may manifest as procrastination, especially in bureaucratic tasks such as filling out forms or responding to emails, as well as in problems in meeting deadlines, multitasking, or planning long-term personal processes. However, some autistics may exhibit the opposite tendency—of overorganizing—leading to an excessive adherence to schedules and routines. Some may oscillate between overorganizing and under-organizing, creating confusion for themselves and their surroundings.

Attention and Concentration Problems—Many autistics have concentration problems and high distractibility stemming from their rich and overly active inner world, as well as heightened sensitivities. However, as in ADHD, alongside being often distracted they may also have the opposite tendency of overfocusing, which may be a real advantage in the medical world.

Inflexibility—Autistics often exhibit inflexibility, as they tend to adhere to their own problem-solving approaches. Although these can sometimes prove advantageous, they may also lead to incorrect decisions or evoke resentment from others. In addition, many autistics display a strong adherence to routines, which can be beneficial for maintaining order but may hinder flexibility, especially when adaptation to new environments is needed.

Difficulties in Emotional Regulation—Autistics frequently have challenges in emotional regulation, often experiencing emotions intensely, with a tendency toward "black or white" thinking. For example, they may react strongly to mistakes, blaming themselves or the system unreasonably.

High Levels of Anxiety—Autistics have a high level of anxiety, which may be linked to physiological characteristics such as an enlarged amygdala (Grandin, 2013b, p. 32) or a high level of cortisol (Taylor & Corbett, 2014). Many of their behaviors may be regarded as defenses against anxiety, including adherence to routines, repetitive movements, meltdowns, or shutdowns. Nevertheless, anxieties can occasionally function as a positive driving force, motivating them to uphold high standards of work.

Sleep and Fatigue Problems—Because autistics invest considerable efforts in social, emotional, and mental struggles, tasks that neurotypicals perform automatically, many of them suffer from almost chronic fatigue. Insufficient sleep often results from psychological factors such as stress, executive dysfunctions, and challenges in perceiving body sensations, alongside potential physiological factors such as a different biological clock, low melatonin production, or medication.

Mood Problems—Due to the numerous challenges they face and criticism from their environment, many autistics suffer from poor self-esteem and depression, being unable to see things from a more objective and integrative perspective. The suicide rate among autistics is nine times higher than in the general population (Doherty, 2020); considering that the suicide rates among doctors are increased anyway, this poses a double risk.

Shutdowns, Meltdowns, and Burnout—The abundance of difficulties and stresses may lead autistics to experience the following phenomena: meltdowns, which involve eruptions of anger, shouting, crying, destroying objects or harming themselves or others (mostly in the domestic area); shutdowns, in which they isolate themselves in a stimuli-free environment such as a dark and quiet room with no communication, for a period of hours, days, or more; burnout, a condition characterized by exhaustion, withdrawal, and reduced functioning, often leading individuals to resign from work environments. Due to these phenomena, autistics are often misdiagnosed with depression, though sometimes what they truly need is understanding and respite from their efforts.

Sensory Sensitivities—Most autistic people experience hypersensitivity or hyposensitivity across all senses: In the sense of hearing—they may be sensitive to sudden noises, which may cause them great discomfort, especially in medical settings with monitors or alarms. In the sense of sight—they may be sensitive to strong or artificial lights such as neon lights or LED screens. In the sense of smell—they may react negatively to strong smells such as body smells, chemicals, garbage, and so on. In the sense of taste—many are picky eaters, which may affect their functioning. In the sense of touch—many are sensitive to various textures or touch; many are also hyposensitive or hypersensitive to pain or to temperature. Autistics may also have other sensory problems, such as difficulty in processing certain auditory or visual stimuli, including faces (known as prosopagnosia) (see Bogdashina, 2003, pp. 51–156; Attwood, 2007, pp. 271–291).

Health Problems—Autistics often contend with concurrent health issues, including psychosomatic problems, allergies, drug sensitivities, autoimmune diseases, or various syndromes such as fibromyalgia, candida, or Irlen Syndrome. Unfortunately, they also have a higher prevalence of cancer (e.g., see Chiang et al., 2015).

Additional Difficulties—Alongside the aforementioned challenges, autistic doctors may experience typical difficulties such as a difficulty in expressing emotions (alexithymia); unusual way of speech (unclear/slow/fast/weak/loud/high/low/monotonous speech); problems with spatial orientation, balance, coordination, proprioception, and more.

In conclusion, autistic doctors often exhibit extreme gaps—between exceptional abilities and substantial challenges, between outstanding skills and difficulties in actualizing them, between how they see themselves and how society sees them—leading to confusion, frustration, or resentment in themselves or in others, especially in the absence of a formal autism diagnosis.

JULIE'S CASE

Background

Julie, a medical doctor in her mid-40s, sought a diagnosis for autism after her daughter was diagnosed, a common occurrence among the "lost generation of autism." During the diagnosis process, Julie displayed impressive expressiveness, radiating brilliance, and inner richness. Julie refrained from social niceties or small talk but, rather, focused on answering my questions very openly and honestly. She fired her words quickly yet managed to be very precise. She often avoided direct eye contact, especially when she was trying to concentrate on what she was saying.

Julie was born in the United States and immigrated to Israel as a baby. Both of her parents are physicians. In her early development, she exhibited typical autistic characteristics, including delays in motor and verbal skills, though eventually making significant progress in both areas. As a child, she often retreated into her inner world, enjoying sensory stimuli, such as playing with water or sand. Occasionally, she acted impulsively, for instance in jumping into a pool without knowing how to swim, leading her mother to comment "how such a smart girl can be so stupid?"—reflecting the difficulties many autistics face in foreplanning their actions. Julie's intelligence stood out from a young age, and she displayed high curiosity and an early ability to read.

As a child, Julie had notable sensory sensitivities, including aversions to certain fabrics, clothing labels, certain foods, bright lights, strong smells, and unpleasant sounds. She also experienced anxieties and fears related to insects, evil people, and scary characters.

Julie had a special bond with her grandmother, a Holocaust survivor, who used to share stories about the family's losses during that dark period; these stories captured Julie's imagination, stirring in her intense emotions and anxieties. She even used to imagine how the notorious Nazi Mengele might break through her window. Julie believes that these stories may have influenced her deep interest in death and her strong desire to help people.

In kindergarten, Julie did not know how to make friends and often imitated her older sister. In elementary school, she was immersed in her inner world and found it challenging to interact with classmates. She found it easier to connect with boys, as their behavior seemed more understandable to her, and engaged in physical games with them. Despite being easily distracted in class, Julie excelled academically due to her high intelligence. In her free time, she enjoyed reading, particularly books about the Holocaust or biographies of inventors, explorers, or politicians. She developed a particular fondness for the life stories of Albert Einstein, Ignaz Semmelweis, and Franz Kafka, realizing in hindsight that all three had traits that could be related to autism, such as being incomprehensible geniuses, facing social difficulties, and seeking absolute truths.

During high school, Julie felt different from other girls because she did not know how to dress fashionably or apply makeup and lacked social skills. She faced challenges in forming friendships and tended to correct others' mistakes, often leading to negative feelings directed at her. Julie attributed these challenges to her immigrant background, feeling that she didn't understand local habits. She attempted to improve her social adjustment by imitating others or by preparing conversations in advance. Academically, Julie was unorganized and prone to procrastination, but her intellectual abilities enabled her to excel, particularly in science, whereas in the humanities she faced difficulties in interpreting hidden meanings. In her spare time, she enjoyed reading philosophy books and was pondering profound questions.

Julie chose to study medicine with the goal of helping others. She completed her medical studies with great honors and achieved high esteem in her professional career. She played a role in establishing and managing several medical units in Israel. In addition to her professional accomplishments, Julie married and became a mother, offering her opportunities for breaks from work and personal fulfillment.

Receiving an autism diagnosis was a liberating experience for Julie. It allowed her to gain new insights into the origins of her difficulties and to reconsider, in this new light, what she accepts about herself and what she may want to change. She feels that this diagnosis has freed up lots of energies that she used to invest in self-criticism and enabled her to embrace her true self. However, Julie acknowledges that it can be challenging for her to fully identify as "autistic," and she sometimes prefers to see herself as having "autistic features," recognizing that her support needs differ from those of other autistics who require more substantial assistance.

Julie's Academic Journey

In the medical school admission interview, Julie demonstrated remarkable honesty. When prompted to identify her shortcomings, she openly highlighted her struggles with being organized. Despite this, she was accepted, based on her excellent grades and impressive personality. Julie reflects that a few decades ago, the admission process was much less stringent and focused mainly on grades. Nowadays, she believes she may not have passed the screening interview, which places more emphasis on social skills, potentially excluding many highly capable autistic candidates.

Studying medicine presented challenges for Julie. Driven by her strong desire to succeed and her exceptional abilities, she excelled in the end, but along the way she faced obstacles related to autism. Adjusting and understanding expectations took her longer at each stage. In class, she often struggled to concentrate, as her thoughts frequently wandered to her inner world. She also experienced constant fatigue, making her sometimes fall asleep during lectures.

Because her notebooks remained incomplete, she had to rely heavily on studying from books. She also had problems in planning and organizing and in submitting paperwork on time. She could not stand writing assignments, particularly creating bibliographic lists, but at least medical school involved relatively few writing assignments.

In exams, Julie generally performed well, particularly in multiple-choice formats, thanks to her strong memory and her ability to eliminate incorrect options. Open-ended questionnaires posed more challenges, as she often struggled to grasp the implicit intentions behind the questions or delved into excessive details. Fortunately, most exams in medical school were multiple choice. Julie excelled in practical exams, especially in her advanced years, due to her excellent ability to describe the development of diseases as if they were tangible entities. On the other hand, memorizing facts, figures, and data proved more difficult for her. It should be noted that autistics vary in their ability to remember factual information; there are those who excel in it, whereas Julie was better with narrative materials.

In the practical parts of her training Julie often took longer than average to understand expectations. She sometimes missed instructions that others automatically absorbed, resulting in incidents such as forgetting to close the protective cover of an ultraviolet lamp and burning her eyes. However, Julie's difficulties lessened as she progressed through each stage as she found ways to bridge these gaps.

Julie experienced anxiety when presenting in front of others (in this respect, too, autistics tend to belong to extremes; quite a few have no audience anxiety at all, perhaps because they overlook the feelings of those in front of them, whereas others may be at the opposite extreme). However, she never considered avoiding these tasks or seeking help and always managed to complete them. Over time, Julie grew more accustomed to appearing in public and relies on medication to manage her anxiety.

Socially, Julie experienced insecurity throughout her studies, often perceiving herself as different and inferior. She sought comfort in a small group of fringe students. During the clinical years, she felt more at ease, as some friends embraced her, assisting her in understanding and navigating social dynamics, as is common for autistic girls and women.

Professional Path

Julie chose a medical field that deeply interests her, requiring high diagnostic skills, meaningful interactions with patients and their families, and coping with death, which continues to fascinate her. She has also been selected to establish and manage several medical units and appreciates the diversity in her professional responsibilities. Julie's notable accomplishments have positioned her as a highly esteemed figure in her field.

As a diagnostician, Julie possesses exceptional abilities and often has been hailed as a "genius" in her field. She can assimilate vast amounts of data and construct a unique disease narrative for each patient, almost personifying diseases in her mind. This enables her to "sense" a patient's condition and predict the future progression of their illness. Julie excels at identifying situations requiring further examination or treatment due to her proficiency in recognizing patterns and deviations. In addition, she has strong visual skills and can derive valuable information from medical images. Julie also excels in "corridor medicine," swiftly identifying patients' issues through chance encounters. She relies heavily on her strong intuitions and gut feelings, preferring to examine patients herself rather than relying solely on others' reports.

Julie is less likely to remember numerical data but has an excellent memory for visual or emotionally significant information. Nevertheless, she knows when it's important to verify numerical data—for instance, when prescribing medications—and thereby compensates for her tendency to overlook them.

Another area where Julie excels is in executing large projects, working tirelessly and paying meticulous attention to every detail. However, she faces challenges in dealing with bureaucratic obstacles, which she finds cumbersome. Julie acknowledges that her greatest professional challenge lies in her difficulties with executive functions, such as planning her schedule, completing forms, or responding to emails. Fortunately, she now has a secretary who assists her in managing her responsibilities, reminding her of her duties, scheduling appointments for her, and helping her establish necessary boundaries with patients. Julie sees this support as invaluable help. In addition, her executive dysfunctions hinder her ability to produce academic papers, somewhat impeding her professional progress.

Dealing with Patients

Julie often forges strong relationships with her patients and their families, thanks to her unwavering professionalism, logical thinking, honesty, dedication, and heightened emotional empathy, as she has actively honed her communication skills over the years. Initially, she tended to speak in a distant, factual manner, but now she is more open to listening, engaging in small talk, and adopting a softer tone. Patients have discovered that Julie possesses a genuine and unconventional sense of humor that helps alleviate stress. She also enjoys listening to her patients and demonstrates a profound interest in their emotional stories, believing that they deeply influence their illness. Connecting with her patients' emotions also helps her explore her own feelings and gain insights into the complex subject of death, which deeply intrigues her. Julie has formed some deep emotional bonds with her patients, particularly with women, though she finds it easier to work with male patients due to their more direct communication style.

Patients frequently compliment Julie on her sincerity and reliability. She believes that people value honesty, especially when facing death. Julie treats her patients with utmost respect, refraining from imposing solutions, and instead, sharing her professional considerations while remaining open to hearing their opinions. Nonetheless, Julie maintains clinical assertiveness and can make decisions and take responsibility when necessary. Julie treats all patients equally, without discrimination based on fame or commonality. Over time, she has observed her inclination to be drawn to patients with unique psychological or psychosocial backgrounds. Although initially she attributed this to her general curiosity about people, she now recognizes that it may also be connected to her being on the autism spectrum herself.

Julie demonstrates immense dedication to her patients, immersing herself in the details of their illnesses and providing compassionate care. However, due to her difficulty in setting boundaries she has been overly devoted in the past and was often feeling exhausted. To address this, her personal secretary now helps her establish more reasonable limits.

In conclusion, although Julie may initially come across as tough due to her logical, matter-of-fact speech and her restrained facial expressions, patients are often impressed by her high level of professionalism, unwavering dedication, and respectful, compassionate attitude. Occasionally, patients express their gratitude by referring to Julie as an "angel," but she surely corrects them by stating that she is "not an angel," as being accurate is so important for her.

Dealing with the System

Julie finds the main difficulty in her work life to be in her interactions with fellow staff members and the overarching system. This is a common experience for autistic doctors, as they have to navigate neurotypical norms that they may not find logical or easily understood (Doherty et al., 2021; Bury Simon et al., 2021). Indeed, Julie has a keen perception of system malfunctions and, in the past, frequently voiced criticisms, earning her reputation as a "bone in the system's throat." However, due to her great value for the system, she was not fired. Over time, Julie has learned how to soften her criticism, gaining a deeper understanding of the system's constraints and the importance of adapting to its intricacies.

Ethics are of paramount importance to Julie in her work. For instance, she refuses to participate in clinical experiments conducted by pharmaceutical companies that may involve data manipulation or false indications of improvement. This stance occasionally places her in a tense position within the system.

Staff meetings pose another major difficulty for Julie. She struggles to have patience with others' opinions and often regrets things she had said. As a result, she has chosen to exempt herself from attending staff meetings, a decision somehow accepted by her supervisor. Interestingly, when Julie is in a managerial position and conducts staff meetings herself, she feels more comfortable expressing her genuine thoughts.

Asserting her rights is another challenge for Julie. For many years, she prioritized her work and neglected her rights in terms of salary, conditions, or promotion opportunities. Only recently did she become aware of the importance of personal negotiations within the differential reward system. Fortunately, when Julie relocated to work in the country's periphery, her conditions improved. In the past, she sometimes relinquished managerial positions when things did not go her way, realizing in hindsight that she may have conceded too easily. Julie acknowledges her tendency to oscillate between staunchly standing by her opinions and yielding too readily, a pattern that has led to challenges and confusion, both for herself and those around her.

Dealing with Staff Members

Interacting with other staff members has been a challenge for Julie, but she has made progress over time. Social niceties such as greetings, smiling, or small talk feel artificial and tiresome to her. Nevertheless, a colleague-friend offered her a valuable insight into the importance of fostering positive relationships with colleagues, especially as a manager, and advised her to treat employees with greater consideration, pay attention to their emotional experiences, and initiate social activities. Julie implemented these tips, experiencing a notable improvement in her relationships. Nevertheless, certain aspects continue to be difficult for her, such as engaging in small talk, which she finds trivial and boring, or knowing how to act in specific situations such as parties. Julie was surprised to discover how important she can be to others and noticed that people often seek her out for conversations, appreciating her honesty and wisdom. She has learned to listen more, refrain from giving unnecessary advice, and to connect emotionally in such situations.

Colleagues often perceive Julie as assertive and opinionated because she doesn't hesitate to comment about things she finds inappropriate. However, over time, they have come to realize that beneath her tough exterior, she is soft and empathetic. Her staff members greatly appreciate her and often seek her advice on complex professional issues due to her sound judgment. She has been told on multiple occasions that they would prefer to see her if they were ill.

Julie is not competitive and strives to help her colleagues as much as possible. However, she sometimes feels jealous of those who navigate the political and social landscape more successfully. She finds it challenging to collaborate with people she dislikes but is happy to work with those she respects and values for their attitude and professionalism. Over time, she has built a small network of people she trusts and enjoys consulting and collaborating with. Julie particularly enjoys working with doctors whom she suspects are on the autistic spectrum as well—and she believes that there are quite a few of them—appreciating their excellent professional level, high ethical standards, originality, and generosity. However, she is now more aware and critical of the challenges that rigidity may pose, especially when these individuals hold managerial positions.

Julie treats junior staff, interns, and students the same way she treats high-ranking executives, as autistics do not follow regular social norms. However, as an instructor for students or interns, Julie often struggles with conveying knowledge in an orderly manner due to her divergent, fluid thinking. She notices that at times, they find it difficult to comprehend her distinct communication style. Presentations are also frequently challenging for Julie because of her difficulty in presenting information in a clear, organized manner. Nevertheless, when given the opportunity to freely discuss topics that truly interest her, she can genuinely captivate others.

Julie's General Feelings as an Autistic Doctor

Julie believes that being autistic is wearying, being a doctor is tiring, and being an autistic doctor is even more exhausting, as autistic doctors must cope constantly with incessant internal noises stemming from being constantly preoccupied with questions regarding possible ways of behavior, attempts to understand things, and constant self-criticism. She feels that all these internal noises often deplete her energy. The intense focus and hyper-attention contribute to her success but may also lead to feelings of burnout. To manage this challenge, Julie has developed strategies such as taking breaks and engaging in activities that bring her joy, such as music, spiritual studies, and spending time with her family. Julie finds practicing medicine advantageous as it allows her to channel her constant inner noise into purposeful action. Being an autistic doctor imparts a profound sense of professionalism to Julie, grounded in her knowledge, curiosity, intuition, patient care, and playfulness, providing her with a sense of security and purpose. Despite the advantages, Julie feels that there is a split between her image as a highly successful doctor who possesses special abilities, excels in relationships, and knows what to do and who she is in the "real" world, where she often feels unassertive and misunderstood. Embracing her autism diagnosis is gradually facilitating more integration between these "two Julies."

Julie believes it is crucial for the health-care system to support and promote autistic doctors, recognizing their unique skills, creativity, ethical approach, and compassion, which can contribute greatly to the medical field. However, she fears that convincing the system to embrace this idea may be challenging, as conservative standards and hierarchies still prevail, and she worries that raising awareness about autistic doctors might lead to discriminatory practices against them.

In conclusion, Julie's story sheds light on her individual journey, yet resonates with the experiences of many other autistic doctors. Despite the substantial challenges stemming from her autism, Julie has achieved undeniable success, illustrating the abundant assets and advantages that autistic doctors can bring to the medical world.

SUGGESTIONS FOR COPING AND SUPPORT

Various courses of action can be considered to assist autistic doctors in navigating the challenges mentioned above, benefiting both their well-being and the overall functioning of the system.

Coping on the Personal Level

Obtaining the Appropriate Autism Diagnosis—Numerous studies and personal reports suggest that getting the appropriate diagnosis of autism can have numerous benefits for autistics. It may help them understand themselves better, reduce feelings of guilt and shame, and develop self-acceptance. They may gain more awareness of their strengths and challenges and seek suitable medical and psychological support. Diagnosis also enables them to exercise their legal rights and form connections with other autistics for mutual support and empowerment. Moreover, awareness of the diagnosis fosters understanding from others, mitigating negative and unjust attributions such as laziness or selfishness.

Occasionally, depression or fear of negative societal reactions may arise following an autism diagnosis. Nevertheless, substantial evidence indicates that in the majority of cases, the advantages of such a diagnosis outweigh the drawbacks.

Following the autism diagnosis, acquiring knowledge about autism through self-studies or engaging in psychotherapy proves highly beneficial. Such efforts can aid in processing past hurts, rehabilitating bruised self-esteem, mitigating rigid thinking, alleviating anxieties, and enhancing emotional regulation, executive functions, and decision-making skills.

Determining whether to disclose an autism diagnosis poses a significant challenge. On one hand, it may elicit criticism from others or require extensive explanations and clarifications. On the other hand, concealing the diagnosis may prove challenging for autistics, who inherently value honesty, and may impede opportunities for understanding and support from their peers. Selective disclosure to understanding individuals or sharing specific difficulties can be a solution. Naturally, each autistic doctor should consider the worthwhileness of disclosure based on personal circumstances and comfort level.

In preparing for medical school interviews, autistics should be aware of potential pitfalls related to social manners, such as challenges with making eye contact, speaking too excessively or too sparingly, being overly candid, or presenting too much self-doubt or overconfidence. Engaging in tutorials or role-plays is recommended for practicing and refining these social skills. It should be noted that such endeavors are aimed at enhancing interview performance and not indicative of severe inner limitations.

During their studies and training, autistics should be aware of potential difficulties and take appropriate measures. These include managing time effectively (e.g., by planning schedules, allowing enough time for sleep or rest); coping with study-related difficulties (e.g., by breaking tasks into smaller components, using aids such as lists or cards, obtaining the necessary study materials, and seeking support from teachers or colleagues); addressing cognitive impairments (e.g., difficulties in understanding instructions or specific learning disabilities); dealing with social difficulties, sensory sensitivities, attention and concentration problems, emotional regulation, anxiety and depression. Contacting disabled student services for academic and social assistance, as well as accommodations in exams—such as extra time, being examined in a separate and quiet room, using headphones to minimize noise—are also recommended.

During their medical practice, autistic doctors are recommended to be aware of and effectively manage the following challenges:

Learning Social Norms—Acquiring an understanding of social norms including greetings, tact, diplomacy, openness, reciprocity, maintaining appropriate physical distance and eye contact; once aware of these norms, individuals have the autonomy to decide whether to align with them, as they are not obliged to comply with ableist norms. Alternatively, they may choose to leverage their unique assets, such as high intelligence, a special sense of humor, a genuine interest in people, high ethics, and dedication.

Expressing Criticisms Diplomatically—Developing the skill of expressing criticisms diplomatically and discerning when and how to engage in conflicts.

Asserting Rights—Learning to stand up for one's rights by confidently asking questions, setting boundaries, or refusing requests when necessary.

Expressing Emotions and Desires—Developing the ability to better articulate emotions, desires, and personal goals and make choices assertively.

Emotional Regulation—Acquiring techniques for emotional regulation and adopting a more integrative perspective, beyond the initial tendency to perceive things in "black and white."

Improving Executive Functioning—Employing strategies such as lists, schedules, or seeking assistance from others or from secretarial services to enhance executive functioning.

Avoiding Exhaustion—Implementing measures to avoid exhaustion, such as controlling participation in social events, maintaining boundaries, reducing exposure to unnecessary stimuli, taking breaks, and engaging in self-care activities such as sports, yoga, meditation, mindfulness, and writing or sharing with others.

Addressing Sensory Sensitivities—Employing aids such as earplugs, sunglasses, sensory games, or therapies such as sensory integration and desensitization (see Bogdashina, 2003, pp. 153–156; Attwood, 2007, pp. 271–291; Grandin, 2013b, pp. 96–98).

Pharmacological Treatments and Alternative Therapies—Seeking pharmacological treatments for conditions such as anxiety, depression, attention and concentration problems, obsessive-compulsive behaviors, sensory sensitivities, and sleep problems; considering alternative therapies, including art therapy, animal-assisted therapy, hydrotherapy, biofeedback, neurofeedback, among others.

It is crucial to emphasize that the aforementioned efforts may sometimes involve the masking of autistics' natural tendencies, which may lead them to feelings of artificiality, alienation, and potentially depression or self-harm. Hence, it is vital to acknowledge the toll this adaptation can exact and afford individuals the autonomy to choose the degree to which they conform to social norms. Moreover, it is equally imperative for individuals surrounding autistic individuals to actively foster an environment of utmost acceptance and support.

Recommendations for System-Level Efforts

Health-care systems should consider implementing the following measures to support autistic doctors:

Accommodations in Admission to Medical Schools—During this phase, it is recommended to provide appropriate preparation for autistics and their examiners to accommodate their needs, as well as to consider affirmative action, recognizing the valuable contributions autistics can make to the health-care system.

Raising Awareness in Health-Care Environments—It is crucial to increase awareness in medical schools and health-care institutions regarding the challenges that autistic doctors may encounter and to take the following steps:

In light of their sensory sensitivities, it is advised to create an environment that minimizes sensory stimuli, including efforts to reduce noise, unpleasant smells, or textures.

In light of their communication challenges, it is advised to use clear and explicit communication methods, such as detailed and/or written instructions.

In light of their difficulties in social situations, it is advised to foster a more tolerant and accepting attitude toward their social challenges and offer higher understanding and flexibility for their needs. This may include, for instance, allowing them to be exempt from staff meetings sometimes or to take breaks more frequently than usual.

In light of their difficulties in executive functions, it is advised to show understanding and offer assistance or accommodations (e.g., in answering emails, filling out forms, or making phone calls).

Adjustments in the Regulatory Level—It is recommended to institute formal rules and regulations within health-care systems to support autistic doctors. This should encompass matters such as employment equality, safeguards against discrimination, and the provision of psychological support and mentorship opportunities.

CONCLUDING REMARKS

Understanding the psychological profile of autistic individuals, encompassing their strengths and challenges, is essential for both autistic doctors and health-care systems. In this process, autistics must navigate the balance between remaining true to themselves and adapting to the demands of the system. Health-care systems should allocate resources to foster understanding and support for autistic doctors. Beyond the imperative of social justice, such an investment may prove advantageous for health systems, considering the numerous benefits that autistic doctors may bring to the medical world through their exceptional professional skills, unwavering dedication, ethical standards, and creativity.

Chapter 2

Autistic Therapists

> People have been my special interest throughout my life, and even as a young boy I stated, "I am not from this planet, and I was planted here to learn how people feel and think." Throughout my life I have immersed myself in extensive reading, watching movies, and observing other people's behaviors to better understand them. (Hillel, an autistic therapist, cited below)

Common stereotypes surrounding autistics involve misconceptions about their perceived lack of empathy, self-awareness, and appropriate communication skills—qualities crucial to therapeutic professions. Nevertheless, it is essential to recognize that many autistics do possess or actively develop these qualities over time, enabling them to excel in therapeutic professions. This chapter delves into the characteristics that may prove advantageous for autistics in the field of therapy, as well as the challenges that they may encounter along this path. These will be illustrated through the personal narratives of three successful Israeli therapists, Hillel, Gili, and Ruth (pseudonyms), who kindly agreed to be interviewed for this book.

HILLEL'S STORY

Hillel pursued a diagnosis after his son was diagnosed with autism. Despite his decades of experience in the therapy field, he was surprised to find how closely he aligned with the diagnosis, which had never been considered before. Hillel impressed me deeply with his wisdom, heightened self-awareness, and compelling charisma, fueled by his exceptional intelligence, articulate communication, unwavering honesty, and noteworthy professional accomplishments as a successful therapist and author.

The diagnostic meetings with Hillel were particularly interesting because despite his inherent difficulties in expressing emotions, over the years he acquired the ability to formulate his emotions in a very profound and intricate way, surpassing many neurotypical individuals. This ability was honed through his deep interest in people, a trait shared by other autistic individuals, especially women, who observe others endlessly to extract psychological rules about human behavior.

Hillel's diagnostic process was highly instructive due to the stark contrast between his seemingly normative appearance and his profound autistic characteristics, which are even more severe compared to many other autistics, manifesting in both his exceptional skills and his lifelong struggles: Hillel was identified as gifted and demonstrates exceptional talents in writing, painting, and music. However, his difficulties related to autism are also extreme: he has very heightened sensory sensitivities; for instance, his sense of smell is so sensitive, that he can identify people by their scents, and his attitude toward others is deeply influenced by their smells. He is also extremely sensitive to touch, lights, and sounds. Hillel also experiences synesthesia, as emotions and colors automatically translate in his mind into smells and sounds, and numbers and letters automatically trigger different colors. Hillel also has an unusually high pain threshold, barely feeling any pain even when his limbs were broken, much to the astonishment of his doctors. He also has a high tolerance for temperature, not experiencing pain until a burn formed in his fingers after touching a hot surface.

Hillel also possesses a very high emotional empathy (e.g., he avoids watching or listening to the news as it causes him too much pain and he feels sorrow even for plants). He also has fixed habits and routines (such as eating the same breakfast for years and following the same daily route). He is also very naive (e.g., he avoids inviting technicians as they might take advantage of his naiveté). He also has difficulties in forming and maintaining relationships, finding satisfaction in the company of his close family. Due to all these challenges, along with his hesitance to ask for help, Hillel has experienced eating disorders, self-harm behaviors, and suicidal thoughts, especially during his younger years.

Throughout his life, Hillel has developed a controlled, restrained appearance that conceals his internal difficulties related to autism: to compensate for his discomfort with direct eye contact, he focuses on the lips of his interlocutor. Through observations, taking notes, and training, he has learned to engage in mutual dialogue with socially accepted responses. Although his body language is generally reserved in social situations, he displays repetitive movements when alone. Like many other autistics, Hillel is drawn to extremes in various respects: for instance, he can fearlessly address large audiences but experiences intense anxiety in smaller social situations; even during our diagnostic meetings, he sought support by having his partner sit beside him and hold his hands. Hillel's eating habits reflect a similar duality, as on the one hand he used to be very picky and detested lots of foods (especially those with a mushy or lumpy texture), but on the other hand he sometimes consumed inedible substances such as plants, sand, and papers (Pica syndrome). In decision making, Hillel has on the one hand lots of difficulties in making everyday decisions, yet on the other hand he demonstrates ease in arriving at important decisions. In relationships, Hillel has, on the one hand, a keen interest in other people, yet on the other hand, he is not interested in forming new relationships.

People have been Hillel's special interest throughout his life, and already as a very young boy he stated, "I am not from this planet, and I was planted here in order to learn how people feel and think." Throughout his life, he immersed himself in extensive reading and watching movies, focusing on understanding human behaviors, with a heightened interest in profound subjects such as human evil and the Holocaust. At school he used to stare at other kids to grasp their laws of behaviors, and during his military service he upgraded this tendency by creating extensive lists and tables of behaviors, both of himself and others.

Hillel naturally gravitated toward the study of psychology at the university. Although deeply interested in the subject, he often felt he could have absorbed the material much more effectively through independent study. He also detested the excessive sensory stimulation on campus, especially the strong neon lights and strong scents, and had challenges in navigating the campus, even with the aid of maps and illustrations, and often arrived at class overstimulated. Nevertheless, Hillel managed to complete several degrees and training programs in the subsequent years.

Psychotherapy captivates Hillel because it allows him to do what he likes the most—engage in deep conversations and try to understand people and help them. Hillel can work for many consecutive hours due to his love for the work, coupled with his difficulty with transitions. During these extended work periods, Hillel frequently skips eating, drinking, and even bathroom breaks due to his tendency to focus on a singular task, as is typical of autistics.

The fixed and predefined rules and setting of psychotherapy provide a sense of security for Hillel, as he does not have to worry about social expectations or making social mistakes. He feels relaxed because the purpose of therapy is well-defined: to discuss meaningful topics, distill the truth about a patient's psyche, and help him recognize behavior patterns for potential change. Viewing therapy as a collaborative endeavor, he operates on the assumption that his patients are truthful, in contrast to everyday situations where discerning between truth and lies proves challenging for him. Nevertheless, Hillel encounters difficulties when dealing with manipulative or deceitful patients.

Hillel possesses an extraordinary memory, effortlessly recalling details such as the names of his patients' friends, children, life events, and even their recounted dreams. This remarkable ability not only fosters a sense of deep care among his patients but also aids him in discerning psychological patterns, such as tendencies toward passive-aggressiveness or pleasing people. Hillel is also adept at noticing subtle changes in his patients' appearance, although he has learned to be selective in sharing such information to avoid shocking them or invading their privacy. Hillel's excellent memory also enables him to remember theoretical knowledge and techniques and apply them effectively in his therapeutic work.

Another trait that helps Hillel a lot as a therapist is his ability to meet people "where they are" in a nonjudgmental manner, understanding his patients from a "bottom-up" perspective, which is typical of autistics. Consequently, he is not afraid to work with challenging patients, including those with severe personality disorders or criminals, and he worked in prison for a period. Hillel sees all his patients as individuals in need of help and relies on rational rather than emotional reactions. This also enables him to compartmentalize his personal life from therapy without difficulty.

In therapy, Hillel is less inclined toward overt emotional expressions. For instance, when a patient expresses pain, rather than responding emotionally, he focuses on aiding him in understanding his experiences and finding ways to overcome them. However, Hillel emphasizes that this does not mean that he lacks empathy. He can genuinely identify with his patients, even sensing their physical and emotional feelings with no language, through a "primary process" mode, akin to that of animals. Hillel recounts:

> Most of my patients felt that no one has ever understood them as I did because I let things pass through my body, so that I knew them from the inside, and that's why they felt understood.

This special ability can be attributed to Hillel's proclivity to mirror-emotion or mirror-touch synesthesia, enabling him to sense other peoples' emotions and physical sensations through the body automatically, like a kind of an echo (Hill, 2022).

Alongside these special abilities, Hillel acknowledges that some autistic traits present substantial challenges for him in his work as a therapist:

Hillel's heightened sensory sensitivities present challenges, particularly his acute sense of smell, which can disrupt his concentration. For instance, he used to sense a strong acidic odor emanating from a patient with bulimia, which constantly disrupted his attention. One day, when he had a cold and his sense of smell was less acute, he felt more at ease with that patient and realized how much her acidic smell used to bother him. It should be noted that Hillel's strong sense of smell also helped him more than once in his work, as it helped him identify, for instance, patients suffering from eating disorders or from trauma only by dint of their smell. He typically waited a few minutes before addressing the issue with them so as not to astonish them. Once a patient came to Hillel for therapy to treat his anxiety attacks, and Hillel immediately recognized that his skin smelled very strongly of coffee. Hillel asked him how many cups of coffee he had been drinking a day, and he replied about 20–30, so Hillel suggested that he had better stop drinking coffee before seeking therapy, as caffeine in itself increases anxiety. The patient told Hillel that no psychiatrist had ever thought in this direction, which proved highly helpful for him.

To mitigate sensory challenges, Hillel takes measures to create a working environment that minimizes noises and replaces white or neon lights with softer yellow lighting. He also requests that patients avoid using strong perfumes or deodorants. Previously, when commuting via public transportation, Hillel would experience sensory and emotional overload, impending his ability to rely on his feelings and intuition in therapy. Since relocating closer to his clinic, he feels more attuned to his emotions and intuition.

Despite Hillel's general ability to pick up things intuitively, he has a fundamental difficulty in recognizing when his patients are untruthful. As an autistic, he tends to believe what he hears and naively assumes that patients will cooperate and speak honestly. He has also struggled to recognize when patients developed romantic feelings for him, often realizing it only through supervision.

Another autistic characteristic of Hillel is his tendency to be very direct and occasionally blunt. In the past, he would bluntly say to patients as they entered the room things like "What did you eat?" or "there's a really strange smell here," or correct their mistakes in Hebrew. Although some patients appreciated his frankness, others found it offensive. Hillel now makes an effort to moderate this tendency and communicate more tactfully.

Another challenge for Hillel as an autistic therapist is linked to his inclination to prioritize others' interests over his own, stemming from his tendency to perceive things literally and his struggle to simultaneously hold opposing interests. For example, when patients requested changes in payment or appointments, he would promptly agree without hesitation. His supervisors had to repeatedly urge him to consider different perspectives before responding to such requests.

Due to Hillel's typical difficulties with executive functions, he more than once missed giving receipts or maintaining orderly records of his meetings and more than once he scheduled double meetings. He now makes a conscious effort to prevent such situations.

Despite his autism-related difficulties, Hillel is highly regarded as an excellent therapist and is consistently fully booked. Although his supervisors have been impressed by his extraordinary skills and successes, they have also perceived him as unconventional and advised him to take better care of his physical well-being and avoid automatically aligning with patients' requests. Hillel believes that his supervisors would have understood him better if they had been aware of his autism.

In retrospect, armed with his current understanding of autism, Hillel recognizes that many of his patients were also autistic. He acknowledges that he felt a stronger connection to them compared to his neurotypical patients, who appeared more mysterious to him. This allowed him to better understand their motivations, establish significant and enduring relationships, and facilitate substantial positive changes for them. Hillel firmly believes that autistic patients are undeniably capable of deep, lasting relationships, sometimes even more so than neurotypicals.

Overall, Hillel believes that autism enhances his abilities as a therapist thanks to his heightened sensitivity, attention to detail, pattern recognition, curiosity, creativity, and a strong desire for meaningful, beneficial relationships. These qualities have enabled him to help numerous patients. However, he acknowledges that he did not adequately protect himself from sensory overloads, excessive workloads, and excessive compliance with patient requests, leading to burnout. Presently, with his growing awareness, he actively tries to address these factors.

Hillel discovered that receiving an autism diagnosis significantly contributed to a better understanding of himself and an acceptance of his diversity, which had been a source of internal struggle for most of his life. He now embraces himself more fully and is more attuned to his needs. For instance, he allows himself the agency to choose where to work, with clearer justifications for controlling his sensory environment.

GILI'S STORY

Gili, a clinical psychologist in her early forties, recently discovered her autism diagnosis. Throughout our interviews, she demonstrated remarkable intelligence, precision, and depth, using fascinating metaphors to articulate her thoughts.

Gili's parents were white-collar workers who spent long hours at work, leaving her to explore realms of imagination filled with fairies and princesses. From a young age, she displayed high intelligence and exceptional visual abilities, particularly excelling at completing complex jigsaw puzzles. All her life she has grappled with heightened sensory sensitivities and anxieties, including fears of the dark and cockroaches. Gili's parents frequently reproached her, and she internalized their anger, experiencing it as physical pain. Throughout her life, Gili has experienced physical reactions in response to others. For example, when someone mentions being hit, she immediately visualizes it and feels a corresponding physical sensation within herself. Witnessing violence or disrespect are always challenging for her. Gili describes herself as a sensitive sensor in an energy field, where negativity creates powerful vibrations within her.

Until around the age of 12, Gili perceived things almost exclusively on a sensory level, akin to a video camera, without actively processing them. However, after overhearing some friends analyzing a ballet performance, she became fascinated by the concept of assigning meaning to things. Since then, she has made it her mission to process information to comprehend it, as a jigsaw puzzle that she must assemble until it feels complete and understandable.

In school, Gili often felt bored and had challenges in concentrating and doing homework. It wasn't until the end of high school, when she decided to become a psychologist, that she studied independently for her exams and achieved very high grades. Socially, Gili had conflicting desires; she craved solitude and personal space, yet also desired to be part of a larger whole. Her involvement in the Scouts kept her busy but disconnected from her personal needs, feeling as if she were incessantly juggling. Gili was also an outstanding officer in the army, constantly in a frantic effort to catch the multiple juggling balls without being connected to her emotions.

During her university years, Gili had no learning habits; however, before exams she used to study each course's material in three days, relying on her photographic memory. She successfully earned her BA and MA in clinical psychology while caring for her ill mother. Cannabis provided her with a temporary escape from the weight of her hectic activities. Gili enjoyed her clinical studies and found great interest in her internship. However, she always longed for moments of solitude.

After completing her internship, Gili established her own independent clinic and became successful in her work. She continuously seeks to expand her knowledge in psychology, thoroughly immersing herself in learning new subjects. Gili finds the therapeutic profession well-suited for her, because she always strives to understand people and has a high capacity for empathy, exceptional listening skills, analytical ability, and keen intuition. Her intuition enables her to grasp "the psychological structure" of her patients, encompassing their deep nature, relationship, and defensive strategies. As she tends to think in pictures, she transforms patients' words into vivid images, describing them as "the treasure map of the real person." Their narratives about their homes, deeds, and dreams are automatically transformed in her mind into movies, allowing her to remember them effortlessly.

Gili has worked hard to develop her emotional abilities: about a decade ago, after her therapist had asked her what she was feeling and she could hardly answer that, Gili delved into the field of emotions and adopted learned techniques of "compassionate communication" to better identify and express her emotions. This has helped her feel more integrated and connected to her own truth and authenticity.

Gili is very sensitive to the extent to which her patients speak from their authentic selves: when a patient is connected to his inner essence and speaks from a genuine place, she senses it as an energy of life present in the room, causing her to be more present, too. Conversely, when a patient distances himself, she finds herself drawing inward. Gili describes this sensitivity as a delicate radar, gauging the depth of connection that patients have with their true essence. She often reflects these feelings back to her patients, thereby assisting them in becoming more connected to themselves.

During treatments, Gili grapples with her inclination to retreat into her inner world of images and associations ("like a vacuum that tries to suck you in") as well as with her desire to be left alone. This happens more often when she is in a negative mood. She also sometimes finds it challenging to be tolerant of her patients' psychological defenses, given her naturally honest and open disposition. Nevertheless, over time, she has learned to be more understanding and respectful of their discomfort in exposing vulnerable aspects of themselves.

Gili is primarily rational and less inclined to experience things emotionally in the presence of her patients. However, her supervisor, using mind-body psychotherapy techniques such as Hakomi, assists her in connecting with her underlying feelings toward the patients, such as empathy, care, anger, or frustration, which may be present within her during the therapeutic sessions, but in a split way, therefore not always readily accessible. Gili likens this experience to a video camera typically focused outward that is suddenly turned inward.

Because Gili tends to refrain from displaying emotional reactions in front of her patients and assumes that they come to therapy with a generally positive attitude, she is less inclined to analyze their feelings in the "here and now" or the transference and countertransference patterns. At times, she may attempt to do so in a forced manner, but overall, she perceives herself as less skilled in this aspect. However, Gili's detached stance allows her to avoid being judgmental toward her patients and to handle their negative expressions or criticisms in a constructive manner, feeling satisfied that they can express various facets in them. Moreover, Gili's affinity for the subterranean realms allows her to easily contain difficult emotions such as depression or anxiety. Due to her detached approach, she does not frequently think about her patients outside of treatment hours.

Over the past decade, Gili has undergone spiritual development, expanding her understanding of relationships beyond the human realm to an expanded relationship with the cosmos. This perspective provides her with a sense of connection, relieves her anxieties, and may be related to the autistic search for unity as a way to overcome the anxiety-inducing trauma of separation from the mother's body (Tustin, 1994). This cosmic perspective also enables her to approach her patients' processes without fear and view them as part of a larger cosmic process.

Gili highly values the depth and intimacy inherent in her work as a psychologist. The structured environment of the treatment room, with clear rules and control, allows her to manage her schedule effectively, accommodating personal needs such as sports, family time, and solitude. However, the fixed setting has exacerbated Gili's feelings of burnout, prompting her to seek a new therapeutic environment that resonates with her authenticity and truth—a quest she describes as "looking for my yellow brick road." Gili feels that as an autistic she is more worn out because her brain does not cease to process the inner and outer reality, and this is very tiring for her.

Gili expresses regret that she was not diagnosed as autistic many years earlier, believing it could have spared her years of masking and conforming to external expectations rather than prioritizing her own needs. Over the years, Gili has undergone various psychological treatments that helped her in connecting with her feelings but did not fully address her difficulties, which she now understands are related to autism. She feels that gaining a deeper understanding of her autism has brought clarity to the intricate puzzle of her life. Gili is still at the beginning of the process, often amazed to realize that others do not experience things as she does ("Don't you see everything people tell you like in a movie?"). This ongoing discovery marks the beginning of her journey toward deeper self-awareness.

RUTH'S STORY

Ruth is a 50-year-old clinical social worker. She grew up in Jerusalem as the second of three children. As a child, she had a quiet, curious temperament, enjoying watching TV and learning to read at a preschool age. In kindergarten, she often felt more mature than her peers, preferring adult conversations over their games. She experienced sensory sensitivities and anxieties typical of autism, such as fear of darkness, doctors, and imagined creatures. In elementary school, Ruth excelled academically but struggled to fit in socially, often spending breaks alone in the library, engrossed in books about the Holocaust or fantasy literature. At age 12, her autistic brother once violated her boundaries, leaving her emotionally hurt. She did not tell her parents because she took his warning literally that they would never let him come back home if she did.

Ruth attended a high school for the gifted, where she finally found like-minded peers with whom she could bond over shared interests such as logic puzzles, musicals, and Beatles songs. Despite executive function challenges, she excelled in her matriculation exams, always studying at the last minute.

During her bachelor's and master's degrees in social work, Ruth managed her tendency to procrastinate with self-help books and many lists and reminders. She did her practical training at a shelter for battered women, where she showcased her caring nature and ability to act calmly and logically in crisis situations. However, she often overextended herself due to her high concern for her patients, and her blunt communication style strained workplace relationships. Successful therapy helped her navigate these challenges. Ruth often felt exhausted after work and spent many hours in bed, frequently watching the series *Friends* over and over.

(Interestingly, I found that many autistics are drawn to this show. Initially, I thought it was because it offers opportunities to learn about social skills and relationships. However, an autistic patient once told me that the show's appeal for him lay in the fact that each main character exhibits autistic traits—such as Ross's intense fascination with dinosaurs; Phoebe's dreamy, associative nature; Monica's compulsive need for order; and Rachel's frequent clumsiness and cluelessness. I guess that this unique blend of sociable and autistic models of behavior may be the secret to the show's popularity among autistics, along with the predictable yet amusing behaviors and reactions of each character that create a sense of comfort and understanding for the viewers.)

For the past 10 years, Ruth has been working as a clinical social worker in a mental health clinic, often handling the most difficult and complex cases, especially those involving sexual assault survivors. She continually learns new therapy techniques, boosting her confidence in her professional efficacy and helping her patients in creative ways. She listens attentively to her patients, providing high acceptance, understanding, and empathy, often feeling over-empathy for her patients' concerns after therapy hours. Although Ruth struggles with dynamic aspects such as interpreting the nuances of transference, she has an intuitive perception of her patients' emotions, which her supervisor helps her verbalize after sessions.

Ruth believes that autism provides her with many advantages in her work as a therapist, alongside several challenges: she is often bothered by the smells of others' foods and by noises in the clinic and is frequently startled by knocks on her office door, struggling to refocus afterward. She finds small talk with colleagues very challenging and often overshares personal information, such as her former borderline personality disorder diagnosis, which she later understood was given mistakenly instead of the correct autism diagnosis. Ruth also struggles with bureaucratic tasks, and when she finally manages to write reports, they are always too long. These challenges contribute to her frequent sense of burnout, prompting her to take many days off to recharge through solitary activities such as watching TV, reading, or listening to podcasts.

About three years ago, after her child was diagnosed as autistic, Ruth realized that she was autistic, too. This realization brought her a high sense of relief and self-acceptance. Since then, autism has become a focal point of her interest, and she continues to gain extensive knowledge on the subject. She also joined various Facebook groups for autistics and was happy to find validation and resonance in them.

This newfound awareness of her autism has also catalyzed a significant professional transformation for Ruth: she now aspires to focus on supporting autistics, providing affirmative treatments, and running support groups for them. Ruth states,

> There is so much to do in this area, so many people who can be helped by raising their awareness and helping them to embrace their autism. I would have been so happy if someone like me had helped me through all these years when I felt so different from everyone else and felt that no one could understand me. I feel that we live in a special period, where many autistics discover their true psychological identity and need help in empowering them to embrace their new identity and to define and realize their own goals. I see this and advocating for autistics' rights as a most important and fascinating personal mission for me.

AUTISTICS' STRENGTHS AND CHALLENGES IN THE THERAPEUTIC PROFESSION

I will now outline the major advantages and challenges that autistics may encounter in their careers as therapists, drawing from the evidence provided above and additional sources.

Typical Strengths

The Human Psyche as a "Special Interest"—Many autistics have a special interest in the human psyche, which may become their favorite field of study, in which they may accumulate lots of knowledge. Many of them are keen observers of human behaviors in real life as well as in books, movies, and TV series. Many autistics are interested in psychological disorders, including autism, or in deciphering the complexities of human cruelty, evident in a frequent special interest in wars, crime, and historical events such as the

Holocaust. Autistic therapists demonstrate genuine curiosity in their patients' lives, actively seeking to comprehend their inner motives.

High Intuition and Sensitivity—Despite their challenges in deciphering social cues, many autistics possess heightened intuition and sensibility. Some of them are endowed with a special ability, present in about 2% of the general population, to feel other people's emotional and physical sensations within their own bodies: this phenomenon, known as "mirror-emotion or mirror-touch synesthesia," refers to the ability to sense emotional and physical sensations automatically, as a kind of an echo (Hill, 2022). In the case of "mirror-touch synesthesia," individuals may feel physical sensations in the same body part as the person in front of them. For instance, Hill describes a therapist who experienced dizziness or throat constriction, or visualized specific images immediately upon a patient's entry, aligning with the patient's condition (Hill, 2022).

Heightened Empathy—Contrary to common beliefs, autistics typically have high levels of compassion and emotional empathy, also known as "hyper-empathy" (Hill, 2022; Smith, 2009). Autistic therapists may deeply empathize with their patients' difficulties, sometimes drawing from their own struggles with anxiety, depression, and trauma. They may also obsess with their patients' problems outside therapy hours due to their extreme empathy and proclivity for overthinking. In contrast, some autistic therapists easily disconnect and would not think about their patients outside their designated working hours.

Keen Attention to Details and Exceptional Pattern Recognition—Many autistics are endowed with remarkable aptitude for observing minute details and recognizing recurrent patterns (Baron-Cohen et al., 2009; Gollwitzer et al., 2019). These assets may sometimes be considered as hyperawareness, hyper-perception and hyper-memory (Hill, 2022). In psychotherapy these attributes empower autistic therapists to discern subtle nuances and changes in their patients' behaviors, as well as identify repetitive patterns, all of which play a pivotal role in an effective psychological treatment.

Problem-Solving Skills—Autistics may excel in problem solving, leveraging their ability to analyze multiple data, focus on details, and identify patterns in their patients' behaviors. In addition, their unique perspective, unbound by conventional frameworks, allows them to provide solutions tailored to each patient's specific circumstances, often offering unconventional and creative approaches. Moreover, their capacity to calmly navigate emergency situations, stemming from their inclination to separate emotion from reason, can prove highly beneficial for patients in tense circumstances.

Elevated Self-Awareness—Many autistics exhibit a heightened level of self-observance, driven by their innate inclination to seek truth. Their heightened self-awareness is an asset in the therapeutic professions, enabling them to meticulously monitor their own reactions and behaviors, thereby enhancing their effectiveness as therapists.

High Ethical Standards—Autistics most often uphold elevated ethical standards and possess a genuine desire to help and to contribute their knowledge for the betterment of others.

Mastering Communication Skills—Autistic therapists frequently excel in mastering the fundamental principles of effective communication with their patients, as the guidelines in this realm are generally clear (e.g., how and when to initiate a conversation, respond, commence and conclude meetings, etc.), and in this way they conscientiously adopt behaviors that neurotypical therapists may perform more instinctively. They can become adept listeners (see Baker & Shelly, 2015) and engage in deep conversations, showing a preference for and excelling in meaningful conversations over small talk.

An Accepting, Nonjudgmental Approach—Because autistics are not prone to look at things through conventional lenses, they tend to present an accepting, nonjudgmental approach toward their patients. They may also be willing to work with individuals who have severe disorders or disabilities that other therapists are more hesitant to work with. Drawing from personal experiences, they can suggest coping strategies and deeper understanding of the needs of autistic patients and their families.

Beyond these personality traits, autistics may be attracted to the therapeutic vocation due to the independent work environment, flexible hours, and the ability to control sensory stimuli in the clinic, such as lights, sounds, and smells.

Typical Challenges

Alongside their valuable assets, autistic therapists may encounter typical challenges throughout their studies, training, and work as therapists. These include:

In their studies and training, autistics may succeed due to their keen interest, high intelligence, and good memory. However, they must overcome typical difficulties with executive functions, sensory sensitivities, getting along with colleagues, and more.

While searching for a job, autistics may struggle with executive function difficulties, which may manifest, for example, in procrastination in sending letters, making phone calls, or completing forms. In addition, they may face hurdles in successfully navigating job interviews.

In shared work environments, autistic therapists must navigate various challenges, such as deciphering the implicit rules of behavior in interpersonal interactions. They may also tend to criticize the system or other staff members too bluntly or undiplomatically. Difficulties in emotion regulation can lead them to emotional overwhelm, burnout, and shutdowns. Sensory sensitivities to noises, lights, or smells can also pose challenges.

Autistics also must deal with a series of difficulties and challenges related to the therapeutic work itself: they should be mindful of potential communication pitfalls, such as being too silent or talking too excessively. They should avoid being blunt, offensive, or one-dimensional toward their patients. They should also be aware of the danger of being emotionally dysregulated, which may be expressed, for example, in overconcern, over-vulnerability, or unregulated anger. Conversely, due to their inclination toward extremes of either excessive emotional engagement or excessive rationality, autistics may also experience or display emotional detachment or aloofness. Another danger lies in relying too heavily on techniques, questionnaires, and external criteria rather than genuine human responses. Missing cues such as body language, facial expressions, or insinuations can also be a challenge. Recognizing manipulations or lies may also be difficult for them.

Another danger lies in autistics' tendency to overextend themselves by taking on excessive workloads, being constantly reachable, or continuously pursing further education, leading to exhaustion and burnout.

Another kind of difficulty lies in autistics' high sensory sensitivities: autistic therapists can be easily distracted by smells (e.g., many cannot stand body odors or potent perfumes), strong lights (such as neon lights), noises, or textures that their patients may bring.

CONCLUDING REMARKS

The chapter highlighted the assets and challenges that autistics bring to the field of psychotherapy. To address the challenges, autistic therapists are encouraged to pursue a formal autism diagnosis, fostering a deeper understanding of their strengths and challenges and facilitating the development of effective coping strategies. It is recommended that they work on enhancing their interpretation of nonverbal cues, establishing clearer boundaries, refining communication skills to be less blunt and more nuanced, cultivating flexibility and emotional support and emotional regulation without neglecting personal interests. Self-awareness, supervision, or collaboration with colleagues can aid in this process.

Autistic therapists may also grapple with the dilemma of whether to disclose their autism openly with patients and colleagues. Unfortunately, societal prejudices and limited awareness about autism can lead to criticism or disdain in certain environments. The hope is for societal understanding and acceptance to evolve, recognizing the myriad advantages that autistic therapists bring to the profession.

Overall, many autistic therapists feel that autism provides them with more advantages than disadvantages as therapists, and some even view it as a kind of superpower (Hill, 2022; Pretorius, 2020; Englebrecht, 2020). The narratives above illustrate how adept autistic therapists can be in their field.

Chapter 3

Autistic Musicians

> For me, music is not just about sounds; it serves as a gateway to entire worlds . . . Music floods me with emotions, feelings, thoughts, insights, images, situations . . . I find myself captivated by a brief musical line for weeks and enter a whole world through it. Eventually, this little line may become the seed of a huge creation. (Amit, an autistic musician, cited below)

Studies indicate that many autistics possess heightened musical skills and have a strong attraction to music (Masataka, 2017; Wenhart et al., 2019; Heaton, 2009). Already Leo Kanner, who was one of the first to describe high-functioning autism contemporaneously with Hans Asperger, pointed out that 6 of the 11 children he diagnosed with autism displayed exceptional musical talents. Autistics may exhibit musical abilities such as absolute or relative hearing, proficiency with musical instruments, the ability to memorize and play entire pieces by heart, sometimes even only after one hearing, and more.

Research on the musical talents of autistics has centered predominantly around absolute hearing, denoting the ability to accurately recognize musical sounds without external cues. Numerous studies indicate a high prevalence of absolute hearing among autistics (see a summary of studies in Wenhart et al., 2019). This musical aptitude has been attributed to factors such as heightened perceptual function (Stanutz et al., 2014; Brown et al., 2003; Masataka, 2017), a detail-oriented cognitive style (Stanutz et al., 2014; Wenhart et al., 2019; Mottron et al., 2006), a strong memory, and either over-connectivity or under-connectivity between different brain areas (see Wenhart et al., 2019; Bouvet et al., 2014). In addition, musical tendencies have been linked to the dominance of the right hemisphere, which is associated with associativity and creativity, particularly in the realm of music (Lyons & Fitzgerald, 2012).

Although many autistics possess high musical skills, among them are also those who lack musical ability, a condition known as amusia (see Dohn et al., 2012; Wenhart et al., 2019), aligning with autistics' broader tendency to exhibit extremes, apparently stemming from over-connectivity or under-connectivity in their brains.

Autistics' attraction to music often manifests as a special interest in the field, leading them to devote significant time to listening, acquiring knowledge, or creating music. Some autistics choose to pursue music professionally, taking on roles as singers, instrumentalists, composers, producers, conductors, or music therapists. Noteworthy musicians diagnosed with autism include David Byrne, Lady Hawk, Courtney Love, Eminem, Gary Numan, Craig Nichols, Travis Meeks, Marty Balin, James Durbin, Susan Boyle, and others. In addition, historical figures such as Glenn Gould, Mozart, or Beethoven, are believed to have been autistic (Fitzgerald, 2005; Bryar, 2015). It is likely that numerous autistic musicians remain undiagnosed due to underdiagnosis of autism.

Despite the notable prevalence of autistic musicians, the absence of studies that delve into their experiences with music is notable. Although studies conducted by Bakan (2018) and Bryar (2015) offer insights through interviews with small samples of autistic musicians, a clear need exists for more extensive and comprehensive research in this domain.

To explore the connection between autistics and music, I conducted a group discussion with three talented autistic Israeli musicians, for whom music is a central focus in their lives. The joint conversation allowed for collaborative brainstorming, in which I presented general questions, and each musician shared his or her unique perspective.

I will briefly introduce these three musicians, who have chosen to remain anonymous:

Amit, a young woman of approximately 30 years, has exhibited extraordinary musical talents alongside high intelligence and creativity since her early years. Proficient in playing multiple instruments, she excels as a singer, songwriter, composer, and music producer. Amit earned a prestigious music degree from a renowned European university and received her autism diagnosis about a year ago.

Rotem, in her early thirties, demonstrated a natural affinity for singing, playing, and composing from an early age. Possessing perfect pitch and skilled in various instruments, Rotem holds multiple music degrees, including one in classical music. She currently engages in composing, singing, playing, and teaching music. She received her autism diagnosis approximately two years ago.

Ron, in his mid-fifties, has harbored a deep connection to music throughout his life, dedicating most of his time and energy to it. A seasoned performer in well-known ensembles in Israel, he works as a singer, instrumentalist, songwriter, composer, music producer, and critic. Ron is widely revered as one of the most esteemed musicians in Israel and received his autism diagnosis about a year ago.

We gathered in the summer of 2022 at a beautiful house in the Tel Aviv area. The ensuing conversation was remarkably engaging, as the musicians gave candid, insightful responses that provided a glimpse into their profound experiences with music. I was particularly impressed by their ability to articulate profound insights effortlessly on the first try, often enriched with vivid examples or captivating imagery. Contrary to common misconceptions about autistics, they displayed remarkable focus for many hours and listened attentively to each other which can be attributed to their truth-seeking and preference for deep conversations rather than superficial small talk. Noteworthy was the observation that everyone appeared about 10 years younger than their actual age, as observed in many autistics. In the room, there were also stuffed dolls for stimming, and one participant found relaxation in holding a guitar as well. At least one animal was present to contribute to the sense of well-being.

SPECIAL MUSICAL SKILLS

Sagit: Could you share your musical skills and abilities? This may include aspects like perfect pitch, synesthesia, or a robust memory for musical pieces.

Ron: I don't believe I possess perfect pitch. It's a skill that typically develops with early-age guidance, and without that, it might not naturally develop. Personally, when tuning a guitar, I always appreciate having a tuner on hand.

Amit: I don't have perfect pitch either, but I do have a relative hearing.

Rotem: I do have a perfect pitch. I was tested for it as a child. Besides, I have a really good memory of musical pieces. All my recitals were performed from memory.

Ron: I also have a strong memory for musical pieces. On numerous occasions, I've heard a song just once and retained it in my memory for an extended period. For example, I once heard a particular song at a concert which I really liked and couldn't find it on any of the band's albums, and 15 years later I interviewed the singer and hummed that song to him, much to his surprise.

Rotem: I have synesthesia—I see music in colors. For me, for example, C is blue and D is green, in all kinds of shades.

Ron: Is C in the same blue in every octave?

Rotem: No. In different octaves it will be in different shades of blue.

Sagit: I met an autistic musician who has synesthesia, and images automatically translate in her mind into music. She leverages this extraordinary gift as a film composer, and her success in this field is truly awe-inspiring. She herself refers to it as a superpower.

Amit: For me, music is not just about sounds; it serves as a gateway to entire worlds. I find myself captivated by a brief musical line for weeks and enter a whole world through it. It's a very spiritual experience. That line holds deep meanings for me, like a story, and I can adhere to it for weeks or more. Then it may become the seed for a huge creation.

Ron: I deeply relate to what you just said. Sometimes a combination of a few notes carries a certain energy that gets me captivated, and I feel that there is a song surrounding it. I once sat with a musician friend and I was stuck on two notes that I replayed over and over, till she was freaked out. Those 2–3 seconds were for me the seed for a complete work. Likewise, when I produce music, very often parts of a song get stuck in my head, looping for a day or two.

Rotem: I can also get stuck on a musical line for hours. Sometimes, I consciously choose not to develop certain lines further and leave them as they are because they carry so much meaning for me.

Ron: I've maintained since a young age that musical pieces can be as short as 10–15 seconds.

Amit: I agree.

Rotem: I carry musical ideas within me for 10 years or more, each carrying significant meanings for me and serving as a creative anchor. This is quite beneficial for me, as a kind of a psychological therapy.

Amit: It's exactly the same for me. There are certain lines or sounds that I always go back to when I want to get back "to my zone." When I was a child, I had many difficulties and didn't know how to express them, but then I came to my guitar and played those simple chords over and over again, and they provided me with both emotional and sensory regulation, like a psychological treatment, or a kind of a mantra or meditation.

Rotem: Musitation.

[All nod in agreement.]

SELF-TEACHING VERSUS FORMAL TEACHING

Sagit: I've noticed that many autistics learn to play instruments on their own.

Ron: Yes, when I was a kid, my brother taught me a few things on the guitar, and from there, I continued on my own. I never learned formally.

Amit: I taught myself to play the guitar as a child. I'm not good with organized systems; though I was considered talented in high school, it was challenging for me to attend classes or to practice. Besides, because it's important for me to always tell the truth, I was perceived as blunt or tactless, particularly during my studies abroad. My unfiltered responses lowered my grades, despite being one of the top students in my class.

Sagit: I have noticed that many autistics tend not to read sheet music. What are your thoughts on this?

Ron: After my brother showed me how to play the guitar, I became accustomed to playing without sheet music, and since then, I don't need it.

Rotem: Same for me.

Sagit: Is it because you have challenges in reading notes or maybe you see it as unnecessary, or is it too difficult for you to do multiple tasks simultaneously?

Rotem: The music is in my head, so I don't see the need to look at the notes.

Amit: Perhaps many people, not just autistics, don't feel the need to read from sheets?

Rotem: Yes, but I have also found that many autistics encounter difficulties in learning notes. I've come across it frequently with my students.

REPETITIVE MOVEMENTS

Sagit: For you, does playing music involve an element of repetitive movements or stimming?

Everyone: Yes.

Rotem: Sometimes people ask me why I don't use specs while playing the guitar, and I explain that I need to feel the guitar with my fingers. Even when I don't feel like playing, I hold my guitar and move my fingers on it.

Ron: I also need to feel the guitar and to make movements. Sometimes I make movements on my guitar while watching TV, and then I stop the TV to listen to what I just played. I used to play while chatting with people, but then I realized that it was offensive to them, so I stopped.

Amit: I stim with my voice, as this is my instrument. I often repeat phrases or words because I feel compelled to. Words come to my mind all the time even with no connection to music.

Rotem: I read that repeating words involuntarily is called "musical behavior," even if it's not directly related to music.

Amit: When I ride my scooter, words come to my mind all the time, and I can't stop muttering to myself. Luckily people think I'm talking on my cellphone.

Rotem: Words always jump to my mind while shopping at the supermarket.

Ron: It happens to me, too, both at the supermarket and while riding my bike. I keep saying words or singing, and sometimes it can be very embarrassing, so I pretend I was just humming a song.

Amit: Even when I'm alone at home, I talk to myself a lot.

Ron: At times, I find myself concerned that someday someone will invent a time machine that will come around and see me humming to myself.

LOOKING FOR THE BEAT

Sagit: Autistics are often drawn to rhythm or beat, which has a calming effect on them. Do you experience that?

Rotem: Yes, I constantly tap my body to the beat.

Amit: From a very young age, I was drawn to drumming on things or on myself. I have a strong sense of rhythm. Even my stimming is more musical and rhythmical compared to others.

Ron: I also make drumming movements all the time. Rhythm is the foundation of music for me, and my ideas often start out from rhythm. However, my coordination is not so great, so I wouldn't fare well with a drum set.

Rotem: I'm actually a very good drummer. I'm immensely attracted to rhythm and can discern it in diverse contexts. For instance, I can recognize rhythms in birds' chirping or even my cat's drinking.

[Ron and Amit nod with identification.]

Amit: I'm generally clumsy and struggle with both gross and fine motor skills. However, when I play the guitar, I have no problems or awkwardness at all.

WAYS OF EXPERIENCING MUSIC

Sagit: Do you think you experience music differently from non-autistic individuals?

Amit: Music overwhelms me with emotions and brings up vivid images, stories, and memories in me. When I hear a song, I imagine an entire event. And when I return later to that song, it's as if I was returning to the same event. So, music is for me an entire world, flooding me with emotions, physical sensations, thoughts, and insights.

Ron: For me, too, music is much more than music. It automatically translates in my mind into figures, landscapes, and stories. I convert musical pieces into narratives. Sometimes I share those with musicians who work with me.

Rotem: I resonate deeply with that. When I listen to music, it activates all my senses and takes me to various places. Music also helps me gain new insights: in my everyday life, I often struggle to understand situations, but when I listen to music, it makes me reflect on things and improves my understanding. When I want to know how I feel about something, I often turn to music as it helps me gain insight.

Sagit: Can you give an example, please?

Rotem: Last Wednesday, I found myself in a social situation where I wasn't sure if I had been too blunt or not, and it left me feeling upset. On my way home, I listened to the song "I Worry," and it helped me reflect on myself from a more compassionate perspective and move forward.

Sagit: Can you describe how music evokes emotions in you?

Rotem: In everyday life, my emotions are all mixed up, but through music I can feel each emotion distinctly. Music separates and intensifies emotions, allowing me to experience them more strongly.

Amit: I can relate to this completely. For me, too, everyday life is like a fan of emotions, stirring in me many feelings and past experiences. For example, at a friend's wedding, if I am happy, there are always many other emotions present, and it can be overwhelming. In music, on the other hand, there are pure emotions.

Sagit: I'm just trying to understand better—you said that in everyday experiences your feelings are always mixed, but isn't music a kind of a human experience as well?

Rotem: I think music is something more absolute.

Amit: Yes, music is more objective and purer, without all the complexities of interpersonal relationships. It's also easier to gain insights through sounds than through words.

Ron: I can be immensely overwhelmed by a song. I often experience a mix of strong emotions, such as an intense energy, sadness, and amazement at the beauty of the song, all at once. I believe that music evokes something very pure within me, a force that is both energetic and emotionally intense. It also evokes emotions and memories. About once every two or three months, a musical piece can completely overwhelm me, and I'm grateful that no one sees me. I may even shed tears because it's so beautiful and deeply moving.

Amit: I also experience emotions through music in a profound way. It floods me with insights, feelings, memories, tastes, smells, and hopes. I lose track of time. It helps me put things in perspective, as Rotem described before.

Sagit: Is there a difference in the way you experience instrumental music versus the way you experience music with lyrics?

Ron: Over 95% of the music I create starts as instrumental, and even when words are incorporated, I treat them as another layer of music. The goal is always the music. Turning it into a song with lyrics is more challenging for me. That's why I often collaborate with writers who connect with my music. Sometimes I leave the music instrumental, with no lyrics. Many of my songs have a significant instrumental part.

Rotem: As a child, words were like music to me. I reacted to their tangible qualities and found repetition highly amusing.

Sagit: This may be related to autistics' tendency to experience words through "primary processes," that is, to relate to their outer qualities rather than their inner meanings.

Rotem: Yes. Instrumental music was easier for me to understand compared to words that were meant to take me to places that I didn't always comprehend. Only as I grew older and understood word meanings better could I relate more to lyrics' meanings. Music with words can help me a lot when I need to organize emotional situations. When I write, I usually combine melody and words in a holistic process. Sometimes words come first, and other times the melody comes first—there is no fixed pattern.

Amit: For me it depends on my mood. On one hand, I have a strong need for words. On the other hand, when I listen to rich instrumental music, like classical music or jazz, which has multiple layers and instruments, it can take me to spiritual places and help me regulate my emotions. For example, today I was bothered by many things, and listening to classical music in my car calmed me down. Sometimes that's all I want. When I was a child, my parents pushed me to listen to classical music, which created some resistance in me, but I'm trying to overcome that now. On the other hand, the intellectual side in me often needs words. Sometimes music alone is very meaningful to me, but to really express how I feel I have to add words.

Rotem: Music helps me get into certain roles. For instance, two weeks ago, I had to give a lecture that made me fearful. After practicing many times what I would say and how to say it, I listened to the song "Giant Heart," and it really helped me to connect to the feeling of being part of the world. Then, I came to the lecture as a different person and was able to do the masking much more easily.

Amit: Music takes me out of the need to mask. It's a world without masking.

Ron: For me, too. However, I use music to relax before meetings or interviews, especially extreme and energetic music.

Sagit: Do you feel that you express emotions through music?

Rotem: I struggle with expressing emotions outside of music, because for me they are always mixed together. Through music I can express emotions in a neurotypical way—that is, separately.

Ron: For me, playing music is a necessity, ever since I have started playing. I can't go a day without playing. If I'm on vacation without a guitar, I'll usually buy one. It's a genuine need.

Rotem: I feel the same way. A vacation without playing is a punishment for me.

Amit: I can do without a guitar because my voice is my instrument, so I always have it with me.

UNDERSTANDING AND EVALUATING MUSICAL WORKS

Sagit: Do you believe your understanding of music aligns with that of neurotypicals, particularly in deciphering the intentions of the artists?

Rotem: I believe I can understand no less than neurotypicals. I once participated in a study that tested this, and my answers were similar to those of the other participants. In fact, I believe I can recognize more complexities than others can.

Sagit: How good are you at evaluating other people's music?

Amit: Songs take me through processes and evoke emotions within me. Others may judge if a piece is beautiful or interesting, but for me it's a holistic experience.

Sagit: I'm trying to understand if your assessments would have reliability and potential objectivity. For example, would there be an agreement between different assessors?

Rotem: I feel that there will be an agreement between us.

Amit: We can identify if something is ordinary or unique and expresses something significant. I think this is an important criterion for art.

Ron: I agree. I used to work as a music critic, and I believe I did well in that role.

Amit: Same here. People often seek my opinions on music.

Rotem: People also consult with me a lot.

MUSICAL PREFERENCES

Sagit: Let's talk about musical preferences. I would start with a question that has been bothering me for a while, regarding the relationship between autistics and jazz music: I know autistics who really love jazz music while I know others can't stand it. What are your thoughts on this?

Amit: I studied jazz music, but it didn't always resonate with me. For me the problem with jazz is that it requires too many executive functions—you need to acquire lots of knowledge and techniques and learn many rules and obey them in order to play jazz—and that doesn't appeal to me.

Sagit: I thought that jazz was more about improvisation?

Amit: Yes, but improvisation is within certain rules and patterns. As a student, you have to follow specific rules when improvising. This didn't suit me. Sometimes I enjoy listening to jazz music, but at other times I find it too sophisticated or trying too hard to be sophisticated. I prefer simplicity.

Ron: I don't connect to jazz. The only times I enjoyed jazz were at live concerts, simply because I love live performances. A friend once took me to a jazz concert, and I liked it, but afterwards, when he sent me the CD, it didn't evoke any emotions in me. I don't understand the rules or harmonies of jazz.

Rotem: I don't like jazz either. I can appreciate the music and the musicians, but the unexpected changes in jazz are beyond my comfort zone. For me it's too unpredictable, and it can even make me cry.

Ron: I feel the same way. Jazz has too many unexpected elements for my taste. I prefer a more repetitive and minimalistic music.

Rotem: Another aspect of jazz that I don't like is its heavy reliance on communication between the players. There are moments when everyone plays together, while at other times each player does their own thing. It's too challenging and difficult for me to understand. Jazz, to me, feels like a foreign and incomprehensible language. Sometimes I sympathize and identify with it, as I am an outsider myself, but the unclear and undefined flow can really bother me. It also sometimes feels like a kind of self-indulgence on stage.

Amit: Yes, there is an expression for it—"swinging the Mickeys."

Sagit: How do you feel about trance, house, and techno music?

Amit: The noise bothers me, and I don't connect with it.

Rotem: I feel the same way.

Ron: I can't understand the appeal of it either. However, a peculiar incident occurred to me recently. I experimented with a very small amount of MD

[MDMA; psychoactive drug] and noticed a significant reduction in my social anxiety, along with a decrease in other autistic characteristics, similar to the effects of medication. Interestingly, while under the influence, I heard trance music from a nearby house, and for the first time in my life, I could enjoy the trance experience.

Rotem: I've read about MD helping with social anxiety, but I steer clear of drugs.

Ron: Absolutely, it's risky, and I have no intention of continuing. Yet, it was like an experiment that provided me insights into the relationship between autism and a distaste for trance music, and vice versa.

Sagit: Maybe autistics dislike this kind of music because it's too technical, as they are often more drawn to things closer to nature. I think exploring autistics' preferences in music could be quite fascinating. Now, what genres do you enjoy?

Amit: I appreciate music of high quality, regardless of genre. It can be Oriental, pop, indie, classical, jazz, or folk music, or specific songs by various artists in different languages. The important thing is that it meets the criteria of being unique and of high quality.

Ron: I, too, cannot say that I have a preference for specific genres. There are certain qualities that touch me, and they can be found in any genre. Even in regard to a specific band I may only like some specific songs. I don't have sentimental attachments to any band or genre. I judge everything based on its merits.

Sagit: This may be related to the fact that autistics do not judge things based on preconceptions, just as they do not judge people by their origin, age, or status.

Amit: Yes, I just wanted to say that we judge music regardless of religion, race, or gender.

Ron: Aren't all musicians like that?

Sagit: I think neurotypicals are less open to listening to different genres.

Rotem: I also think that neurotypicals tend to stick to genres they already know. My musical taste, too, is very broad but specific. I listen to a variety of genres, but I like specific works based on their quality. I grew up on classical music, but now I listen to many genres, like indie, rock, Balkan music, and more. I consider myself open-minded but always seeking high quality.

Ron: I also value diversity. In my role as a DJ, I blend songs from various eras and styles. Another phenomenon I've noticed since being diagnosed as autistic is my tendency to go down a "rabbit hole" after encountering certain artists or songs. Once I discover a new song that captures my interest, I become utterly obsessed. I start reading extensively about the singer or band and listen to all their songs. This deep immersion can persist for weeks.

Rotem: I, too, do a lot of research about singers I like and often listen to all their songs. In high school, I was particularly obsessed with The Beatles and Edith Piaf. I even went as far as learning complete songs by heart in French without even understanding the language.

Amit: I also had extreme obsessions. In high school, I knew everything about The Rebels, Nirvana, and Avril Lavigne. I would search for information about them on the internet, not only about their music but also about their personal lives and culture. I would even dress like them, sing like them, and fill my room with posters of them. I still have similar obsessions today with singers I like.

COOPERATING WITH OTHER PEOPLE

Sagit: What are your experiences working with others in the field of music?

Amit: It can be both fun and challenging for me. I bring enthusiasm and high energy, but I might come across as difficult and domineering, as I tend to focus on small details, and others may perceive me as rigid or arrogant. I demand a lot from my coworkers and may impose my methods. Sometimes, my mind wanders during rehearsals, and others may get frustrated when I disconnect. However, I also inspire people and create unique experiences with them through music, forming meaningful friendships.

Ron: Working with other musicians has its ups and downs for me. On one hand, I enjoy collaborating with others who resonate with my vibe and provide a platform for inspiration. But there are certain challenges. I prefer playing with minimal breaks, which can be difficult for others. In band meetings, if someone shouts, I get up and leave the room because it's unbearable for me. Or sometimes I get tired and need to sleep. And sometimes I may remain silent for hours. I fear hurting others with my words as I sometimes say things I later regret. I often feel very problematic and wonder how people manage to get along with me. I often experience intense internal dramas, but I usually keep them to myself.

Amit: I always strive to speak the truth, but it can be hard when it hurts people I care about.

Rotem: I feel the same way. I try to find ways to express things in a less offensive manner.

Ron: I've noticed that people often appreciate honesty, but it can be overwhelming for some.

Rotem: I've also discovered that people appreciate honesty. Over time, I've learned to express myself in a way that is less objectionable.

Amit: My problem is that I can't stay silent, and I always feel the need to warn about problems or dangers, and sometimes it's too much for other people. For example, in my current job I criticize the system too often, and I know that it may make me lose my job.

Sagit: I have noticed this is often the primary reason why autistics lose their jobs.

Ron: Another aspect related to honesty is that people often seek my opinion on their work, and I consistently offer honest feedback, even if it may be difficult to hear. For instance, if I think they are not "baked enough," I always tell them that and explain in detail how it can be improved. I know that other people may produce such stuff and charge lots of money for it, but I don't want to take advantage of other people's lack of awareness.

Rotem: I also provide honest feedback, sometimes brutally so. I believe that being a musician requires dedication and talent, and not everyone is cut out for it. I am also much more meticulous about small things than other people. When I had a band, if the performances weren't going perfectly according to my plans, I could be quite hard with the other band members. When I teach young students, I'm very stringent about how they put their hands on the guitar and in what angle, and I can stop everything and tell someone, "Can you please tune your C?"

Ron: I am also very strict about details. There are things that drive me crazy that no one else even notices.

Rotem: Musical communication is much easier for me than verbal communication. If we could not talk but just play, it would be much easier for us, since it is much easier for us to communicate through the language of music.

Amit: Exactly. In speech, each word may carry several meanings and may seem unclear to me, but in music having several meanings is fine with me.

Rotem: When I was the head of a band playing my materials, I was unbearable, as I was always dissatisfied with what happened during rehearsals. After each rehearsal, I felt enormously tensed and couldn't understand why—it was before I was diagnosed with autism, so I couldn't understand that it was because of my autism—and I constantly felt guilty and blamed myself for destroying everything, and it really drained all my energy. Over time, I learned to express myself in a less rigid manner and to consider others' emotions, too, and not just the musical piece; however, it required lots of energy and attention on my part.

Ron: I also have a part in me that seeks perfection, but I also have another part in me that tries to help others make the most out of themselves. My perfectionism is both in paying attention to details and in receiving energy from other people and letting others express themselves, too.

Amit: I also know how to bring out the best in people. I ask them to "learn my language and improvise within it"—that is, to express themselves in my world.

Ron: Exactly.

Rotem: It's like allowing others to enter your cocoon.

Ron: When people try to play my pieces, they often tell me at first that they are too difficult because they lack symmetry or conventional harmonies. I don't understand what they are talking about, because they seem easy to me, but then, after I explain to them the repeating parts and other aspects, they suddenly grasp it, get into it, and love it.

Amit: Our compositions may seem complex to others in terms of harmony and rhythm because our thinking is different. Yet, for us, it feels natural and easy.

Rotem: Our stuff may appear complex to others, but we perceive it as simple.

Amit: Once, during a high-school harmony class, my teacher gazed at what I had written for a few minutes, visibly shocked, and then said, "It really goes against the rules, but it's so incredibly creative."

Rotem: I had a strikingly similar experience in high-school harmony class. I always had problems doing homework, as my mind was always wandering in various directions, but once I presented something I had written, and the teacher played it in front of the class, and said, "It's totally different from what you were supposed to do, but it's stunning."

Ron: I used to play with a bassist who had a strong classical background. When I once showed him a new song that I had written, he said, "What you wrote is really illegal harmonically, but it is so beautiful."

Sagit: How would you describe the music you make in terms of innovation versus repetition?

Ron: I aim for each project to be entirely different, reflecting the changes happening in my life.

Rotem: I also strive for diversity in my music, but being strongly rooted in classical music, there are always some repeating sequences, too, but always with variations.

Amit: I also incorporate recurring motifs in my music, but I also introduce twists and creativity.

Sagit: Autistics shouldn't be stereotyped as only repetitive, as they possess a great deal of creativity.

PLAYING IN FRONT OF AN AUDIENCE

Sagit: How do you feel about performing in front of an audience?

Ron: In the beginning, it was incredibly difficult for me to play or sing in front of even one person. It felt like a nightmare, filled with anxieties such as audience anxiety, performance anxiety, and social anxiety. I was using alcohol to cope with the stress. But after years of performing, I started to enjoy it. I still experience some stress, but I am much happier on stage now compared to before. However, the administrative aspects of performing are still challenging for me. If even a minor issue arises, I tend to give up everything, which is why I seldom handle it myself.

Amit: I also struggle with everything surrounding a show. I have a specific way of doing things, and if there are even minor changes, I may give up entirely. Making decisions and considering whether people will attend or not overwhelms me. That's why I haven't performed in three years. Recently, I regained the desire to perform again. On stage, though, I have no fear at all. It's as if I have a superpower of having no fear, as if there is a kind of screen between me and the audience, and I don't feel the audience at all but only music itself.

Rotem: I, too, don't experience audience anxiety. It's as if I create a barrier between myself and the audience, caring little about what they may think. There were even performances in which I was sitting staring and didn't really care about it. I used to perform quite frequently, but then I realized that applause isn't that important to me and that music is a much more personal and meaningful experience for me, so I decided to stop performing on stage.

Ron: I practice a lot before shows to feel relatively confident. I need to get to the point where I feel as if the music is in my fingers' memory. I practice intensively in order to avoid having blackouts. The problem is that sometimes during a performance my mind is already in the next song, and I'm getting distracted.

Rotem: It happened to me, too.

Amit: It also happened to me during concerts. But I have the ability to improvise and handle unexpected situations. The best moments in performances are when something goes wrong, but I manage to smile or say something that uplifts everyone. It's like my superpower in action.

Ron: If it happens to me in the middle of a song, I can manage it because I'm skilled at playing guitar. But if I miss starting a new song, it's a problem. Fortunately, I can rely on other musicians for assistance.

Sagit: Do you prefer to sing with a guitar or without a guitar?

Amit: When I sing, I need the guitar. Initially, it was a way for me to hold something and hide behind it. It's a combination of insecurity and the need to fiddle with something. I feel vulnerable without the guitar, unsure of what to do with my hands.

Sagit: This may be related to autistics' challenges with the proprioceptive system, which affects body positioning in space.

Ron: I also struggled with knowing what to do with my limbs on stage. I always prefer to have a guitar in my hands when performing.

TECHNICAL VERSUS EMOTIONAL PERFORMANCE

Sagit: I would like to ask honestly, and I'd appreciate it if you could correct me or help me understand: is it possible that autistics' music tends sometimes to be more technical? I once heard an autistic singer with an exceptionally angelic voice, but when I purchased her CD, I was so disappointed to find it sounding too technical and lacking emotions.

Rotem: There might have been a problem with the production. Sometimes, after too many rehearsals, the recording can become overly technical. In general, it's not true to say that autistics' music lacks emotions. There is an abundance of emotions in it.

Ron: I believe the opposite is true. My music is filled with emotions. When I learn a new piece, I practice it repeatedly until I master the technical side, and then I infuse it with emotion to express my feelings.

Amit: As a counterpoint, I must admit that sometimes as a defense mechanism I may go to the technical side.

Rotem: That's true. Sometimes, when you fear being overwhelmed by emotions, you resort to the technical extreme to avoid it.

Ron: It's true that being emotionally exposed in front of others can feel too vulnerable. So maybe it's only about 70% of the time.

Sagit: I think it's important to be aware of this in order to avoid falling into this trap. You helped me understand that autistics can perform in a highly emotional way, but sometimes, as a defense mechanism, they may veer toward the technical side.

COPING WITH CRITICISM

Sagit: How do you handle criticism?
Amit: I can be deeply hurt or angered by a negative criticism. While I may later reflect on that feedback, my initial reaction can be harsh. It may be connected to feelings of being misunderstood and rejected.

Rotem: I can relate to this. Criticism triggers a feeling of rejection in me, and I tend to respond defensively, thinking, *Why is this happening to me in an area in which I excel?* or *You don't understand my language; go away*. There is a real dissonance within me between being self-critical and insecure and having such a hard time receiving criticism. When I'm being criticized it really shuts me down, and I go into shock.

Ron: I also have a hard time with negative reviews, even if I believe the critic lacks understanding. Of course, it's even worse when I sense that they do understand and expose my weaknesses. In any case, dealing with criticism can be really tough for me, too.

Sagit: I guess it stems from autistics' black-and-white thinking and their common fear of fall and failure.

Amit: I have a hard time with compliments, too. They make me think things like *excuse me, wasn't that obvious and self-evident?* or *How haven't you noticed this before?* but also *yes, please say it again* [all laughing].

Ron: I often feel that compliments don't truly reflect my abilities. Even when I collaborate with first league musicians, I tend to feel that others have a more conventional musical education, whereas I come from a self-taught, raw background. Even in high school, I couldn't comprehend why they asked me to perform since I was so closed in my cocoon until then.

Rotem: It's called the "impostor syndrome," and I believe we experience it more.

Sagit: Yes. I believe autistics experience it more because they feel a continuous gap between their authentic selves and how society perceives them, as they tend to mask their true identities. It may also be linked to the confusion and discomfort felt when stepping out of the autistic cocoon or comfort zone.

RELATING TO OTHER MUSICIANS ON THE SPECTRUM

Sagit: Do you know other musicians on the spectrum? Do you feel a stronger connection with them?

Ron: I wasn't even aware of autism until about a year ago, when I started considering whether I might be autistic. That's when I discovered that one of my favorite musicians, David Byrne (the lead singer of Talking Heads), is also autistic. I've always identified with various elements of his music, such as its content, repetitions, complexity, and his adoption of different personas both on stage and in his songs, which I now recognize as a form of masking. I also relate to his introverted yet unconventional behavior in interviews and the unique interactions he creates. Finding out that someone I admire and draw inspiration from, who has achieved great success, is also on the spectrum was very empowering.

Rotem: I was raised in the world of classical music, where numerous musicians, including notable figures like Mozart, Beethoven, and possibly Chopin, could have been on the autism spectrum. I also encountered many classical music players who may have been on the autistic spectrum. Playing classical music requires immense dedication, bordering on obsession, which is not only socially accepted but often deemed necessary for success in this field. Consequently, in this realm you don't even ask yourself whether you are on the spectrum or not.

Sagit: Is there a specific autistic musician you identify with?

Rotem: When I was a child, I almost exclusively listened to Mozart, who is believed to have been autistic. There was something in his music that resonated with me and made me feel at home. In fourth grade, when I had to write a paper about him, I struggled to write in the past tense because he felt so alive within me. I then wrote, "I wish Mozart would come to visit Tel Aviv," and my teacher asked if I understood that he was no longer living with us.

Amit: Because I was diagnosed only less than a year ago, I don't have enough experience in identifying autistic musicians yet. However, I really love Rotem's music videos and deeply connect with them.

Sagit: Can you recognize other autistic musicians around you?

Rotem: Yes, there are many.

Ron: I can't diagnose others, but I often notice certain characteristics shared by autistic musicians like David Byrne or Gary Numan. What may seem natural and obvious to them in terms of structure, harmony, or rhythm may appear unique or unusual to others because their brains work differently.

Amit: I believe that many music students, particularly those labeled as "geniuses," might be on the spectrum. I remember a talented guitarist at my school abroad who was perceived as rigid and childlike and who was socially rejected. Looking back, I'm sure he was on the spectrum. I also believe my sister is on the spectrum as she has a remarkable ability to identify specific sounds, like a squeaking chair.

ADVANTAGES AND DISADVANTAGES OF BEING AN AUTISTIC MUSICIAN

Sagit: So, what are the advantages and disadvantages of being an autistic musician?

Rotem: For me, the advantages include hyperfocus, precision, perfectionism, a deep understanding of music, openness, and exploration. The disadvantages are being too obsessive and struggling with social aspects.

Amit: I agree with Rotem. I also have a very complex relationship with music: it can be overwhelming at times, but it also gives me strength, positive energy, resilience, and a creative urge not only in music but also in other areas of life.

Ron: Grace Jones quotes in one of her songs Edith Piaf, who famously said, "Use your faults, use your defects, then you're gonna be a star." This resonates with me as someone who often feels flawed; realizing that my faults can also be an asset is empowering. Without a doubt, I have leveraged the advantages of being autistic, even before I had a name for it. In an interview, Gary Numan expressed that autism was his greatest gift, enabling him to be hyperfocused and obsessive. While I'm not sure if autism makes me a better musician, it certainly enables me to do what I do. On the other hand, I observe others who can juggle multiple projects simultaneously, which is a superpower that I lack. I also believe that others experience less stress than I do.

DISCUSSION

The evidence above provides us a glimpse into the experiences of autistics in the world of music, though they present only an initial exploration in a vast space that has yet to be thoroughly investigated. Here are some key points that emerge, complemented by relevant research findings on the subject:

It appears that many autistics are naturally drawn to music, often showcasing remarkable musical sensibilities and abilities such as perfect pitch, exceptional musical memory, and synesthesia. Moreover, music frequently becomes a special interest for autistics, in which they may express their auditory talents, curiosity, inquisitiveness, and depth.

It seems that autistics experience music in a distinctive manner, marked by the generation within them of numerous associations, such as feelings, memories, images, landscapes, and stories. For them even a brief musical combination can carry multiple deep meanings. Bakan also describes how autistics tend to focus on a certain piece of music that evokes a wide range of associations in them (Levy, 2018). It seems that this unique mode of experience is related to the dominance of the right hemisphere and primary processes in autistics, in which a wide network of emotional and sensory associations is activated, as opposed to the more linear, conventional, and rational processing style associated with the left hemisphere and secondary processes (see chapter 13).

In general, autistics' musicality seems to align with the characteristics of the "primary processes" in the brain (see Noy, 1999, pp. 123–180), which are the dominant processes in autistics' thinking (for a detailed description of the characteristics of the primary processes, see chapter 13): Their tendency to displace emotional meanings to the musical medium is related to the primary process of *displacement*. Their tendency to condense different contents into a singular image is related to the primary process of *condensation*. Their tendency to attach multiple meanings to one object is related to the primary process of *multi-determination*. Their tendency to switch between opposites may be related to the primary process of *representation by the opposite*. Their tendency to focus on the tangible qualities of words, such as sound, shape, rhythm and so on, instead or alongside their meanings, is related to the primary process of *loosening of associations*. Their tendency to experience things primarily through the senses is related to the primary process of *concretization*. Thus, the important psychoanalytic framework of primary processes aids in illuminating the internal cognitive processes that autistics entail in their musical creativity.

Music provides numerous benefits for autistics, serving as a medium for expressing emotions—which they often struggle with in everyday life—and facilitating sensory stimming and relaxation. Music may also help them in gaining insights and enhancing their self-awareness and understanding of the world and in reducing anxieties. In addition, it creates opportunities for social connections, fostering shared "magical moments" and inspiration.

It appears that autistics do not fall short of neurotypicals in their ability to comprehend musical works. They can grasp rather well the emotional meanings of musical works, as reported by the above musicians as well as by other studies. Molnar-Szakacs and Heaton (2012) indicate that studies show that autistics exhibit adeptness in comprehending both simple and complex emotional contents in music. Autistic musician Dotan Nitzberg affirms, drawing from his own experience, that autistics have no difficulty in identifying the emotions behind musical pieces (Levy, 2018; see also Bhatara et al., 2013). Moreover, their heightened attention to detail allows them to absorb intricate aspects of music, thereby enriching their comprehension and appreciation of musical artistry, as described by Rotem above, or by Bakan (Levy, 2018). It seems that autistics often find it easier to understand instrumental music, as the verbal dimension is often more threatening or ambiguous to them, as suggested in the above interviews. Bakan also notes that the verbal aspect might be more threatening for autistics, because they typically find it hard to decipher hidden layers within it (Levy, 2018). However, they also sometimes may connect with the intellectual aspects of lyrics and derive enjoyment from them, as described above. The above interviewees also report that it is easier for them to express their feelings through music than through verbal means. Bakan underscores that autistics feel more comfortable expressing themselves through music, considering it a purer form of expression, with fewer potential misunderstandings or the need to conform to social expectations or constraints (Levy, 2018); Bryar also asserts that autistics can communicate through music things that they cannot convey through language (Bryar, 2015).

Regarding their musical preferences, autistics may be open to diverse kinds of works, with no specific genre priorities, possibly due to their "bottom-up" thinking style. In the limited sample above, they shared a disinterest in electronic music genres such as trance, house, or techno. This tendency may be explained by autistics' general inclination toward the "natural" and "nonindustrialized," though this assumption warrants further examination in future studies. In addition, a polarized attitude toward jazz music is observed, with some autistics being deeply drawn to it, whereas others detest it, because of the unexpected changes, the need to communicate with other musicians, and the complex rules in it. Again, it would be interesting to explore these ideas in further studies.

In their musical endeavors, autistic musicians may leverage their unique talents and assets, including high sensibilities, hyperfocus, meticulous attention to detail, originality, and creativity. Renowned figures such as Mozart, Beethoven, and Glenn Gould, presumed to be autistic, serve as striking examples of the extraordinary creativity achievable by autistic musicians. Their remarkable creativity may be attributed to an internal wealth and unruled thinking that propels them in novel directions, often disregarding conventional norms and rules, particularly in terms of harmony or rhythm. Along with their creativity, autistic musicians may also exhibit a penchant for repetitive elements, finding order and comfort in them, showcasing in their compositions intriguing blends of inventiveness and repetition.

In terms of working with others, contrary to common stigmas, autistics are often attracted to working with others, as they may derive from them inspiration, a platform for creativity, mutual nourishment, and meaningful connections. However, challenges may arise in collaborative settings due to their adherence to strict standards, distinct work pace (which can be either too intense or too slow), emotional dysregulation, and communication difficulties, as they may at times be too distant or too blunt. Nevertheless, their contributions to collaborative efforts can be substantial, as they bring enthusiasm, depth of thought, perfectionism, honesty, and a distinctive ability to elicit high-quality contributions from others.

In terms of performing in front of an audience, it appears that many autistics tend to exhibit opposing poles of either having a high level of audience anxiety or none at all (see also Bryar, 2015). Autistics' anxieties may sometimes lead them to perform more "technically," as a psychological defense against feeling too exposed or emotionally overwhelmed, and it's crucial for them to be aware of this potential pitfall to avoid falling into it. Autistics may also encounter other challenges related to performances, such as difficulties in initiation, coordination, and coping with unexpected obstacles, which may make them abandon entire projects. In addition, they may be hypersensitive to criticism, due to their tendency to view things in black and white. To navigate these challenges, they should endeavor to adopt a more integrated perspective.

In conclusion, autism grants individuals certain advantages in the realm of music, including heightened musical skills, attention to detail, hyperfocus, creativity, curiosity, and openness. Nevertheless, they also face challenges such as obsessiveness, rigidity, anxieties, executive dysfunctions, and susceptibility to criticism. It is essential for society to foster greater understanding and provide support to empower autistic musicians, enabling them to contribute their unique creations and enrich the world with their musical talents.

Chapter 4

Autistic Teachers

> Being a teacher is an excellent profession for me because I can freely discuss the topics I'm most passionate about. (Sharon, an autistic teacher, cited below)

Many autistics are naturally drawn to teaching, where their abilities range from being charismatic and outstanding educators who captivate students with creative teaching styles and profound knowledge, to individuals who encounter challenges fitting into the system, interacting with colleagues, or connecting with students. The underdiagnosis of autism, especially among women who constitute a substantial portion of the teaching workforce, often means that many autistic teachers remain undiagnosed. Research on this topic is still limited and has only recently begun to emerge.

The opening section of this chapter begins with real-life experiences, presenting the personal stories of Reut, Sharon, and Galit (pseudonyms), who graciously agreed to be interviewed for this book, followed by the insights of two autistic authors, Donna Williams and Gunnila Gerland, who detailed their personal experiences as autistic teachers in their autobiographical books. The subsequent section explores common characteristics of autistic teachers, including their motivations for choosing the teaching profession and the advantages and challenges they face as autistics in this profession. In addition, it delves into potential strategies to address the difficulties they may encounter.

PERSONAL RECOUNTS OF AUTISTIC TEACHERS

Reut

Reut, a special education teacher diagnosed with autism at the age of 40, stands out for her extroverted and energetic personality, along with a determined focus on achieving her goals. For instance, during her university studies, she always ensured that she submitted assignments before deadlines to counter her natural inclination to procrastinate. However, as an autistic, she often encountered difficulties with open-ended tests, struggling to grasp expectations and frequently providing excessive details.

After graduating, Reut initially transitioned to working in the field of art, hesitating to start a professional career as a teacher. Like many other autistics, she did not have a predetermined career plan but, rather, embraced opportunities as they presented themselves. Ultimately, she reentered the teaching profession and developed a distinctive and successful teaching style, characterized by meticulous attention to detail. For instance, when planning her lessons, she always considers the class type and student nature, skillfully adapting each lesson to cater to these changing factors.

Drawing from her personal struggles with attention and concentration challenges, Reut advises her students to participate in activities such as coloring, knitting, or folding paper while listening and takes the time to teach them these techniques. She has observed that such activities contribute to increased attentiveness, a sense of calm, and improved absorption of the material. In addition, Reut permits students to stand or swing during class. However, she insists on absolute silence, as noise can be particularly disruptive for her and potentially for others. Acknowledging students' difficulties with order and organization, Reut imparts algorithms to assist them in establishing and maintaining order in the classroom, aiding them in developing such essential habits.

Reut fosters a serene and accepting atmosphere in her class, providing a space for her students to feel comfortable being themselves. She arranges the class tables together to create one large table, allowing her to sit at the same level as her students and engage in discussions with them. During breaks, Reut chooses to remain in her classroom, playing music and gradually attracting a community of students who appreciate her alternative and accepting style, and who choose to spend their breaks with her.

Reut invests considerable personal attention in each student, employing a "bottom-up" thinking style to better understand them. She goes the extra mile by visiting their homes to gain a deeper insight into their backgrounds. With a wealth of knowledge in special education, coupled with her high curiosity and intuition, Reut adeptly identifies and addresses her students' challenges, even those deemed most challenging by the system. Establishing positive relationships extends to students' parents, who value her understanding, dedication, and personal care. They also commend her clear communication with both them and their children.

Reut's primary challenges arise in her interactions with fellow staff members and within the broader system. As she tends to avoid socializing or engaging in small talks with colleagues, she is often perceived as overly distant, direct, or critical. Her reluctance to partake in social gatherings has also impeded her professional advancement. Reut has transitioned through various educational settings before finding one where her abilities are appreciated, and where the school principal is understanding of her weaknesses.

Sharon

Sharon, diagnosed with autism at almost 60, has built a successful career giving private lessons in mathematics over many years and has earned an excellent reputation in this field. She chose this profession for the autonomy it offers, as she strongly resents conforming to rules, principles, and values within systems that she often finds challenging to understand or agree with. Sharon has crafted her own teaching materials, aligning them with her unique logic and preferences. She favors one-on-one communication, finding it more manageable than addressing a large group.

Sharon has distinctive characteristics in her teaching approach. She holds a passion for stickers and uses them as rewards for her students. She humorously claims that teaching is merely an excuse for her to continue indulging in buying stickers, reserving the best ones for herself. Sharon's creativity shines through as she crafts special teaching aids and practice sheets. Further, she has developed an innovative card game aimed at facilitating enjoyable learning experiences, although she faced challenges in successfully marketing it due to her executive dysfunctions.

Patience stands out as one of Sharon's strengths, and she consistently responds to her students' questions with respect and understanding. This stems from her own experience of being criticized in her youth for asking what others deemed "silly questions" when she did not comprehend things that appeared obvious to everyone else. As a teacher, she values and respects every question and endeavors to provide thoughtful responses to her students' inquiries. Sharon is also skilled at identifying areas where her students struggle, thanks to her intuition, extensive knowledge and experience, and attention to detail.

Galit

Galit, diagnosed with autism in her early fifties, had a successful and cherished career as a kindergarten teacher for many years. In this role, she exhibited a deep affection for engaging in conversations with the children, caring deeply, and enjoying singing and dancing with them. She found communication with children to be much more straightforward and easier for her compared to interactions with adults. Daily exchanges with parents and other staff members proved more challenging for her, as she perceived superficial conversations and adherence to social etiquette as pointless. Galit has maintained a pleasant and efficient facade for many years, upholding her reputation as an exceptional kindergartener. Nevertheless, the mental stress and constant exhaustion resulting from the necessity to consistently mask her autistic traits eventually prompted her to leave that job.

Donna Williams

Donna Williams, a renowned Australian autistic writer, known for her writings about autism, briefly worked as a teacher, as described in her book *Somebody Somewhere* (1994).

Williams describes in her book how even while working as an assistant in kindergarten, before starting her formal studies in education, she intuitively grasped the children's difficulties and devised unique and effective ways to cope with them. For example, with one autistic child who could hardly communicate with anyone she established a connection by repeatedly handing him objects, coaxing him to step out a little from his autistic cocoon. Recognizing another girl's sensitivity to overstimulation, she refrained from subjecting her to excessive stimuli, unlike other staff members. In the case of yet another girl, she engaged in repetitive movements, which helped her to calm down. Williams performed these actions effortlessly, drawing on her ability to empathize with the children, intuitively discern their needs, and share their sensory sensitivities. This fostered a sense of closeness, empathy, and vitality.

However, during her training period Williams encountered significant challenges: she struggled to understand situations and determine appropriate behavior, often attempting to navigate these difficulties by imitating her colleagues' behaviors. When questioned about her personal thoughts or feelings, she frequently responded with general answers or redirected the conversation. Seeking help from others posed difficulties for her, and she often felt lost and isolated. During breaks, she sought hiding places to conceal her loneliness. In addition, her sensory sensitivities made her feel overstimulated, prompting her to use earplugs and sunglasses, even during classes. To manage tactile sensitivity, she employed a puppet glove in classes involving physical contact, such as dance, drama, or physical education. On the positive side, Williams's sensory sensitivities drew her to provide her students with extensive sensory experiences in music, drama, art, and science classes, enriching her students with vivid and lasting experiences.

Williams points to several assets she had as an autistic teacher: her voice was strong and calm; she was very methodical in her work and was sensitive to all parts of the class:

> Intuitively I knew what was going on in all peripheries and even behind me, and directed children by name who were out of sight. I was so calm and tuned out that I was totally tuned in. I felt I was not teaching but conducting and directing and learning along with the children. (Williams, 1994, p. 161)

Williams also notes that the well-structured nature of the teaching profession suited her well as an autistic person: "I was protected within the structure of being the language teacher. I knew how long each session would last. I knew I could say stop or change the topic" (Williams, 1994, p. 122).

Gunilla Gerland

The Swedish author Gunilla Gerland wrote several books detailing her experiences as an autistic person, including her remarkable book *A Real Person* (Gerland, 1996), in which she portrays her experiences as a kindergarten teacher.

Gerland highlights her strengths as a kindergarten teacher: Her tendency to adhere to rules made her punctual and responsible in carrying out her duties. She displayed tremendous patience in dealing with children's complaints, repeated requests, and stubbornness. For example, one girl repeatedly asked for the same word to be repeated again and again; although others gave up after a few tries, Gerland patiently continued for an entire hour because she recognized that it was what the girl needed. Garland states:

> My endless patience and my ability to put myself into the children's situation were what made me good with them. I had no training and no theoretical basis to go on. Whenever I felt that I really was helping, I also felt great satisfaction with my work. (p. 214)

The children felt comfortable confiding in Gerland because she treated them with utter empathy and respect. Similar to Williams's description, Gerland describes how she had a very keen perception of everything that was happening around her:

> As nothing escaped me, I could hear a conflict as it arose and intervene at once. I could see if someone was about to fall, and I knew what was happening in the next room. In other words, I usually had an overall view. (p. 216)

Gerland describes that other staff members liked and appreciated her:

> My status was quite good, and they often asked my opinion, because I was a good observer. I would notice details the others might have overlooked, and they were pleased to listen to me, for everything I said had been thoroughly thought through and I never rushed things. As I never became emotionally involved in anything, they often turned to me for mediation. I had no need for prestige, nor had I any competitive instinct, any pride to lose. I got on with everyone. Most of the children also liked me very much although, being predictable and always the same, I perhaps did not respond to the need that healthy children have for excitement. (p. 219)

Despite her success as a teacher, Gerland encountered various challenges, with her main struggle being communication with the children's parents, often leading her to avoid such interactions whenever possible. She also struggled with the constant noise in the kindergarten and found it challenging to supervise many children during outdoor activities in new settings. These demands drained her energy, ultimately leading her to quit the job.

GENERAL CHARACTERISTICS OF AUTISTIC TEACHERS

Drawing on the evidence presented above, as well as insights from other autistic teachers I have encountered and recent research on the topic (Baird, 2020; Damian, 2021; Lawrence, 2019; Martin, 2020; Wood & Happé, 2021), I will outline some general characteristics of autistics in their roles as teachers.

Autistics' Attraction to Teaching

Autistics may be drawn to teaching for various reasons: It allows them to engage in their favorite areas of interest, deepen their knowledge of them and discuss them with others. Teaching provides a platform in which they can find eager listeners, even legitimizing the "monological" speech to which many of them are prone. Teaching offers opportunities to form relationships, which autistics often crave but typically struggle with forming. Their role as teachers is clear and well-defined, in contrast to their challenges in navigating most other social settings. Teaching fosters order alongside creativity, both aligning with autistics tendencies. In addition, autistics may be drawn to teaching for ideological reasons, driven by a desire to assist others or improve the educational system, often stemming from their desire to address challenges they had encountered within the system.

Working with children holds a special allure for autistic teachers: they perceive them as open, natural, and less judgmental than adults. Autistics often feel a greater sense of freedom and experience less judgment for deviating from social codes when interacting with children.

Autistic teachers may specialize in diverse areas aligned with their special interests, such as math, language, art, history, or music. Some may be inclined toward special needs education, particularly educating autistics, where their inherent understanding facilitates a respectful, empowering approach. Moreover, the small-group settings commonly found in special needs education might offer autistic teachers a less stressful alternative compared to larger groups.

Strengths of Autistics in the Teaching Profession

Autistics bring some significant advantages to their roles as teachers:

High Professional Expertise—Autistic teachers often possess extensive knowledge in their areas of interest and may be well-informed in myriad details (e.g., a biology teacher who can identify every plant). They typically strive for proficiency both in their selected field of knowledge and in teaching itself, which may become another specific interest for them, prompting a continuous quest for refining and perfecting their instructional methods. Autistic teachers also naturally gravitate toward providing sensory experiences for their students through music, dance, art, or other mediums. Their extensive knowledge, articulate communication, enthusiasm, creativity, and often unique sense of humor frequently render them as charismatic and inspiring educators.

High Dedication—Autistic teachers often exhibit remarkable dedication to their work, owing to their intense focus and meticulous attention to detail. They may invest substantial time in meticulously preparing lessons and make themselves readily available for students for extended hours. Nonetheless, it is crucial for them to be mindful of potential overwork and prioritize balancing their commitment to work with attention to their personal interests.

Order versus Creativity—Some autistics are highly organized and adhere strictly to lists and timetables, whereas others embrace a more creative, unstructured style. Those inclined toward meticulous planning should be cautious of becoming overly rigid. Conversely, those drawn to creative, free-flowing activities such as listening to music, engaging in art, or interacting with animals should also be mindful of achieving a balance. Autistics may find themselves leaning toward either extreme or oscillating between them in their work and in their personal lives.

A Rational Approach—A rational approach is a common tendency among autistics, offering distinct advantages in their role as teachers. For instance, they often display exceptional patience with students, willingly listening and calmly repeating instructions or actions without succumbing to emotions such as impatience or boredom. They can also be adept at handling emergencies, including accidents, injuries, or emotional outbursts from students with a serene and rational approach. Nevertheless, it is crucial for them to be mindful of the potential pitfalls of excessive rationality, ensuring that they acknowledge and address emotions both in their students and within themselves.

Advantages in the Relationships with Students—Autistic teachers tend to be accepting, respectful, and nonjudgmental, as in general they tend not to look at other people through conventional lenses. Their high curiosity, intuition, and attention to detail enable them to excel in grasping their students' skills and challenges, although they may occasionally overlook their emotional states if they are not clearly expressed and may have a hard time in recognizing manipulations. Their elevated emotional empathy and personalized problem-solving approach, looking at each situation from a "bottom-up" regard, combined with innovative teaching methods, may highly benefit their students.

Working with Special Needs Students—Autistic teachers typically possess a profound understanding of the challenges that students with special needs face. Through effective communication, clear instructions, and skillful use of sensory and nonverbal cues, they can create a supportive learning environment, making special needs students feel understood, accepted, and empowered. In addition, autistic teachers can play a crucial role as advocates, fostering communication between students, fellow staff members, and families.

Challenges Autistics May Face in the Teaching Professions

Along with their multiple advantages, autistics may also have typical challenges in their work as teachers:

Challenges in the Training Process—Typical challenges are in interacting with peers, deciphering implicit or unclear instructions, and prioritizing and executing tasks due to executive function difficulties, learning disabilities, and heightened sensory sensitivities. In addition, adapting to new environments and understanding unwritten rules can be particularly challenging. Although some autistics manage to navigate these challenges with considerable effort, others may opt for alternative paths, such as informal or private teaching, or withdraw from the conventional training itinerary.

Challenges with Colleagues—Autistics typically experience difficulties in understanding and navigating social situations, making staff meetings particularly anxiety-inducing and often leading to intense self-criticism. Some may attempt to mask their challenges or imitate others to fit in, but this typically results in mental exhaustion and a need to withdraw or "shut down." Further, autistics' tendency to prioritize others' interests over their own can lead to taking on excessive tasks and feeling taken advantage of. In addition, seeking assistance or collaborating with others poses challenges, often resulting in overwork and feelings of exhaustion.

Challenges with Students' Parents—Autistic teachers may feel uncomfortable with students' parents due to various reasons: Because of their difficulties in social situations, they may be perceived as distant or strange. They may tend to postpone or avoid tasks they dislike, such as answering messages, letters, or phone calls, which can provoke frustration and anger. They may come across as overly blunt or direct. Despite these challenges, autistic teachers often win parents over through their sincerity, dedication, caring approach, and ability to provide accurate and creative answers.

Challenges in Accommodating to the System—Driven by high ethical and work standards, autistics frequently engage in critiquing system shortcomings, often in a one-sided manner and nondiplomatically, without taking into account wider considerations or constraints and therefore often are perceived as overly critical or insolent. Besides, they are often naive and tend to refrain from asserting their rights in terms of employment conditions, salary, or promotions.

Professional Challenges—Due to executive dysfunctions, autistic teachers may encounter difficulties in handling administrative tasks such as submitting grades or reports, potentially eliciting negative sentiments from their surroundings. Conversely, some may veer toward the opposite extreme of overplanning and meticulous attention to details, which may make them perceived as too rigid, for instance, in expecting specific answers and displaying inflexibility toward their students. Moreover, due to challenges in prioritization, autistic teachers may allocate an excessive time to work at the expense of their private lives. Adapting to changes in curriculum, schedules, or job definitions can also be problematic, triggering discomfort, anxiety, and anger. These cumulative challenges frequently leave them feeling overwhelmed and exhausted, resulting in frequent absences from work.

Sensory Sensitivities—Autistic teachers often experience heightened sensitivities across all their senses. For instance, they may struggle with the noise in classrooms or during recess, or find the sound of the school bell overwhelming. Bright lights, be it sunlight or fluorescent bulbs, may pose challenges. Strong smells, such as food odors or perfumes, can also be discomforting. Further, some autistic teachers may find physical contact from students or colleagues uncomfortable.

Difficulties in Relationships with Students—Despite the numerous advantages autistic teachers bring to their interactions with students, certain challenges may arise. Difficulties in reading emotions may cause them to overlook certain emotional aspects that their students experience. Conversely, hyperempathy, anxiety, and challenges with emotion regulation could lead to an excessive concern about their students' difficulties. In addition, identifying students' manipulations or lies might prove challenging. Autistic teachers may also face ridicule due to their unique mannerisms, unconventional dress style, repetitive movements, or unconventional tone of voice.

Emotional Challenges—Autistics commonly grapple with difficulties in emotion regulation, resulting in intense reactions and challenges in gaining perspective. Unmanaged emotions can contribute to anxiety and depression, sometimes manifested in psychosomatic symptoms. Autistic teachers may also become fixated on specific matters and be obsessed about them for extended periods. All these challenges can potentially lead them to frequent absences, burnout, or even prompt them to leave the teaching profession.

COPING STRATEGIES FOR AUTISTIC TEACHERS

First, obtaining a formal autism diagnosis can significantly enhance the self-awareness of autistic teachers, fostering increased self-acceptance and diminishing feelings of inferiority, self-blame, distress, and depression. In addition, it may equip them with tools to better manage outbursts, withdrawal, frequent absences from work, and burnout.

Following the confirmation of an autism diagnosis, the question arises whether to disclose it to others within the system. On one hand, revealing it may lead to more understanding and support from others. It may also align with autistics' inclination for honesty and reduce the need to mask difficulties. In addition, they may serve as role models for students and teachers in embracing diversity. On the other hand, disclosure can result in negative reactions such as disdain, exclusion, pity, and hinder career advancement. Moreover, because autism is not widely understood, explaining the diagnosis often requires significant effort and can be exhausting. It is hopeful that with increased awareness and understanding of autism over time, disclosure will elicit more acceptance, support, and understanding.

After receiving a diagnosis, it is advisable for autistic teachers to continue expanding their knowledge of autism through self-study or with the assistance of psychotherapy. This may facilitate a deeper understanding of their autism-related challenges and provide them with effective strategies for managing them. It is important to emphasize that autistics need not necessarily conform to societal norms, as this "ableist" approach can be unnatural and draining. Instead, they should prioritize what aligns with their well-being. A supportive environment that recognizes their challenges and offers assistance is essential for their overall success.

The education system and school environments should extend support to autistic teachers through various measures: During their studies they can benefit from special accommodations and adjustments, such as extended time for tasks, clear instructions, the option for a quiet room, as well as mentors who provide emotional and practical guidance. In the work environment, accommodating special needs is essential, encompassing provisions such as allowing breaks, providing autonomy in teaching methods, offering flexible timetables, reminders, and assistance with paperwork. Proactive communication about anticipated changes can also prove beneficial. Sensory adjustments, including reducing the volume of the school bell or dimming overly bright lights, can contribute to a more comfortable environment. In addition, appointing a mediator within the system to enhance understanding of unwritten rules and mediate between autistic teachers and other staff members is advisable.

By actively integrating autistic teachers into the school system and implementing these supportive measures, the educational system can harness the exceptional contributions of these individuals as outstanding teachers.

CONCLUDING REMARKS

As presented, autistics can excel as teachers, displaying dedication, diligence, vast knowledge, and a respectful approach. Hence, they often become outstanding and highly appreciated teachers who leave a strong mark in their environment. However, they must navigate the various social, professional, sensory, and emotional difficulties described above. When weighing the advantages and disadvantages, it appears that, for the most part, the benefits outweigh the challenges. For example, in Wood and Happé's study, 16% of participants believed that autism positively influenced their teaching, whereas only 5% felt that it hindered their work (Wood & Happé, 2021). It is recommended that autistic teachers obtain an autism diagnosis to enhance self-understanding and self-acceptance, as well as an increased awareness of their strengths and potential obstacles and develop strategies to overcome them to fulfill their exceptional potential as outstanding teachers.

Chapter 5

Other Professional Arenas Where Autistics May Be Found

Beyond the professional arenas discussed thus far, there are numerous others where autistics may excel, each of which could merit a captivating chapter in this book. I will briefly highlight some of these professional domains that may align with the interests and abilities of autistics.

Computers, Engineering, and High-Tech—Autistics may be drawn to careers in the fields of computers, engineering, and high-tech, finding fulfillment in roles such as programming, software testing, and software development. They often excel in these professions due to their skills in analyzing complex systems, recognizing patterns, attention to detail, logical thinking, problem-solving abilities, and out-of-the-box thinking. These professions frequently require less emphasis on social skills, and individuals may encounter in them fellow autistics and experience a sense of acceptance without feeling out of place. (Silberman describes the high numbers of autistics in high-tech centers such as Silicon Valley; Silberman, 2015.) Many autistics are also attracted to the gaming industry, where they can harness their rich imagination, creativity, visual abilities, and often their experience of numerous hours' playing.

Research and Academia—Many autistics are naturally inclined toward research, as they are deeply driven to unravel the mysteries of the physical or human world and accumulate knowledge in their specific areas of interest. They may be drawn to a broad spectrum of research fields, encompassing natural sciences (physics, chemistry, biology), mathematics, earth sciences (geography, geology, ecology), atmospheric and space sciences, social sciences (economics, sociology, anthropology, psychology), as well as the humanities (history, archaeology, ancient cultures, linguistics, literature). Plausibly, many researchers, past and present (e.g., Isaac Newton, Albert

Einstein, or Charles Darwin, who are presumed to have been autistics)[1] are or were on the autistic spectrum, indicating the importance for further studies to explore these assumptions.

Inventions and Discoveries—By virtue of their high curiosity, vast knowledge, unconventional regard, and creativity, autistics have the potential to enrich the world through innovative breakthroughs, inventions, and discoveries. Notable figures such as Alexander Graham Bell, Thomas Edison, Nikola Tesla, and others, who are believed to have been autistic, or Elon Musk, who was officially diagnosed as such, exemplify the impact autistics can make in this area.

Numbers and Finances—Autistics with a strong affinity for numbers and pattern recognition may find careers in fields such as mathematics, accounting, statistics, economics, and business. They may also be outstanding entrepreneurs thanks to their unconventional approach, creativity, and high focus. Evident success stories, such as those of Bill Gates, Steve Jobs, and Richard Branson, who are believed to be autistic, exemplify the achievements that autistics can attain in these domains.

Language and Writing—Autistics with strong verbal skills may gravitate toward careers in writing, editing, translating, and proofreading. Many autistics are drawn to writing poetry, prose, and various kinds of literature, where they can express their rich imagination, creativity, insights, and verbal abilities. Notable writers believed to be autistic include Lewis Carroll, Hans Christian Andersen (the author of *The Ugly Duckling*, with whom many autistics can identify), William Butler Yeats, and Emily Dickinson.

Animal World—Due to their keen interest and love for animals, autistics may pursue careers in areas such as veterinary medicine, zoological research, animal care, animal training, or advocating for animal rights.

Nature World—Autistics may immerse themselves in occupations related to nature, including forestry, gardening, agriculture, exploration, nature conservation, or environmental advocacy.

Art—Autistics often are drawn to various forms of artistic expression, allowing them to convey their rich inner lives, creativity, sensual sensitivities, and high technical or visual skills. Whether creating realistic, expressionist, abstract, or surreal art, they often use their artwork to express the dynamic interplay between emotion and intellect within them. Their works are often characterized by richness and colorfulness, reflecting the vivid

[1] Despite the challenges of retrospectively diagnosing individuals who are no longer alive, this chapter presents carefully considered hypotheses about well-known figures who have apparently exhibited traits on the autistic spectrum. These hypotheses are based on their documented life stories and suggested by reputable sources (e.g., Baron-Cohen, 2020; Grandin, 2022). However, it is crucial to emphasize that these hypotheses should be viewed solely as careful conjectures and not as definitive diagnoses.

and colorful spectrum within them. Notable artists believed to be autistics include Vladimir Kandinsky, Piet Mondrian, Joseph Cornell, and Andy Warhol.

Crafts—Autistics may find fulfillment in various crafts, including making jewelry, weaving, knitting, embroidery, and ceramics. In these crafts they may express their affinity for patterns and repetitions, attention to detail, creativity, and heightened sensual sensitivities while also addressing their tactile needs and their need for repetitive movements.

Design—Many autistics are naturally drawn to different fields of design, including fashion design, interior design, and architecture. Their designs often tend to be unconventional or colorful and reflect their unique perspectives.

Animation and Comics—Autistics frequently gravitate toward animation and comics, which align with their special interests and provide a platform for expressing their artistic talents. Notable figures such as Satoshi Tajiri, the creator of Pokémon, and Charles Schulz, the creator of Peanuts, are believed to have been on the autistic spectrum.

Photography and Cinema—Autistics often display a keen interest in photography, showcasing their high visual sensitivity, attention to detail, high focus, technical prowess, and enchantment with various areas of interest, such as animals or nature. The film industry also attracts many autistics, allowing them to express their creative imagination, high focus, attention to detail, and tendency to transgress time and place boundaries. Leading filmmakers such as Stanley Kubrick, Tim Burton, Woody Allen, Steven Spielberg, and Alfred Hitchcock are believed to have been autistic.

Acting—Many autistics are drawn to acting, as they naturally tend to observe and imitate others' behaviors in their efforts to decipher and align with human behaviors. For instance, many autistics engage in pretend play from an early age. Some prominent actors, such as Dan Aykroyd, Daryl Hannah, and Anthony Hopkins, have been officially diagnosed as autistic, and it is plausible to assume that plenty of other autistic actors are undiagnosed.

Humor and Stand-Up Comedy—Contrary to common stereotypes, autistics frequently possess a highly developed sense of humor. They can excel in stand-up comedy, using their unique and honest observations of human behavior, stemming from their initial struggle to decipher its rules, along with their distinct sense of humor and creativity. Several outstanding stand-up comedians such as Hannah Gadsby, Andy Kaufman, Roseanne Barr, and Robert Witt were officially diagnosed as autistic, and even Jerry Seinfeld has indicated that he might be on the autistic spectrum.

Fantasy—Autistics may be attracted to occupations related to fantasy, imagination, or science fiction. They often find appeal in role-playing or customs games, gatherings, and festivals, deriving pleasure from navigating between past and future, reality and imagination, through immersive experiences.

Technical Jobs—Autistics often excel in professions that require high technical dexterity, meticulous attention to detail, and problem-solving abilities, often finding success in careers as technicians of various kinds. In addition, many autistics have a keen interest in vehicles and transportation, making them well-suited to jobs related to transportation, driving, vehicle building, and maintenance.

Libraries, Archives, and Collections—Autistics are often drawn to work in libraries and archives due to their highly organized nature and a natural attraction to collections. They also typically appreciate the quiet environments that such professions typically provide.

Law—Autistics may be drawn to the field of law due to their pursuit of truth and justice, as well as their high logical and verbal abilities.

Politics and Activism—Autistics may channel their pursuit of justice, inclination to protect others' rights, and tendency to criticize existing systems into social or political activism, aligning with either the left or right wings of politics. They may advocate passionately for various causes, including the protection of minority rights, such as those of women, LGBT individuals, or animals, as well as other social or environmental struggles. For instance, well-known Swedish activist Greta Thunberg, diagnosed as autistic, has made significant contributions to raising awareness about climate change.

Therapy and Counseling—Autistics' curiosity and desire to help others make them well suited for therapy, alternative health, nutrition, and counseling professions. They may also be attracted to alternative or mystical pursuits that supposedly provide explanations for various world phenomena, such as astrology, meditation, yoga, or herbology. Autistics may also pursue vocations in health care, including medicine, pharmacy, or nursing, where their ability to remain rational, calm, and caring, even in stressful situations, may shine through.

Telemarketing—Even though autistics most often do not like to talk on the phone (as they find it too difficult to follow unwritten rules of communication) they may find surprising success in jobs such as telemarketing or conducting surveys, in which they can follow predesigned scripts and satisfy their desire for human contact.

Investigations—Autistics may excel in roles such as detectives, spies, police investigators, intelligence officers, and similar professions, leveraging their innate ability to seek truth, solve mysteries, and use skills such as attention to detail, thinking outside the box, photographic memory, analytical thinking, high focus, determination, and a strong sense of justice. For instance, Sherlock Holmes, the renowned literary detective, may be considered to embody many autistic characteristics.

Sports—Autistics can excel in sports by virtue of high motor skills (as they often belong to extremes in this regard), intense focus, determination, and a natural attraction to physical activity to alleviate anxiety. They often prefer individual sports such as swimming, diving, rowing, surfing, floor exercise, martial arts, dancing, riding, climbing, parkour, jumping, weightlifting, golf, bowling, snooker, marathon running, and so on (see Notbohm & Zysk, 2010, p. 9). Autistics may also pursue careers as sports teachers or trainers.

Chess and Poker—Autistics may excel in chess due to their logical and analytical abilities, exceptional memory, ability to focus, and high intelligence. Notably, Bobby Fischer, a former world chess champion, was believed to be autistic. Autistics may also demonstrate high calculative abilities, excellent memory, and attention to detail in poker, with their sealed facial expressions providing a strategic advantage.

Occupations Related to the Senses—Autistics may find fulfilling careers in occupations that leverage their heightened sensory sensitivities, such as music, cooking, baking, or within the perfume, food, or wine industries, which provide avenues for their unique sensory profiles. In addition, autistics may be drawn to the cosmetics and beauty industries, where their acute sensory awareness can contribute to their success.

Modeling—Modeling can be a fitting career for some individuals on the autism spectrum, as autistics have been observed to sometimes possess extraordinary beauty, which can be explained by a remarkable symmetry in their looks (see Attwood, 2007, p. 303).

Part II

CHALLENGES IN THE LIVES OF AUTISTIC ADULTS

Chapter 6

Autism and Eating Disorders

> Anorexia became the only way for me to address the unnamed distress and anxieties, providing a semblance of control to manage the chaos that the world aroused in me . . . Anorexia was supposed to bring me the appropriate treatment but it brought upon me a futile treatment that just wrapped me, who in any case suffers from masks, with more things that were not mine. (Shira, cited below)

Autistics commonly encounter challenges related to eating throughout their lives, which can be broadly divided into two categories. The first category, observed in roughly 90% of autistics mainly during childhood, is characterized by selective eating patterns stemming primarily from sensory sensitivities, rigidity, and adherence to routines (Volkert & Petula, 2010). These patterns tend to diminish to some extent in adulthood. The second category is linked to emotional factors, leading to attempts to control eating behaviors and falling under the category of eating disorders. Typically emerging during adolescence, it affects around 27% of autistics, indicating that autism can be considered a predisposing factor for developing eating disorders (Kerr-Gaffney et al., 2021).

Given the heightened vulnerability of autistics to developing eating disorders, they constitute a significant portion of individuals affected by such disorders. Although the overall prevalence of autism in the population is estimated at approximately 2% (Maenner et al., 2020), the rate of autistics or individuals with high levels of autistic traits constitutes about 20–30% of those suffering from eating disorders, as consistently shown in numerous studies and meta-analyses (see Kinnaird et al., 2019; Brede et al., 2020; Arnold, 2016; Harrison et al., 2020). Despite potential critiques regarding sample size or measurement tool validity, these consistent findings underscore the importance of addressing this co-occurrence.

This chapter emphasizes the significance of identifying autistics suffering from eating disorders to provide them with the appropriate support and understanding. A novel model for understanding the etiology of eating disorders in autistics will be proposed, differing in several fundamental respects from the classical model explaining eating disorders. In addition, tailored therapy guidelines, designed to address the distinctive characteristics of individuals with this co-occurrence, will be proposed. Last, a clinical example will illustrate the experiences of a patient who has grappled with this co-occurrence.

The chapter primarily focuses on autistics who are often referred to as high-functioning, and primarily on anorexia, which has been the central focus of most research in the field of eating disorders, unless otherwise specified.

IDENTIFYING AUTISM AMONG THOSE SUFFERING FROM EATING DISORDERS

Despite the significant prevalence of autism among individuals with eating disorders, a significant number remain undiagnosed as autistics (Kinnaird et al., 2019). This is due primarily to the underdiagnosis of high-functioning autism, especially among females, who make up the majority of those affected by eating disorders (with a ratio of 1:3–1:10, Kerr-Gaffney et al., 2021). In addition, shared characteristics between anorexia and autism pose challenges in distinguishing between the two conditions. Various studies have underscored such common characteristics, including mental rigidity, perfectionism, a need for control, high anxiety levels, difficulties in emotion regulation, adherence to routines, attention to details, discomfort in social situations, and more (Kerr-Gaffney et al., 2021; Kinnaird et al., 2019; Brede et al., 2020; Arnold, 2016; Harrison et al., 2020; Vuillier et al., 2020). Further, studies suggest that starvation can induce physiological changes in the brain, resulting in "autistic-like" behaviors such as cognitive rigidity, social withdrawal, and emotion dysregulation (Brede et al., 2020). Therefore, a professional diagnostic process is essential to determine whether autism is present, including the examination of the existence of autistic characteristics since early childhood. In addition, autistic traits are supposed to persist even after recovery from the eating disorder (regarding differential diagnoses between anorexia and autism, see, e.g., Kerr-Gaffney et al., 2021; Brede et al., 2020; Vuillier et al., 2020).

Identifying autism in individuals with eating disorders is crucially important for several reasons. First, recognizing the autism diagnosis can provide them with more psychological understanding, liberating them from self-criticism and self-blame, particularly because a sense of being misunderstood may have contributed to the development of the eating disorder (Brede et al.,

2020; Arnold, 2016). Moreover, the diagnosis can aid parents in understanding their children better and alleviate unwarranted feelings of guilt. Further, it can empower therapists to tailor their treatment approaches to better align with the individual's characteristics and specific needs. Identifying autistics among those suffering from eating disorders is also essential because studies indicate that their eating disorders are more difficult to treat, with lower recovery rates compared to their non-autistic counterparts (Kinnaird et al., 2019; Brede et al., 2020; Vuillier et al., 2020; Moseley & Renshaw-Vuillier, 2020; Kinnaird et al., 2017). They also face a higher risk of mortality (Vuillier et al., 2020; Moseley & Renshaw-Vuillier, 2020).

Eating disorders tend to be more severe and resistant in autistics due to several autistic characteristics: Their rigidity may lead them to fixed eating habits and excessive physical activity. Attention to detail and adherence to certain beliefs may result in picky eating behaviors. Difficulties in attending to bodily sensations (interoception) may lead to prolonged ignorance of hunger or thirst. Sensory sensitivities may also contribute to food restrictions. Finally, their challenges in expressing needs and emotions further complicate their treatment (Kinnaird et al., 2019). Given all these reasons, it is crucial to identify autistics among those with eating disorders to ensure that they receive the appropriate understanding and therapy.

AN EXPLANATORY MODEL FOR EATING DISORDERS IN AUTISTICS

An explanatory model for eating disorders in autistics is being proposed, differing from the classical causal model of eating disorders in several fundamental ways. The classical causal model for eating disorders in non-autistics encompasses psychodynamic, family, and cultural factors: Psychodynamic explanations posit that eating disorders typically stem from the internalization of a domineering and devaluing maternal object (see Vuillier et al., 2020; Caparrotta & Ghaffari, 2006), leading to feelings of powerlessness (Selvini-Palazzoli, 1974) and the desire for control through food (Bruch, 1973). Self-psychology emphasizes the impact of parents' difficulties in meeting their children's needs for empathic and idealized self-objects, resulting in problems in the cohesiveness of the self, with the eating disorder serving as a revolt against these difficulties (Bachar, 2001). Puberty-related changes can trigger separation anxiety, prompting individuals to maintain a pre-adolescent body and create a compensatory identity through the eating disorder (Goodsitt, 1977; Geist, 1989). Distorted body perception, denial of thinness, and fear of obesity are also highlighted as contributing factors (Selvini-Palazzoli, 1974; Bruch, 1973; Gabbard, 2000). Psychological traumas, such as experiencing losses, violence, or sexual abuse, may also play a role. For instance, Ross found in her study that 40% of the women who experienced childhood sexual trauma suffered from eating disorders, stemming from their need to maintain control, fears of specific foods (e.g., those associated with oral sexual abuse), attempts to halt the menstrual cycle or to die in order to purify the body, or turning to binge eating to supposedly fill inner emptiness, create isolation from others, or suppress sexuality (Ross, 2009). The family dynamics of those with eating disorders are often characterized by poor communication, disregard of feelings, insufficient or excessive attention, domineering and intrusiveness, especially on the part of the mother, and a problematic attitude toward weight loss (Selvini-Palazzoli, 1974; Minuchin et al., 1978). Cultural factors, such as the idealization of low weight in Western society, further contribute to the pressure to lose weight (Boniel-Nissim & Latzer, 2011). Social networks may also encourage self-starvation, sometimes by providing practical instructions (Boniel-Nissim & Latzer, 2011).

In contrast to the classical causal model mentioned above, the proposed explanatory model for eating disorders in autistics differs in several key aspects:

Primarily, the onset of eating disorders among autistics is frequently linked to challenges associated with the autism, encompassing social, emotional, sensory, perceptual, and learning difficulties. In addition, psychological traumas such as bullying or exploitation further contribute to the development of eating disorders. These challenges are frequently exacerbated by struggles in expressing emotions, a common feature in autism known as alexithymia.

Second, weight loss is not always the predominant objective for autistics with eating disorders. Research indicates that factors such as the desire to lose weight or body image concerns play a less prominent role in the development of eating disorders among autistics when compared to characteristics associated with autism itself (Brede et al., 2020; Kinnaird et al., 2019; Arnold, 2016). According to the DSM criteria for anorexia (criterion B), one should have an intense fear of weight gain or of being fat *or* a persistent behavior that prevents weight gain—meaning that even those who are not necessarily motivated by a fear of gaining weight may answer this criterion.

Further, eating disorders in autistics may be exacerbated by factors intrinsic to autism, including sensory sensitivities, rigid thinking, executive dysfunctions, and the eating disorder becoming a "special interest," which can significantly contribute to both the emergence and persistence of eating disorders in autistics.

The proposed causal model for eating disorders in autistics, based on studies conducted by Kerr-Gaffney et al. (2021), Kinnaird et al. (2019), Brede et al. (2020), and others, incorporates both "direct" factors, linked with the inherent characteristics of autism, and "indirect" factors, encompassing emotional influences contributing to the development of eating disorders in autistics (the distinction between direct and indirect factors was suggested by Brede and colleagues, 2020).

"Direct" Causes for Eating Problems among Autistics

Approximately 90% of autistics experience picky eating, especially during childhood (Volkert & Petula, 2010). Picky eating in autistics can be categorized under the category of Avoidant/Restrictive Food Intake Disorder (ARFID) in the *DSM-5* (307.59), characterized by food avoidance, without a strong focus on weight loss or body image concerns, which are often predominant in anorexia. Several factors may contribute to such picky eating in autistics:

Heightened Sensory Sensitivities—Most autistics experience intense sensitivities to the textures, tastes, smells, or appearances of certain foods. They may avoid fibrous, viscous, mushy, lumpy, or uneven textures and have specific requirements for how their food is served (e.g., cut to small pieces or not touching other foods) and at what temperature. This often makes them stick to a limited choice of foods and boycott entire food groups, such as vegetables, fruits, meat, or fish, often with a preference for more uniform and either soft or hard/crunchy foods, such as "fast food."

Need for Routine and Control—Autistics tend to rely on routines and habits to establish a sense of control over anxieties. This can manifest in consistently choosing the same type of food over extended periods, adhering to regular eating schedules, and following specific routines, sequences, and methods of eating.

Social Challenges—Autistics may avoid communal meals due to challenges in navigating social situations, fear of criticism, and heightened sensitivities to sounds, smells, and lights.

Executive Function Hurdles—Challenges with planning and organization, which are common among autistics, can lead to an avoidance of preparing meals that require tasks such as shopping, cooking, and cleaning.

Physiological Challenges—Autistics might refrain from eating due to various bodily problems and sensitivities. These can include allergies or sensitivities to certain foods (such as gluten, casein, or lactose), and digestion problems (such as ulcers, reflux, or irritable bowel syndrome), which are more prevalent within the autistic population. In addition, some autistics may be sensitive to the sensations that may arise after eating, such as bloating or digestion problems. Some may also develop aversions to foods after experiencing vomiting or choking.

Inattentiveness to Body Sensations—Autistics may occasionally skip meals because they are not always in tune with their hunger or thirst signals, particularly when they are engrossed in other activities. This can also lead to irritability, headaches, and dehydration.

Special Interest in Dietary Habits—The inclination of autistics to immerse themselves in specific areas of interest and meticulously attend to details can lead them to be particular about the food components and overall quality of their food. Their commitment to broader agendas, such as vegetarianism, veganism, or environmental protection, can also significantly influence their dietary choices and habits.

Intense Physical Activity—Autistics may engage in intense physical activity, such as running, swimming, dancing, or martial arts, to unwind and alleviate anxiety, potentially resulting in a negative calorie balance.

Although overeating is less common in autistics compared to undereating, it can still occur due to challenges in attending to body sensations, the use of appetite-increasing medications, and resorting to emotional eating to suppress distress ("emotional eating"). It is noteworthy that alongside the picky eating of most autistics, some autistics exhibit the opposite extreme, displaying a remarkable openness to various foods. An extreme manifestation of this can be observed in Pica syndrome (*DSM-5*, 307.52), in which nonedible items such as dirt, paper, or sand are consumed. Notably, Pica syndrome is more commonly seen in low-functioning autistics (Vuillier et al., 2020).

"Indirect" or Emotional Factors for Eating Disorders in Autistics

Numerous "indirect"/emotional factors may contribute to the development of eating disorders in autistics, typically beginning during their teenage years:

As self-awareness grows during adolescence, autistics often become more conscious of their challenges in navigating social situations. The ensuing experiences of ridicule, bullying, ignoring, or rejection often foster profound feelings of rejection, loneliness, and depression in them. In an attempt to improve their social standing, some may emulate their peers, yet this often leads to a sense of inauthenticity and self-hatred. Particularly without a formal autism diagnosis, many autistics contend with feelings of being different, strange, and incomprehensible and questions about their identity and, at times, their sexual identity. Moreover, their difficulty in discerning others' intentions renders them vulnerable to various forms of abuse, including sexual abuse. School tasks may pose additional hurdles, in light of their executive disfunctions, attention and concentration problems, and sometimes specific learning disabilities such as dyslexia or dyscalculia, difficulties in working memory, and a slower work pace. All these may contribute to a pervasive sense of failure and loneliness, depression, anger and despair, which are often further amplified by their difficulties in emotional regulation, heightened anxieties, and the hormonal shifts of adolescence. This heightened emotional intensity sets the stage for the development of eating disorders, alongside self-harm behaviors and psychosomatic ailments, diverting the focus from the intricacies of these challenging emotions (Kinnaird et al., 2019; Arnold, 2016).

A pivotal factor exacerbating emotional challenges in autistics and predisposing them to eating disorders is alexithymia—a difficulty in identifying and expressing emotions—acknowledged by researchers as a significant contributor to the development of eating disorders in this population (see Brede et al., 2020; Vuillier et al., 2020; Moseley & Renshaw-Vuillier, 2020). Autistics have challenges in expressing emotions due to their deficient connectivity between the right and left hemispheres, hindering the necessary integration for recognizing and processing emotions (see chapter 13). Although they can experience basic emotions such as sadness, anger, or fear, often intensely and in an unregulated manner, expressing more intricate emotions that require greater integration proves challenging for them. These challenges, coupled with their difficulties in asking others for help, impede their ability to receive emotional support, prompting them to turn to eating disorders as a more accessible outlet for their complex emotions.

Numerous researchers have pointed out the connection between eating disorders and difficulties in expressing emotions, even beyond the context of autism: Masterson (1978) and Lawrence (2001) have noted that individuals with eating disorders have difficulties in symbolizing; McDougall (1989) elucidates how anorexia functions as a means to express emotional conflicts of which there is no conscious recognition, by way of concretization; Hason Rozenstein and colleagues (2011) describe how anorectics have difficulties in recognizing and understanding both their own and others' emotions. However, whereas alexithymia in allistic (non-autistic) individuals may stem from psychological factors, particularly a parental failure to assist in identifying and processing emotions (Petterson, 2004; Levy-Shiff & Rothschild-Yakar, 2013), in autistics it is primarily rooted in physiological constraints of limited connectivity. As a side note, a question arises as to how many of the descriptions in research literature of individuals with eating disorders and alexithymia were based on autistics who were not officially diagnosed as such.

Another emotional factor involves autistics' tendency to deeply engage in dieting as a special interest, focusing intensely on elements such as food ingredients, eating habits, and schedules, as well as incorporating sports as a special interest. This immersion can serve as a means to regain a sense of control, compensating for autistics' prevailing feeling of lack of control in their lives and in the world. Their so-called success in managing the eating disorder may contribute to an elevated sense of self-worth, and weight loss may be seen as a strategy to enhance social standing (Asada et al., 2018) and mitigate criticism or bullying directed toward them (Storch et al., 2012). The eating disorder may also serve autistics as a platform for establishing connections, either in the virtual world or in reality, sometimes through hospitalization in eating disorder units.

Autistics may inadvertently develop eating disorders, sometimes as a result of casual comments about their weight or haphazard exposure to information on the subject. Due to their inclination to interpret things literally and perceive situations in "black and white," they may take such remarks or information very seriously. For instance, one of my patients was told, "If you lose weight, you will be successful with boys," and she wholeheartedly believed it. Abstaining from eating may later evolve into a rigid pattern, due to autistics' tendency to strictly adhere to routines. For example, some participants in Kinnaird and colleagues' study noted that autism led them to establish inflexible rituals and routines around eating, making it challenging for them to later modify these patterns (Kinnaird et al., 2019).

In summary, autistics may turn to eating disorders to cope with the many emotional challenges associated with autism, psychological traumas, and identity struggles. Difficulties in expressing emotions, alongside the need for control and distraction from depression and anxieties, play a role in both the onset and perpetuation of eating disorders. Autistic characteristics, including mental rigidity, meticulous attention to details, executive dysfunctions, sensory sensitivities, health concerns, aversion to communal eating, and a tendency to seek stress relief through physical activity, can make overcoming the eating disorder even more challenging for autistics.

THERAPY GUIDELINES FOR AUTISTICS STRUGGLING WITH EATING DISORDERS

As awareness of the co-occurrence of autism and eating disorders has only recently grown and research in this field is still in its early stages, a formalized treatment model for this combination is yet to be established (except for general recommendations suggested by Kinnaird et al., 2017, 2019). Such guidelines are crucial in light of the high prevalence of this co-occurrence and the importance of addressing autistic characteristics in treating this population. The following outlines some broad therapeutic suggestions:

First, the diagnosis of autism is a key step in therapy, as it leads to increased self-understanding and self-acceptance. Kinnaird and colleagues found that receiving an autism diagnosis was a very positive experience for patients coping with this co-occurrence, which helped them to better understand their needs and led them to a better treatment experience (Kinnaird et al., 2019). Hence, it is recommended that professionals in this field acquaint themselves with the profile of high-functioning autism to be able to identify it and to share this knowledge with their patients as an essential tool for increasing their self-understanding ("psychoeducation").

Because many autistics resort to eating disorders as a result of alexithymia, it is crucial to assist them in symbolizing their emotions and articulating their distress, anxieties, and traumas. Petterson (2004) writes that clarifying emotions over time reduces problematic eating patterns. Levy-Shiff and Rothschild-Yakar (2013) underscore the significance of addressing alexithymia in individuals with eating disorders by helping them identify their own and others' mental states and uncovering causal explanations for their challenges.

Given that alexithymia in autistics is rooted primarily in an organic deficiency, achieving emotional articulation with them is more challenging, yet feasible. For instance, therapists should be mindful of autistics' challenges in responding to open-ended questions about their emotions, which may evoke feelings of embarrassment and helplessness in them. Instead, employing Socratic dialogue's techniques, involving clear and direct questions and answers, can prove more effective in helping patients clarify their inner experiences. Moreover, many autistics find it easier to express their feelings through writing. As their trust in the therapeutic process grows, they may also become more comfortable expressing their feelings verbally during conversation.

In the treatment of this population, emotional validation and empathy play a pivotal role, as autistics often endure a lifelong struggle with lack of understanding and validation. It is highly recommended to find out with such patients what might help them personally, as many of them possess a high capacity for self-observation.

Further, the emotional stresses at the root of the eating disorders in autistics should be addressed in several ways, such as correcting distorted or negative cognitive patterns, processing psychological traumas within the context of autism, enhancing comprehension of interpersonal situations, fostering the development of supportive and healthy relationships, and managing anxiety and depression through various methods, including medications and complementary therapies like yoga, meditation, or mindfulness.

Autistics suffering from eating disorders may also benefit from group therapies, which may provide them a platform to share their feelings and receive empathy, validation, and a sense of belonging. It's essential, however, to recognize that some autistics may experience anxiety in group settings due to discomfort in social situations. Therefore, it is crucial to assess individual needs and consider creating subgroups for autistic participants, if feasible, to ensure an inclusive and supportive environment.

Family interventions can be particularly beneficial, especially for teenagers and their families, with the goal of fostering open communication and emotional sharing among family members. The autism diagnosis can aid parents in better understanding and accepting their children, potentially reducing feelings of guilt and enhancing cooperation with the treatment process.

In conjunction with psychotherapy, practical interventions such as monitoring eating habits, implementing balanced diets, and teaching self-control strategies can be beneficial. Dietary instructions should be tailored to accommodate autistics' sensory sensitivities to tastes, smells, and textures of foods. For example, Arnold (2016) suggests that it may be more effective to increase the amounts of foods that they like rather than adding foods they dislike, and that one should anticipate very gradual changes, considering autistics' inclination to adhere to routines and fear of change.

From the system's point of view, it is essential to provide training for staff members in eating disorder units to familiarize them with autism characteristics so that they can identify autistics more easily and approach them with more understanding of their challenges, including difficulties in executive functions, expressing emotions, meeting deadlines, and their tendencies toward literal understanding, rigidity, shutdowns, meltdowns, and more. Staff members should be equipped with strategies to meet the unique needs of autistics, employing explicit communication, allowing time and space for withdrawal, and demonstrating sensitivity to their sensory sensitivities to create a more suitable and accommodating environment for them (Kinnaird et al., 2019).

SHIRA'S STORY

Shira, a vibrant and intelligent 28-year-old woman, sought a potential autism diagnosis after undergoing multiple treatments and receiving various other diagnoses. Growing up in Tel Aviv as the eldest of four children, she exhibited early signs of a unique personality. As a baby, she was mostly quiet and immersed in her own world. Throughout her childhood, she exhibited a vibrant imagination and deep curiosity, along with a special fondness for animals, observing them keenly for hours. She was also drawn to nature in general, frequently collecting leaves, acorns, and plants, arranging and exploring them. She also found joy in physical activities such as swinging, spinning, and jumping.

In kindergarten, she faced challenges in making friends and frequently engaged in solitary activities, such as organizing dolls in a specific order. She grappled with numerous anxieties and exhibited heightened sensitivity to sensory stimuli across all senses. In elementary school, despite her dreamy and contemplative nature, she excelled academically due to her high intelligence. Unfortunately, she also experienced bullying as a result of being perceived as peculiar and lacking tact. She developed a keen interest in science fiction, fantasy, animals, and a distinct Spanish TV series, and even learned Spanish to better comprehend the show and explore related internet sites.

In middle school, Shira continued to grapple with making friends and navigating social situations. With few social connections, she often spent her breaks alone in the library, immersed in reading. Her increasing self-awareness intensified her tendency to compare herself to others, resulting in feeling different, lonely, and depressed. School tasks also drained Shira due to her challenges with executive functions and tendency to procrastinate, making her feel unable to adhere to the normal life trajectory. Shira's struggle with an eating disorder began in eighth grade, triggered by a haphazard discussion of the subject in a biology class, which prompted her to delve into blogs and videos on the topic, leading her to restrict her food intake, engage in purging behaviors, and wear weights on her ankles at school. During breaks, she engaged in excessive running or jumping rope, counting in the thousands. Shira believes that her eating disorder developed mainly as a means of distraction and relief from the challenges of social interactions and the sense of not being understood or able to express her distress directly.

When Shira's mother discovered her vomiting, she took her to therapy, which included dietary and parental counseling. Shira's parents had to supervise her meals, often leaving work early, which caused her father to become angry, and this created conflicts and tension at home, exacerbating Shira's distress. Therapy itself was challenging for Shira, as she had problems in verbalizing her emotions and often remained silent. At times, she brought to therapy things she wrote, as writing was an easier way for her to express herself. These writings discussed her difficulties with expressing emotions and navigating social situations, but the therapist failed to connect them to a broader autism spectrum picture. Instead, the therapist repeatedly suggested a potential link to sexual abuse, a disorder she was more familiar with, despite Shira never having experienced such trauma. Feeling misunderstood, Shira continued to lose weight, engage in excessive exercise, and began self-harming as another outlet for her distress.

In 10th grade, after her condition deteriorated, Shira was transferred to a hospital unit specializing in the treatment of eating disorders. She underwent individual, group, family, and medical therapy for a year. Shira often felt different from the other patients as they all had a clear explanation for the development of their eating disorder, whereas she did not. Shira also felt that the treatments she underwent were ineffective and continued to engage in disordered behaviors such as fasting, vomiting, excessive exercise, and pretending to gain weight. After her discharge, Shira resumed therapy with her previous therapist but remained largely silent during sessions. The therapist persistently suggested the possibility of sexual abuse, even going so far as to imply that her father might be the perpetrator. Though untrue, Shira, eager to please others, inadvertently confirmed it, unaware of the potential consequences. The therapist disclosed this information to Shira's mother, resulting in the parents' divorce. Tragically, not long after, Shira did experience a sexual assault due to her difficulties in deciphering others' intentions and in asserting boundaries, which is unfortunately common among individuals on the autism spectrum.

These complications further exacerbated Shira's eating disorder, and after completing high school, she entered a hospital's eating disorders department, where she stayed for approximately one year. Shira struggled with sensory challenges in the department, such as the strong smells, bright lights, and loud noises. She also disliked the taste and smell of the Ensure drink provided. During therapy sessions, Shira remained mostly silent. She often tried to please other girls in the department, for instance by assisting some with their academic papers, but unfortunately, some girls used to mock and bully her. Shira believes that some of the other girls in the department were also autistics, and indeed, at least four of them were later diagnosed as such. After a year, Shira moved to a rehabilitation institute, where she struggled with the demanding schedule and communal meals that inundated her with social, sensory, and emotional stimuli. Consequently, she frequently withdrew and engaged in self-harming behaviors, resulting in multiple hospitalizations in psychiatric units. Eventually, Shira received a permanent recognition of mental disability and an allowance. A few years ago, Shira was also diagnosed with fibromyalgia, a condition that often co-occurs with autism and may be related to the psychological distress associated with it (Asztély et al., 2019).

Several years ago, Shira began a new therapy that she found favorable. Her therapist didn't try to fit her into a preconceived diagnostic box but, instead, adapted to her pace and truly listened to her words and read her writings. She provided Shira with the validation and acceptance that she deeply needed, encouraging her to find her own voice and develop her artistic talents. The empathy and validation received through therapy gradually helped Shira let go of her eating disorder. In addition, she started using medical cannabis to reduce her anxieties and fibromyalgia pain.

Approximately a year ago, Shira started considering the possibility that she might be autistic, and her therapist supported her in exploring this new diagnosis. Shira feels that the diagnosis of autism profoundly improved her life:

> If they had only diagnosed me as autistic when I was young, I could have given a name to my suffering and receive a fitting therapy that might have spared me years of psychological anguish . . . The profound and compelling difference between me and everyone else was always there, yet in the eyes of those around me, it appeared as an invisible nuance . . . after receiving the diagnosis, everything gained meaning. In the past, even with my eyes open, I was in the dark. Now I can see things much more clearly, and that's all I ever truly wanted. Now I can realize that I was afraid of the wrong things—of being myself, of appearing different, of disappointing others . . . now the mask is coming off my face, and I finally know who I am in this world, and I feel a sense of belonging to the lack of belonging.

Following the diagnosis, Shira's relationships with her family members have improved significantly. She feels that they now possess a better understanding of her, and that she, in turn, has become more forgiving of their past misunderstandings.

Shira harbors hard feelings regarding the protracted, expensive treatments she underwent in the past, feeling that her therapists sought to fit her into categories they were familiar with rather than genuinely listening to her. She urges eating disorders' practitioners to acquire the skills to identify autistics among their patients, underscoring the critical need for them to provide the empathetic understanding, validation, and tailored assistance that autistics rightfully deserve.

As Shira is highly intelligent, self-observant, and talented in writing, she could beautifully distill in retrospect deep insights regarding the reasons for her eating disorder: Shira explains that she had turned to anorexia in the first place mainly because she felt lonely, different, and misunderstood, being unable to directly articulate the intense emotional turmoil within her:

> one does not understand how alexithymic pain feels like, when your emotions hit you from within, when you're overwhelmed, and your entire body hurts to the point of physical pain, when you're kicked from side to side chaotically without knowing why . . . and it raises more and more, with no words to express it . . . and you have the urge to discharge it, to let it out somehow.

She describes:

> Anorexia provided me with a sense of control over the situation, offering stability through routines, rules, and rituals. It became the only way for me to address the unnamed distress and anxieties, providing a semblance of control to manage the chaos that the world aroused in me simply from being who I was.

The eating disorder served Shira as an escape from feelings of loneliness and disbelonging: "The eating disorder was for me like an imaginary companion in moments of boundless loneliness and lack of faith in my ability to make friends or get a sense of belonging in this world." Shira believed that the eating disorder was the only thing that could serve her as a substitute for her feelings of self-hatred, guilt, shame, and emptiness and to channel difficulties that she used to mask: "Through the eating disorder I could stop faking and pretending to be 'a good girl,' I could break down and let go. I felt that the prison of anorexia was better than the prison of masking." Shira explains that she intended the eating disorder as a plea for help; however, it failed to achieve that goal, as it created a new form of masking instead of bringing solutions to the original problems: "Anorexia was supposed to bring me the appropriate treatment, but it brought upon me a futile treatment that just wrapped me, who in any case suffers from masks, with more things that were not mine."

Shira's compelling narrative may resonate with other autistics contending with eating disorders. Her story underscores the significance of obtaining a correct autism diagnosis to comprehend and treat such patients effectively.

CONCLUDING REMARKS

This chapter highlighted the significant issue of underdiagnosis of autism among individuals with eating disorders. Despite an estimated prevalence of 20–30% of autistics within this population, many remain undiagnosed as autistics, depriving them of the understanding and assistance they genuinely require.

The chapter introduced a model for understanding eating disorders in autistics, setting it apart from the traditional model in several key aspects. It posits that eating disorders in autistics primarily arise as responses to emotional challenges associated with autism, encompassing social, emotional, sensory, and learning difficulties, in addition to challenges in expressing emotions (alexithymia). The persistence of other autistic traits, such as rigid thinking, executive dysfunctions, sensory sensitivities, and a preference for physical release, can prolong eating disorders and complicate their treatment. Moreover, in contrast to the classical model, autistics typically display fewer distortions in body perception or denial of low body weight.

The chapter delineated overarching treatment guidelines for autistics with eating disorders, underscoring the pivotal role of securing an accurate autism diagnosis. Essential components of therapy involve psychoeducation about autism, facilitating the expression of emotions, addressing cognitive distortions, processing psychological traumas, and enhancing social and interpersonal skills, among other strategies. In addition, it is advisable to equip staff members in eating disorder units with a deeper understanding of autism to enhance their ability to identify autistics among their patients and provide them with heightened understanding and support tailored to their unique needs as autistics.

In light of its high prevalence, the co-occurrence of autism and eating disorders needs further exploration. It is recommended that future studies place emphasis on autistics' personal reports, as they often exhibit high self-observation skills and insights, as Shira's captivating narrative vividly illustrates.

Chapter 7

Autism and Gender Diversity

> My autism and my being trans are intertwined and inseparable. I was a nonbinary child—I didn't feel connected to either gender, and it didn't really concern me. I wore both boys' and girls' clothes and played both boys' and girls' games. I was also an autistic child—I engaged in my special interests, including animals, reading, and mythology, and I behaved in a way that felt natural and right to me, even though others thought it was strange. (Noy, a nonbinary autistic person, cited below)

People familiar with the autistic community can easily observe the notable presence of those who identify as having gender diversity, indicating not conforming to the binary division of male and female or to societal expectations regarding gender behavior. Many of them do not identify with the gender assigned to them at birth and may meet the criteria for gender dysphoria as defined in the *DSM-5*, which replaced the previous definition of "gender identity disorder" in the *DSM-4*, reflecting a positive shift from pathologizing gender diversity to recognizing it as a legitimate identity.

Autistics with gender diversity (hereinafter AGDs), belonging to twice-marginalized groups, often face prejudice, discrimination, criticism, and bullying. Consequently, they are at a higher risk for mental health issues such as depression, anxiety, self-harm, and suicidality (see Warrier et al., 2020; Cooper et al., 2020; Murphy et al., 2020). In light of this, it is crucial for professionals in the fields of autism and gender diversity to enhance their knowledge on this subject to provide appropriate understanding and support.

This chapter delves into the intricate connection between autism and gender diversity, presenting research data, potential explanations for this connection, shared personal experiences from AGDs, and implications for therapy. Personal narratives were assembled from diverse sources, including three insightful qualitative studies—conducted by Coleman-Smith and colleagues in 2020; Strang, Powers, and colleagues in 2018; Cooper and colleagues in 2022—in which AGDs shared their compelling experiences, along with other relevant resources.

To ensure clarity, key terms in this field are:

Sex versus gender—sex refers to a person's physiological affiliation (i.e., male, female, or intersex), whereas *gender* is a social construct that refers to identity (i.e., man, woman, or nonbinary). In addition, there is *gender performance*, which may be either feminine, masculine, or androgynous. For example, there may be a person who was assigned male at birth, has a woman gender identity and a female, male, or androgynous gender performance.

Gender identity—refers to how individuals perceive their own gender.

Gender dysphoria—a condition where there is a significant incongruence between an individual's gender identity and societal perception, causing significant distress (see section 302.85 in *DSM-5*).

Gender diversity—a situation in which the gender identity does not align with binary categories of man and woman, including those who identify as genderqueer, nonbinary, or gender fluid.

Nonbinary—an umbrella term encompassing identities that are not strictly male or female, including genderfluid, agender, bigender, and more.

Gender fluidity—a fluctuating gender identity over time.

Cisgender—someone who identifies with the gender assigned at birth.

Transgender—someone who identifies with a gender different from the one assigned at birth.

Intersex—someone who possesses both male and female physical characteristics (chromosomes, gonads, hormones, genitals). Some intersex conditions may not be apparent at birth and are later discovered or may remain undetected (see, e.g., chapter 8, which deals with those born with Klinefelter [XXY] syndrome).

Gender reassignment—medical procedures aimed at aligning the body with an individual's gender identity, including hormonal treatments and surgeries.

By understanding these terms and concepts, professionals can better support and advocate for individuals with gender diversity within the autistic community.

THE CONNECTION BETWEEN AUTISM AND GENDER DIVERSITY

Many studies from the past few years provide support for the significant connection between autism and gender diversity or gender dysphoria (see reviews of studies on this subject by Warrier et al., 2020; Murphy et al., 2020;

Cooper et al., 2022). In 2010, the first official study on the subject found that out of more than 200 children and adolescents diagnosed with gender dysphoria, 7.8% were autistic (Vries et al., 2010). A 2014 study found that autistics were 7.59 times more likely to be gender diverse than non-autistics (Strang et al., 2014). A 2016 study found that approximately 23% of the subjects with gender dysphoria had Asperger's syndrome (Shumer et al., 2016). A 2019 study found that 22% of 1,178 subjects with gender diversity saw themselves also as neurodivergent (Veale et al., 2019). In 2020, the largest study in this field, conducted by Warrier and colleagues (2020), examined the data of 641,860 people and found that the rate of autistics among those with gender diversity was 24%, and that those with gender diversity had a 3.03–6.36 times higher chance of being autistic. They also found that the rate of those who reported having "autistic traits" among those with gender diversity was five times higher than among those without.

Several explanations have been proposed for the connection between autism and gender diversity or gender dysphoria (see, e.g., Warrier et al., 2020; White, 2016); nonetheless, there isn't yet a universally agreed-upon explanation. Here are some suggested explanations:

The most common explanation is that because autistics tend to disregard social norms, they tend to disregard them in matters of gender expectations as well (see Strang et al., 2014; Gratton, 2019). For example, participant 20 in Cooper et al.'s study (2022) describes: "Being autistic is like everybody else has got the rulebook and you didn't, so you can understand why gender would come into it because that was in the rulebook you do not get." An intriguing yet debatable consequence of this explanation is the suggestion that, without social conditioning, a higher prevalence of gender fluidity may also exist in the neurotypical population (Gratton, 2019).

Another explanation attributes autistics' heightened focus on gender issues to autistic traits, such as an inclination to become intensely absorbed in specific areas of interest (Van der Laan, 2015) or cognitive rigidity (see Jacobs et al., 2014). However, this explanation may be criticized for not taking seriously enough autistics' psychological experience of their gender diversity as stemming from deep internal sources, dismissing it as a passing interest or a mere symptom of autism (see Zupanič et al., 2021; White, 2016).

Other studies have tried to attribute the connection between autism and gender diversity to biological factors, mainly to elevated levels of testosterone during pregnancy; some researchers link it to the notion that autism is associated with an "extreme male brain" (see Baron-Cohen, 2002; Di Ceglie et al., 2014). However, this explanation has not been sufficiently supported in research, nor does it explain the urge for gender change in males, as gender dysphoria manifests in males and females alike (see Warrier et al., 2020; Zupanič et al., 2021).

Overall, it seems that the connection between autism and gender diversity is not yet fully understood and likely involves biological, sociological, and psychological factors (Van der Miesen et al., 2016; Glidden et al., 2016).

To gain valuable insights, it is crucial to consider the perspectives of AGDs on this subject. Many AGDs feel that for them gender reflects external social norms more than an internal identity. Schillace, for example, describes:

> For me, my gender felt wholly outside of, rather than a reflection of, myself. Extrinsic. I had mainly constructed it from other external cues . . . I'm still in the play. But if I don't have a script, I can write my own." (Schillace, 2021)

Brown writes, "For many of us, gender mostly impacts our lives when projected onto us through other people's assumptions, but holds little intrinsic meaning" (Brown, 2016).

Many AGDs feel that they do not belong to a single gender, male or female, but that their gender identities are rather mixed or fluid. Porter describes:

> My abundant confusion with gender is part of who I am as an autistic non/binary-ish person . . . while I know that I am trans because physical dysphoria is a huge part of my experience, I don't know what exactly my gender is because I cannot perceive it . . . Life seems easier when I stop digging into the carousel of failed labels that I've masked myself into to get by and justify my existence to others. (Porter, 2020)

Interestingly, the indetermination or confusion regarding gender among autistics is similar to the one they have regarding emotions: autistics often struggle with prioritizing among various emotions, akin to the difficulty they face in selecting a single gender identity. Porter's description of the challenge in selecting one single gender identity from the "carousel of failed labels," as cited above, resonates strikingly with Rotem's description (in chapter 3) of how autistics experience emotions—as a carousel from which it is difficult to select one emotion, as the different emotions exist simultaneously, and it is difficult for them to prioritize between them. This carousel-like experience is so distinct to AGDs that it may be considered a facet of "an autistic gender identity," as Porter declared: "I am pretty sure that my gender is autistic" (Porter, 2020). Brown points out that some autistics call their unique gender experience "autigender" (Brown, 2016). Autistic activist Linda Brown coined the term "gendervague" to characterize the typical gender identity of autistics, who often resist the assumption that individuals must fit into categories of men and women. For example, participant number 20 in Cooper et al.'s study says, "I don't really want a body at all because it would never be exactly in between" (Cooper et al., 2022).

However, alongside the AGDs who challenge the need to choose a specific gender, some ardently adhere to one specific gender identity, often the one opposed to their assigned gender at birth, and some even undergo gender reassignment. There are also AGDs who identify as nonbinary yet prefer to be perceived as members of the opposite gender.

Therefore, in the realm of gender, autistics may find themselves at the extremes of either gender fluidity or a strong adherence to one gender identity. This mirrors the often-observed extremes in autistics between excessive fluidity and rigid thinking.

Another manifestation of autistics' tendency to belong to extremes is in the way they perceive society's attitude toward their gender diversity: on the one hand, some fundamentally don't care about social norms and expectations (e.g., Zain recounts, "I fit into the category of 'I'm not bothered' which is a blessing, so I've not had any negative experiences. I'm quite happy with my shield of 'this is who I am,' if I don't actually do the 'right' social male thing, tough, I'm used to not fitting in anyway"; Coleman-Smith et al., 2020). On the other hand, some autistics are much occupied with society's negative attitude toward them and may therefore suffer from depression, shame, and self-hatred. These extremes reflect autistics' tendency toward either obliviousness or overthinking. Nevertheless, there are also those who are in between these extremes, experiencing reasonable distress when confronted with transphobia.

Another impact of autism on the experience of gender is that autistics are more prone to thoroughly investigate the subject of gender in the intensive way that characterizes them. Porter, for example, writes, "I am an autistic nonbinary androromantic trans woman, and my journey to these five intersecting labels has been confusing and long" (Porter, 2020). Such thorough explorations may lead AGDs to solidify a well-defined gender identity. For example, participant 22 in Cooper et al.'s study (2022) suggests that autistics are "more in-tune with their gender," as "being autistic allows one to step outside of societal norms and follow one's own path." Receiving an autism diagnosis can also enhance self-validation in this process, as it helps individuals understand that their unique way of perceiving the world is not wrong but simply different.

TYPICAL EXPERIENCES

AGDs naturally possess diverse backgrounds, motivations, and life experiences, but they often encounter typical milestones throughout their gender journey:

Many AGDs recount that from a very young age they do not identify with the gender assigned to them at birth. They may refuse to respond when addressed as belonging to that gender or to behave according to societal expectations attached to it, such as clothing preferences or preferred games. For instance, Sam testifies, "I never felt I was a girl and I never . . . wanted to wear girly clothes or things like that. I always saw myself as being a man . . . [I thought] everyone else was strange 'cause they saw me as being a girl" (Coleman-Smith et al., 2020). Brown also recounts, "I always felt deeply uncomfortable with being labeled a 'girl' or 'woman'" (Brown, 2016).

In Hendrickx's study, 75% of the autistic women she interviewed did not identify with behaviors associated with girls from the beginning of their childhood (Hendrickx, 2015, p. 73). Many autistics assigned females at birth may exhibit tomboy-like behaviors, such as playing boys' games—basketball or hide-and-seek—or climbing trees, whereas those assigned male may not enjoy stereotypical boys' games such as ball games. Many AGDs indicate that they did not identify with either gender from a very young age. For example, Noy, a patient of mine, describes, "My autism and my being trans are intertwined and inseparable. I was a nonbinary child—I didn't feel connected to either gender, and it didn't really concern me. I wore both boys' and girls' clothes and played both boys' and girls' games. I was also an autistic child—I engaged in my special interests, which included animals, reading, and mythology, and I behaved in a way that felt natural and right to me, even though others thought it was strange."

Adolescence can be particularly challenging for AGDs as they become more aware of their neurological and gender diversity, even without an official diagnosis. They may grapple with bodily changes they didn't desire, leading to feelings of hatred toward their bodies or toward specific body elements such as body hair, breasts, or menstruation. The increasing pressure to conform to gender norms, especially for those assigned males at birth, can induce inner turmoil and distress. Some AGDs try to conceal or suppress their gender diverse tendencies due to fears of prejudice or rejection, often resulting in heightened inner conflicts and depression. Many AGDs have difficulties in expressing their distress because of their autism, which also makes it difficult for them to initiate relationships or converse with others to find understanding and support. Kate, for example, describes, "[Autism] makes it really difficult to say how I feel . . . I know lots of trans people who don't have a problem voicing their emotions, and how dysphoria affects them" (cited in Coleman-Smith et al., 2020).

Over time, the feelings of gender diversity tend to intensify for many AGDs, often leading them to investigate the subject intensively. They may seek connection with others experiencing gender diversity through social networks, communities, and organizations, thereby gaining information and a sense of belonging that may assist them in alleviating fears.

Frustration with living inauthentically often pushes AGDs to take action despite potential negative reactions and inner conflicts. They typically begin with a "social transition," which involves changing their name, hairstyle, clothing, and requesting different forms of address. Despite the potential criticism and ridicule that may accompany such transitions, most participants in the studies describe that it significantly enhanced their self-confidence and overall well-being, with some expressing that for them, "life properly began" (see Coleman-Smith et al., 2020; Cooper et al., 2022).

AGDs' "social transition" is typically influenced by their autistic characteristics: autism may make it harder for them to mediate the transition to their environment due to their challenges in communication. In addition, it may make it harder for them to conform to the norms associated with the other gender because of their struggles in adopting social norms in general, as Felix describes:

> I don't feel like I'm fully socially transitioned because I am experiencing more autism barriers than I was as a woman . . . I had thirty odd years to learn how to pretend to be female . . . and I'm still trying to come up with new strategies to be consistently read as male because expectations are different . . . Autism makes this slow. I'm also being read more as autistic because I've not learned the disguises for someone now read as male . . . My confidence is affected . . . so more autistic behavior, like stimming, creeps out. (Coleman-Smith et al., 2020)

Further, autism can either help them disregard social expectations and criticism or make them more vulnerable to criticism due to overthinking.

Many AGDs find satisfaction with their "social transition" and resistance to gender norms, whereas others continue to pursue "physical transition," which may include a range of physical interventions—starting with hormone blockers that suppress hormonal activity; continuing with receiving the hormones of the other sex (estrogen or testosterone); and potentially culminating in surgical procedures that may encompass several stages. It's important to note that many AGDs may undergo only some of these changes and not necessarily all of them.

For a physical transition, AGDs must obtain approvals from mental health and medical professionals. According to World Health Organization, to approve irreversible physical interventions, professionals must be convinced that there is a gender dysphoria, including distress. It is recommended to start these processes with reversible hormone blockers before considering more permanent hormonal or surgical interventions. While seeking the right approvals, various difficulties related to autism may arise:

First, these processes may be hindered by autistics' difficulties with decision making, executive functioning, making phone calls, completing forms and more (although some autistics may undertake all these with full-blown determination); it may also be difficult for them to act without clear instructions (e.g., participant 16 in Cooper et al.'s study describes, "It was very difficult because there's no set of rules, especially with transitioning, there's no kind of checklist well you do this and then you do this"; Cooper et al., 2022). They may have difficulties in expressing what they want or what they need, as well as in understanding professionals' questions or in providing them with the appropriate answers (e.g., participant 18 in Cooper et al.'s study describes: "a lot of their questions were really open-ended and I never really seemed to understand what they were actually asking"; Cooper et al., 2022); and they may also feel uncomfortable in health-care clinics because of their sensory sensitivities (Participant 2 describes: "they had these awful, bright lights that buzz, and then you're in the room with the clinician and they've got their computer on so that's humming away, and then you've got the clock ticking and then the temperature's always way, way too hot and it's just . . . bombard you with all the sensory stuff"; Cooper et al., 2022). As a result of all these, their turning to professionals may be hued by numerous hurdles and anxieties and may involve extensive preparations and overthinking.

Autistics may also encounter difficulties stemming from the attitudes of professionals toward neurological and gender diversity:

First, they may suspect that the desire for gender transition is nothing but a symptom of autism, such as being obsessive or overthinking, which may pass with time, rather than a deep component of their identity. They may perceive them as childish or immature, particularly due to their special interests in subjects such as fantasy, comics, or superheroes, and may therefore refuse their requests for medical interventions (see Strang, Powers et al., 2018; Coleman-Smith et al., 2020; Cooper et al., 2022). One well-known case in the AGDs community is that of Kayden Clarke, whose therapist had refused to approve his hormone therapy until after his autistic disorder "would be healed," treating it as an illness, which led him to end his life by making the police shoot him (White, 2016). Nevertheless, Strang and colleagues emphasize that autism should not invalidate the gender dysphoria diagnosis, and the clinical guidelines published by an international working group in this subject emphasize that autistics' access to gender medical treatments should not be blocked because of their autism (Strang, Meagher et al., 2018).

Research indicates that physical transition can significantly reduce depression, anxiety, and gender dysphoria (see Nobili et al., 2018; Zupanič et al., 2021, Coleman-Smith et al., 2020). However, even after such a change, AGDs still face challenges such as transphobic prejudice, discrimination, and bullying. Studies show that these are more common toward trans women than toward trans men, perhaps because there is a wider acceptance in our society toward masculinity than femininity (see Nobili et al., 2018). Other difficulties may be related to the demeanor of family members, who may react with criticism or sanctions. Research shows that parents' criticism increases AGDs feelings of distress, whereas their support may be an important protective factor, contributing to the self-esteem and psychological well-being (Zupanič et al., 2021).

Another difficulty that AGDs have to cope with is the conflict between their desire to participate in group meetings, parades, or festivals of the LGBT community and their difficulty in doing so due to their heightened sensory and social sensitivities.

Weighing the advantages and disadvantages related to the "physical change" process, participants in the studies referenced consistently reported that this process was their preferred option (see Coleman-Smith et al., 2020; Cooper et al., 2022). Of course, there is room for more studies on this subject. Nonetheless, in light of all the psychological challenges associated with the social and physical transitions, it is important that AGDs receive the appropriate psychological support from mental health services.

IMPLICATIONS FOR THERAPY

Given the significant psychological distress that AGDs experience due to internal conflicts as well as societal challenges such as criticism, bullying, discrimination, and exclusion, it is crucial for professionals to enhance their understanding of autism, gender diversity, and their intersection. This will enable them to provide the necessary support and empathy for AGDs, who often cope with anxiety, depression, self-harm, and suicidal behaviors.

I propose some general guidelines for treating this specific group, drawing from the limited studies that address this issue (Strang, Meagher et al., 2018; Strang, Knauss et al., 2020; Strang, Klomp et al., 2020) as well as my own understandings on the subject. These guidelines can be categorized into three areas—autism-related, gender diversity-related, and the intersection of both:

Autism-Related Guidelines—Professionals should enhance their knowledge of autism and share it with their patients through psychoeducation. They are expected to assist AGDs in coping with challenges related to emotion regulation, executive functions, anxiety, rigidity, emotional challenges, and sensory sensitivities while helping them work through psychological traumas. Validating their experiences and devising effective coping strategies can provide the empathy and understanding that AGDs often seek and benefit from.

Gender Diversity–Related Guidelines—It is important to help AGDs understand their gender identity needs and desires. If they consider gender reassignment procedures, therapists should discuss the risks, benefits, and potential effects of the process with them. Caution and responsibility are very important, particularly when working with teenagers, as gender reassignment can have irreversible psychological and medical consequences. Therapists should be knowledgeable about the medical aspects of gender reassignment, including the effects of hormonal and medical treatments, and be able to refer patients to the relevant experts. Familiarity with patients' legal rights is also recommended. Supporting AGDs and their families in dealing with the psychosocial challenges related to gender diversity and connecting them with relevant resources and communities can also be helpful.

Guidelines Concerning the Intersection of Autism and Gender Diversity—Therapists should be aware of the challenges AGDs encounter in expressing their feelings and of their tendency to approach things rationally or focus on concrete aspects rather than on their emotions. It is recommended to assist them in gaining different perspectives, expressing emotional complexities, identifying their needs and desires, developing flexible thinking, and making future plans. Clear communication and consideration of sensory sensitivities should be maintained, too. Above all, therapists should approach autism and gender diversity respectfully, avoiding a pathologizing perspective, respecting their feelings, desires, and needs, and not trying to "normalize" them.

AGDs may also benefit from group therapy, which can provide them with further knowledge, emotional support, a sense of belonging, and the possibility of forming social relationships. However, they may struggle in such settings with the social aspects and sensory and emotional overload.

Family members, especially parents of AGD teenagers, should be offered help and support to better meet their children's needs and acquire knowledge about autism and gender diversity. Family support can serve as an important protective factor, enhancing self-esteem, satisfaction, and psychological well-being (Strang, Knauss et al., 2020).

CONCLUDING REMARKS

Considering the significant prevalence of individuals who are both autistic and experience gender diversity or gender dysphoria, it is imperative to offer them understanding and suitable treatment. As a "squared" minority group, these individuals encounter discrimination, bullying, and criticism, resulting in mental health challenges such as depression, anxiety, low self-esteem, and heightened risks of self-harm and suicide.

The link between autism and gender diversity or gender dysphoria has been explored, with various explanations suggested, such as relating it to their tendency to disregard social norms or to be obsessed with specific areas of interest or to hormonal influences. However, each explanation has its limitations. It is proposed that autistics may tend to keep different possibilities open and not prioritize one gender identity, leading to a "gendervague" or "autigender" attitude to gender. Alongside this, some autistics with gender dysphoria may choose to adopt the identity of the opposite gender and undergo gender reassignment processes.

Autism can both facilitate and complicate matters related to gender. On one hand, it allows autistics to sometimes disregard social norms or deepen their understanding of gender issues. On the other hand, they may have more challenges in seeking professional help, and they may encounter a lack of understanding and validation from professionals, which hampers their access to essential support.

The chapter underscores the necessity of training health-care professionals to understand autism, gender diversity, and their co-occurrence, enabling better identification of individuals experiencing this combination and providing them with appropriate help. Therapists must be mindful of the unique challenges this population faces, such as difficulties in expressing emotions and considering complex or future perspectives. Supporting family members, especially those of teenage children, is also essential.

As a society, we must strive to overcome disrespect, discrimination, bullying, and transphobia against this group and offer them the medical and psychological services they deserve.

Chapter 8

Klinefelter Syndrome and Autism

This short chapter delves into the intriguing connection between autism and "Klinefelter syndrome," a condition in which individuals assigned male at birth have an extra X chromosome (XXY). Although not rare, occurring in approximately 1 out of 600 male births, about two-thirds of those born with this syndrome remain undiagnosed or are diagnosed later in life, often during fertility treatments (Silva et al., 2022). In Israel, a considerable portion of the diagnoses occurs during medical examinations conducted in the military recruiting process.

Research from the past few decades indicates that 10–27% of individuals with Klinefelter syndrome have been found to be autistic or exhibit a high prevalence of autistic traits (Van Rijn et al., 2006, 2008; Bruining et al., 2009; Samango-Sprouse et al., 2013; see summaries of studies in Jah et al., 2007; Tartaglia et al., 2017). It can be assumed that as awareness of autism characteristics grows and the reliability of diagnostic tools improves, this rate may prove to be even higher.

I have chosen to dedicate a special chapter to exploring the link between Klinefelter syndrome and autism due to its significant prevalence and its potential to uncover a profound connection between autism and sex chromosomes that is not fully understood.

THE LINK BETWEEN KLINEFELTER SYNDROME AND AUTISM

Klinefelter syndrome (XXY) is characterized by deficiencies in the male reproductive system, including small testicles, reduced sperm production, fertility problems, and low testosterone levels. These typically result in a rounded body shape, enlarged breast tissue, and sparse facial and body hair. Research has also highlighted other associated challenges such as learning disabilities, executive dysfunctions, attention disorders, difficulties in emotion regulation, delayed language development, impairments in working memory and decision making, clumsiness, anxiety, and depression. Individuals with Klinefelter syndrome often struggle with social challenges and are frequently described as introverted, quiet, nonassertive, anxious, withdrawn, and vulnerable to bullying (see Geschwind & Dykens, 2004; Jah et al., 2007; Tartaglia et al., 2017).

One may notice a significant overlap between the characteristics of Klinefelter syndrome and those of autism, particularly in terms of social difficulties, attention problems, executive dysfunctions, anxiety, difficulties in problem-solving, low information processing, and motor clumsiness (Geschwind et al., 2000; Jacobs et al., 1988; Tartaglia et al., 2017). Individuals with Klinefelter syndrome also struggle with interpreting social cues such as facial expressions and body language, expressing emotions, and regulating emotions (Van Rijn et al., 2006). Jah et al. (2007) suggest that individuals with Klinefelter syndrome may not always appear to meet the autism criterion of "special interests." However, such special interests may be overlooked in them because they may resemble regular hobbies, such as playing computer games, listening to music, or watching movies or TV series, however the distinction lies in the heightened intensity of such interests, as is often observed in autistic women as well.

The underdiagnosis of autism in individuals with Klinefelter syndrome can be attributed mainly to the limited knowledge professionals have about autism, as well as to their masking of the challenges related to autism to fit better into society, as is also frequently observed in autistic girls and women.

MOSHE'S STORY

Moshe, who was raised in an ultra-Orthodox family in Jerusalem, pursued an autism diagnosis in his mid-twenties. He has delicate facial features and a round body structure. He seems very open, frank, and naive, like a little child, and touched my heart deeply. At the same time, his manners lack consideration, as is evident in behaviors such as sending late-night messages or arriving significantly late for appointments without offering an apology.

Moshe grew up in a large family of 12 children, where attention was scarce. His parents' financial situation was tight, relying on government allowances for their livelihood. Moshe was a quiet, undemanding child, often lost in his own world. He enjoyed playing with sand or water puddles and collecting phone cards and coins. He experienced anxieties related to darkness, medical doctors, and movie characters that haunted his mind for extended periods. Moshe was also highly sensitive to noises, smells, and touch, and had difficulty tolerating clothing labels or seams in his socks.

During elementary school, Moshe remained quiet and absorbed in his own world, and his inner difficulties were hardly noticed. His parents were preoccupied with their own troubles and didn't pay attention to his problems. Moshe rarely initiated contact with others and struggled to understand jokes or social cues. He didn't find joy in ball games like most children did, and often spent breaks alone, engrossed in books or in the company of the school's pets. In higher religious school (yeshiva), Moshe faced difficulties adapting to rules and making friends, and became a target of bullying. He did not do well at his studies and had suicidal thoughts but didn't act on them. He developed a disrupted sleep schedule and eventually was expelled from the yeshiva.

As Moshe was about to recruit to military service, the army doctor referred him to genetic examinations, revealing that he had Klinefelter syndrome. This discovery came as a shock to Moshe, especially when he found out about the fertility problems associated with this condition. Nevertheless, he was drafted into the army and served as a clerk, diligently carrying out his duties, though having problems in fitting socially.

After completing his military service, Moshe undertook several temporary jobs for which he was overqualified, such as a delivery person or a supermarket orderly. His lack of interest in small talk made it difficult for him to get along with coworkers, and he struggled with the loud music played in the car, often becoming the target of ridicule. Although he attempted to mimic others' behaviors at times, he found it exhausting and unnatural. Moreover, his superiors' dissatisfaction with his work exacerbated his anxiety and distress. Consequently, he frequently felt the need to withdraw and disconnect from others, finding solace in reading fantasy and science fiction books and watching movies on his computer.

Over time, Moshe realized that he was attracted to men rather than women. He sought therapy, initially encountering a therapist who aimed to change his sexual orientation, but eventually found another therapist who supported him in accepting himself. Moshe holds liberal views and questions his religious identity but maintains an ultra-Orthodox lifestyle to better fit into his environment.

A family relative advised Moshe to seek an autism diagnosis. This new diagnosis provided him with a better understanding of himself and reduced his feelings of guilt regarding his difficulties. Subsequently, he applied for government support, pursued appropriate therapy, and enrolled in an electronics course to further develop his aptitudes.

DISCUSSION

Research suggests that Klinefelter syndrome is associated with a notable rate of autism or autistic traits, which are often overlooked. Many characteristics of Klinefelter syndrome overlap those found in autism, including social difficulties, executive dysfunction, difficulties in problem solving and information processing, motor clumsiness, attention issues, and anxiety (Jah et al., 2007; Tartaglia et al., 2017).

These findings may raise intriguing possibilities regarding the connection between autism and the sex chromosomes. Some studies indicate a potential link between the X chromosome and social development. For instance, women with Turner syndrome, who have only one sex chromosome (XO), exhibit more social problems and difficulties with reading social cues and facial expressions (Skuse, 2006); Kim Peek, the man who was the inspiration for the main autistic character in the film *Rain Man*, was diagnosed with FG syndrome, a rare X chromosome-linked genetic syndrome (Opitz et al., 2008). However, further investigation into the potential linkage between autism and sex chromosomes is warranted. It is also worth noting that individuals with additional sex chromosomes (beyond XXY) tend to exhibit more pronounced autistic features and are, therefore, more frequently diagnosed with autism. For example, studies on the XXYY population found rates of 33% (Sreedhar et al., 2015) or 52% (Tartaglia et al., 2017) of autism diagnoses. These findings may again indicate a link between the sex chromosomes and autism.

Another interesting idea is that the X chromosomes may be a protective factor against autism, in view of the fact that autistic characteristics do exist but are less prominent in individuals with XXY syndrome. Casanova (2014a) suggests a "female protective factor in autism," hypothesizing that women express autism less severely and are diagnosed less frequently with autism. She proposes that increased estrogen levels may reduce the signs of autism, presenting a case of a person with Klinefelter syndrome who initially received an autism diagnosis in her childhood but had it removed in adolescence, suggesting that the increase in estrogen during adolescence might have diminished autism characteristics (Casanova, 2014b).

From a clinical perspective, it is vital to examine the presence of autism among individuals with Klinefelter syndrome and vice versa. This understanding can assist individuals with these conditions, as well as those around them, in better understanding their mental state and offering the appropriate support.

Further research is needed to explore the links between autism and Klinefelter syndrome, as well as the potential connections between autism and the sex chromosomes. Such findings may validate autistics' feelings that deep internal factors are influencing their gender identity.

Chapter 9

Autistics in the Sex Industry

> I don't see things the way other people do. The attitude towards sex in our culture is mediated by cultural conventions, while I don't see things through conventional lenses. (Sivan, an autistic former sex worker, cited below)

Very rarely during diagnostic assessments did my jaw drop, as happened on several occasions when highly intelligent, successful, and beautiful autistic women disclosed to me that they had been working in the sex industry at certain periods in their lives. I was especially seized by the way they told me about it, quite nonchalantly and with no trace of regret. Several questions instantly jumped into my mind: How did they feel about this work at the time, and how does it affect them today? Should they be seen as victims or as yielding an alternative morality, as they have tried to portray it?

After delving into this topic, I discovered that autistics work in the sex industry, in jobs such as stripping, erotic dancing, erotic calls, videos, or paid sex services, is much more prevalent than one may assume. However, the lack of research on this subject is notable.

Moreover, the engagement of autistics in the sex industry brings forth important psychological, moral, and social justice questions: Should they be viewed as victims, in light of their challenges in finding regular jobs and their increased susceptibility to exploitation due to their naïveté? Is this choice reflective of a lack of integrative judgment or of an alternative moral perspective they hold? Further, what are the psychological ramifications of such work on their well-being, given their distinctive psychological profile? Some of these questions will be discussed in this chapter, even though they do not necessarily yield clear, unequivocal answers.

The chapter will present several personal stories of autistics who used to work in the sex industry, sourced from the internet, published books, and my own encounters. It will discuss the factors leading autistics to choose such a work, the advantages and disadvantages they may find in it, and the dangers and challenges they may face.

PERSONAL STORIES

Reese Piper

Reese Piper, once a stripper in New York strip clubs, has openly shared her experiences from that chapter of her life in various articles and interviews (see Piper 2018a, 2018b, 2019; Sage, 2020; Luterman, 2021).

At 24, Piper turned to work as a stripper to repay a $100,000 loan she had taken to fund her education. After being rejected for other jobs, she turned to that job, which was easier to get into, as she describes: "You don't need to have a degree. You don't need to show that you can multitask . . . You don't necessarily need to be very professional to get hired" (Luterman, 2021). And "sex work has been there while other jobs closed the door on our faces" (Piper, 2018a).

Piper describes that throughout her life she had difficulties in knowing how to behave in a socially acceptable manner, pick up on other people's emotions, read facial expressions and body language, and make eye contact. When she started working at the club she had no idea how to approach customers or interpret their behaviors. She tried to imitate her colleagues' body language and opening lines and gradually learned the job:

> I would say hello, ask how their day is going, ask them a few questions about themselves, relate it to myself, and then ask if they want to buy me drink—that would tell me if they were willing to spend money. Through this job, I learned to have a back-and-forth conversation. (Sage, 2020)

Piper used to plan in advance every detail of the interaction, including how many seconds to look into a man's eyes to create a feeling of intimacy, when to look away to avoid too much intimacy, when to whisper in a customer's ear, and what is appropriate to say exactly (Piper, 2018b). Over time, she became better at interpreting facial expressions and identifying customers who might spend more money. She acknowledges that these are skills that "most people learn unconsciously, but that I'd always struggled with" (Piper, 2018b).

Piper recounts that what helped her in her work was the fact that the conduct rules were clear to her and that she could repeat the same actions over and over. She was also pleased to have control over her working hours. For the first time in her life, that job gave her a sense of competency, boosting her self-confidence. Piper states that the stigma associated with sex work did not affect her in the way it might affect others: "I had less shame and less embarrassment about getting close with others. The dirtiness that is presumed by people outside of sex work . . . I just didn't take it in" (Piper, 2018b). However, she struggled with the long working hours and needed a substantial amount of time to recover (Luterman, 2021).

Piper felt that her work helped her improve her conversational skills and her ability to interpret social cues outside of the club, too. She learned to listen to others and to respond to them appropriately. However, she still felt different from others. Once, desperate for answers, she called an online forum and after describing her characteristics, it was suggested to her for the first time in her life that she might be autistic. Delving deeper into this subject helped her comprehend why she had endured suffering throughout her entire life, ultimately leading to a sense of relief and cessation of self-blame for her difficulties.

Piper retired from sex work as she wanted to develop herself in other directions. Having developed her capacity for forming meaningful relationships, she no longer felt the necessity to fulfill those needs through her work.

Dawn Prince-Hughes

Dawn Prince-Hughes, an American professor of anthropology, is another autistic woman who worked in the sex industry. For a short period she made a living through erotic dancing in clubs, as described in her autobiography (Prince-Hughes, 2004). At around 16 years old, she dropped out of high school and left her parents' home, encountering challenges in finding a job due to her lack of experience and exhibiting extreme anxiety during interviews. After wandering for several years, she came across a dance club where the owner offered her a job as an erotic dancer. Prince-Hughes amusingly describes her experience as a dancer in that club from her very naive perspective at the time: she recounts how she liked dancing due to her strong need to move, which may be connected to autistics' need of repetitive movements; and was especially drawn to animal-like movements such as jumping, rocking, and screaming due to her interest in animals. She was also interested in ritual dances because of her fascination with the tribal origins of culture. Because of her heightened sensory sensitivities, she used to wear leather jackets (as their thickness calmed her), dark glasses (which prevented her from being dazzled by the light), and thick boots (which made her feel more grounded) and was totally unaware of the provocative nature of that appearance. She liked to dance without interacting with other people and loved the music and the surreal look of the club. It did bother her that some men there cursed, shouted, or treated the dancers as objects, but she focused on her work to survive financially until she discovered her passion for working with animals and later pursued a career as an anthropologist and primatologist. It seems that her autistic ability to focus on one thing—the dance—allowed her to ignore the complex context of the sex industry.

Liara Roux

A captivating portrayal of an autistic's experiences as an escort girl is found in Liara Roux's book titled *Whore of New-York* (Roux, 2021). Roux, who was diagnosed as both autistic and a gifted child in her childhood, provides in the book intriguing insights regarding her work in the sex industry:

The book begins by delving into Roux's childhood and youth in New York, highlighting typical experiences of high-functioning autistic girls: as a curious girl with special interests in nature, animals, trains, *Star Wars* movies, computers, Pokémon, and fantasy books, she found it easier to connect with "nerdy" boys who shared those interests and a love for physical activities. She was an excellent pupil almost effortlessly, even though she had concentration problems and sleep issues, as is common among autistics. In adolescence, she became aware of her differences and attempted to imitate her peers' behaviors, read psychology books, and learn to decipher body language and make eye contact to fit in socially.

During college, Roux developed a keen interest in feminist ideas. From a young age, she believed that women may use their sexual power to regain power robbed from them by patriarchy. She discovered ancient texts supporting this view and even wrote a seminar paper on the topic.

To make a living, Roux decided to post an ad on a website for women seeking arrangements after thoroughly researching this topic through books and online articles. She describes her first sexual encounter with a client as a positive experience—"I had wondered if I would feel a sense of shame, of dirtiness. Instead, I felt happy" (p. 88)—because she believed she had made him feel good and earned enough money for the month.

Beyond the financial aspect, Roux provides several other justifications for her work in the sex industry: she writes that her meetings with clients have satisfied her curiosity and need for connection with others:

> Some, like me, get a voyeuristic pleasure from the work. Sex can be more about seeing into someone than about experiencing pleasure . . . I am the type of sex worker, and there are many of us, who delight in strange requests from clients, who read about psychology and sexuality and apply it all in our bookings, approaching the work almost as a type of therapy. (p. 166)

Roux states that for her sex was not solely a physical act but an opportunity for emotional giving, viewing her work almost as a form of therapy, delighting in clients' unusual requests and applying her knowledge of psychology and sexuality. She valued listening to her clients, offering advice, and engaging in activities such as smoking drugs or discussing various topics with them. She recounts:

> For me, the physical aspect is far less interesting than the emotional. I market myself in an attempt to entice clients who want to talk, to be cared for, to work through something. It makes the work fulfilling, something I can look back on and smile. It is, however, far more work. After an emotionally taxing client, I usually need to take the rest of the day off. It's intense. (p. 188)

Roux notes that her favorite clients are "the ones with deep wounds who need a healing touch," such as men who feared touch due to childhood abuse or being a virgin: "I like to hold them, gently caress them, and teach them about the types of touch that can bring pleasure" (p. 187). She notes:

> I love very easily. I can see the best parts of people without trying too hard, the things that make them delightful, their talents, their vulnerabilities. I love making people feel cared for. Perhaps that is a large part of why I started doing sex work in the first place. (p. 165)

Roux explains that she turned to the sex industry because she enjoys giving pleasure to others, among other reasons. She describes how already as a child she had a high level of empathy and loved, for example, petting cats or giving a massage to her mother (p. 27). Roux attributes her heightened empathy to her autism (p. 27). However, she had to learn how not to give too much of herself to others: "I had to learn how to walk away as well. Being generous doesn't mean you need to be a martyr. You can help more people if you nurture yourself" (p. 166)—as many autistics have to learn, because they often concern others' interests over their own.

Typical of autistics, Roux could be emotionally distant at times, proclaiming that for her "sex is something that is less emotional than it is for most" (p. 166) and that the sexual act may feel more "impersonal" for her (p. 166):

> The first few times you orgasm with someone it does feel intense and intimate, of course. But you could say the same thing about going to see a personal trainer, the dentist, or getting your hair cut. Personally, getting my hair cut is far more intimate for me than having sex; this person is going to physically change your body! (p. 168)

Roux describes that she does not feel shame or discomfort as others feel in relation to sex, because her autism allows her to do it from an emotional distance (in an interview with Braiker, 2022). Roux feels satisfied with her ability to stay outside of conventions: "The act of transgression is a thrill, as is teaching my clients to fully embrace their sexuality, to learn how to transmute that shame and disgust into a potent pleasure" (p. 185). She points out that there are cultures in which sex work is not perceived as shameful, as in Hong Kong (p. 193).

As a gifted person, Roux anchors her views in cultural references and, for example, points out that sex workers often admire Lilith, considered Adam's first wife, who had been expelled from the Garden of Eden because she had asked for equality, or believe in Ishtar, the Sumerian goddess who is considered the chaotic and generous goddess of prostitutes (p. 155).

Roux justifies her work choice as a feminist act and as a way for women to regain power from patriarchy (p. 182). She emphasizes the importance of women's financial independence, arguing that many women cannot do what they want in matters of abortions, childbirth, or divorce because they are financially dependent on their partners and are not rewarded for doing housework. Roux condemns the efforts of people in power to regulate spirituality or pleasure by imposing restrictions or prohibitions, particularly in areas such as drugs or sex: "I cannot for the life of me understand the desire to tell someone else that they must live their life in a certain way, especially for decisions that cause no harm to others" (p. 185). Roux appears to somewhat idealize prostitution, viewing it as intertwined with spirituality and pleasure, while overlooking the prevalent elements of violence, exploitation, and pain inherent in this profession.

Roux describes that she tends to see things in "black and white" and to stick only to positive aspects at times (pp. 196–197). This tendency has also manifested in her personal life, particularly in the abusive relationship she had with her partner, who would routinely spend the large sums of money that Roux earned and pressed her to work harder through emotional manipulation. Nonetheless, Roux has continued to regard her partner as benevolent, not picking up her manipulations and lies, which is typical for autistics. Only through the help of her psychotherapist has Roux gradually learned to see that relationship with more intricacy and could eventually separate from that partner. Her therapist assisted her in expressing her needs more effectively and in boosting her self-confidence (pp. 183, 190). Over time, Roux learned to see the sex industry with more complexity as well. In an interview, she emphasized that she is against idealizing sex work; however, she is also against perceiving it as inevitably terrible, and for her the truth lies somewhere in the middle, depending on individual experiences (Specter, 2021).

Similar to her difficulty in setting boundaries in her personal relationship, Roux describes that the most difficult part for her in her work was in setting emotional and physical boundaries for her clients, for instance in asking them to use contraceptives, but over time she learned how to navigate this.

She also highlights additional difficulties in her work, such as physical pains, anxiety attacks before meeting clients she didn't favor, and a sense of burnout ("All I wanted to do was play video games, smoke weed, watch *Star Trek*"; p. 145). Roux has suffered physical violence from a client once, when a drunken customer tried to choke her, and as a result she endured nightmares for several months.

It should be emphasized that Roux's experiences do not represent the broader experiences of sex industry workers, but possibly only those of the few who can filter their clients and choose if, when, and how to work. Roux writes that it is clear to her that most women in the sex industry face much worse experiences, including violence and exploitation, and that most women choose this work because of economic distress, violence, sexual exploitation, or trafficking. Roux has been advocating in the past years for women's rights in the sex industry and has spoken out against restrictions on sex advertising on the internet, believing that such limitations could push women into more dangerous situations rather than controlling their encounters through the internet (see Roux, 2018).

Rona

When Rona came to meet me, she impressed me highly as a beautiful, brilliant young woman who had achieved considerable success in the field of finance. It was inscrutable that for several years she had made her living from working in strip clubs.

Rona grew up in a South American country with her mother, as her father had abandoned them while she was in her mother's womb. As a child Rona was curious and had a keen love for pets and stuffed animals. She shied away from touches and noises and was very picky in her eating. In kindergarten she almost always played alone as she was afraid of other children. At the age of eight, Rona immigrated to Israel with her mother and grandfather, settling in a small provincial town. Her mother worked in low-paying jobs, struggling to make ends meet. Rona found her classmates dirty and had difficulty making friends and hardly spoke with anyone. During breaks, she would sit by herself, reading books and learning Hebrew without speaking at all. Hence, her teachers suspected her of plagiarizing her essays. During adolescence, Rona felt "transparent" and different. She developed an eating disorder and was sent to psychotherapy, but hardly spoke there, felt misunderstood, and left treatment. She had trouble falling asleep at night and would often read or watch TV until late hours and therefore at school often dozed off. She was very beautiful and had several sexual experiences, but no one wanted her as a steady girlfriend, which deeply hurt her. In ninth grade, Rona stopped attending school and completed her studies through an evening school, where she had few contacts with others who were considered "outsiders" like her. She successfully passed the matriculation exams.

Rona had a strong desire to pursue higher education to gain freedom and independence but had no idea how to finance it. A friend from a similar background offered her to join her work as a lap dancer at a club, assuring her that it was an excellent way to earn money, "not terrible at all and actually even fun." The friend provided her detailed guidance on what clothing to buy—suits that were easy to open and close, short skirts, and high-heeled shoes—and where to purchase them. She also instructed her on the work protocol: approaching a man, sitting on his lap, not allowing him to touch anything but the outer parts of her body, smiling, engaging in small talk, and getting up after about one-third of a song, because men were charged per portion of a song. Her friend suggested thinking of the men as pieces of furniture—"you just sit on them and get paid for it"—which Rona, as an autistic, took literally, and thereby that sentence helped her a lot. With these detailed explanations, Rona felt prepared to take on the job.

Rona's first experience at the club was strange for her. The unfamiliar environment with new smells, lights, and music, coupled with her low self-confidence, made her believe that no one would want her to approach them. However, a "cute" man called her, and she followed her friend's instructions as she observed from a distance, confirming with hand gestures that she was doing things right. After about a minute, her friend signaled her to stop, and Rona moved on to another man. She was surprised by how easily she could earn money. In the following weeks, other girls at the club helped Rona by providing guidance, like correcting her overly wide smiles. Rona appreciated these precise instructions because all her life she had been expected to understand things without explanations. Suddenly having step-by-step guidance was extremely helpful to her.

Rona felt secure at her workplace due to the presence of strict rules that protected her: the men were required to wear pants made of hard fabric to minimize sensations and were prohibited from touching intimate parts of the workers' bodies. Guards ensured compliance, and if a woman complained, she was always justified. Sometimes men asked Rona to go up with them to the upper floor rooms to have sex, as other girls in the club did, but Rona was absolutely determined to abstain from such encounters, as she knew she wanted to lead a decent life later on.

Contrary to what one might expect, Rona was not disgusted by the men at the club. She found them mostly clean and tidy. In addition, she had the freedom to choose whom to approach. She noted that in her previous jobs, such as working as a waitress where she had to handle food she didn't like, or in an office with unpleasant smells, she experienced much stronger feelings of repulsion. Rona believed that the men in the club, not herself, should have felt embarrassed because she was the one in control of the situation.

Rona liked the fact that the rules in her work were very clear and that she had fixed working hours. The odors of cigarettes and alcohol in the club were constant and familiar to her, and the music was not too loud. Rona even enjoyed watching the strip shows that took place on stage, appreciating the aesthetic dimension in them.

The most challenging aspect for Rona was engaging in small talks, but she gradually learned to do it through trial and error:

> Before, I was shy and had extreme social anxiety. I had no idea how to start a conversation. With time I learned what was working: for instance, I found out that if I had said to someone, "You're handsome," or asked him, "How was your day?," this would make him want to be with me as much as possible. I've learned that when I saw a ring on someone's finger, I could safely say, "You look like someone who is married and has two kids," or "You seem to me like a very good father," and they felt as if I was reading who they were, making them eager to give me anything. If someone told me that he had given up a football match to come to the club, I could safely ask the next guy, "Did you miss a match in order to see me?," and this made him think that I totally understood him and understood about football. In this way I learned what was working and what wasn't, much as AI bots learn after receiving inputs from 50 people every day.

The men in the club were much impressed by Rona's knowledge and understanding of economic and political topics, setting her apart from other girls in the club.

Although Rona felt completely comfortable at work, she often experienced loneliness outside of it due to a lack of friends. Saving money for her education, she seldom went out or took vacations. During exam seasons, she took breaks from work to concentrate solely on her studies, aligning with the challenges that autistics face with transitions. Working at the club enabled her to manage this without economic stress or anxiety. Rona excelled in her studies and graduated with honors, which otherwise would have been unattainable for her.

Looking back, Rona has no regrets about that chapter in her life. Instead, she remembers it positively, as it paved her way to obtain a respected degree and embark on a promising career at a young age, achievements otherwise unattainable. She believes that during that time she reinvented herself by learning how to communicate, interpret body language, and understand others' intentions and emotions. She maintains that for her it was "the best school of communication." Her self-confidence significantly increased at that time, as she felt liked and desired, in stark contrast to the constant rejection and lack of love she experienced before. Rona believes that no psychological treatment could have achieved such transformative results.

After graduation, Rona left the club and secured a prestigious job in economics after she had learned how to navigate interview pitfalls such as eye contact or over-directness. At first, navigating teamwork and social conventions was challenging for her, but over time she impressed those around her with her high intelligence, meticulous attention to detail, and creative thinking. Rona is highly esteemed in her company as someone who can come up with innovative solutions to intricate problems. She has been promoted several times and earns a substantial salary. Rona is now married with three children, and no one around her has any idea about her previous job.

Sivan

Sivan was brought up in a middle-class family in central Israel. Her parents were emotionally distant and often neglectful of their children's emotional needs. Sivan suspects that her mother may also be autistic, as she never had friends, kept rigid habits and routines, never talked about feelings, and was not involved in her children's lives. Sivan herself exhibited delayed speech, being unable to speak until the age of three. She was a selective eater and rejected feminine attire and dolls, preferring to climb trees and play football with boys. In school, she was straightforward and justice-seeking, which led others to distance themselves from her. During high school, she felt lonely and misunderstood, resulting in self-harm. In the army, she served as a tough commander, often being asked, "Why don't you smile"?, and had no friends.

Sivan pursued a computer science degree, supporting herself through low-paying jobs such as working in security. After completing her studies, her high skills, outgoing nature, and impressive appearance enabled her to secure positions in leading high-tech companies. However, she was consistently fired from these jobs, primarily because of her deficient social skills and a penchant for tactless criticism. For instance, she once scolded her superior for taking extended lunch breaks.

Sivan is exceptionally beautiful and has always attracted numerous admirers and sexual partners of both genders. She considers herself highly sexual, finding it easy to be sexually satisfied with men. Autistic women, she believes, often experience sex as purposeful and enjoyable, similar to men. However, forming emotional connections with men is challenging for her, whereas falling in love with women comes more naturally.

Sivan was briefly married and has one daughter. After her divorce, she could hardly support her daughter due to job terminations and substantial debts. In a casual conversation with a father from her daughter's kindergarten, after she had complained about her financial situation, he jokingly said,

"Go find a sponsor," and she took his words very seriously (in light of the autistic tendency to take things literally). She placed an ad on a dating site and received numerous calls within minutes, which continued to increase daily. Sivan rejected older or vulgar individuals, thereby filtering out problematic clients.

Sivan chose this path primarily out of financial necessity. Moreover, she asserted that in other countries students often funded their studies in this way, while Israeli society was more religious and conservative, and she refused to conform to such social rules. In addition, Sivan genuinely enjoyed sex and knew she was skilled in that area. She proclaims:

> There is a lot of authenticity in my sex appeal. I'm not trying to be a porn star with weird looks, but I do what I do naturally and with lots of energy. There hasn't been a man that I've been with who didn't tell me something like, "You're the sexiest woman I've ever been with." Once a friend who saw me in a bathing suit told his wife that it was insane how sexy I looked, and that what makes me even more so is that I'm not at all aware of it [I told Sivan that in this regard she reminded me of the beautiful actress Daryl Hannah, who was also diagnosed on the autistic spectrum—S. B. S]. For me, sex comes very naturally. Men love women who are liberated and who don't pretend to be innocent girls but rather enjoy sex. A woman who tries to enjoy herself and do what she wants and does not just lie in one position is very sexy. I believe in sexuality that stems from a libidinal drive for creation. Each of us has a divine energy within himself.

However, Sivan emphasizes that her decision to engage in sex work did not stem from high values but, rather, from an economic need, combined with her natural talent in this area. Sivan's attitude to sex was very simple and matter-of-fact: she used to meet clients wearing jeans and a T-shirt, sharing her personal phone number with them, and often hosting at her own home. During the encounters Sivan used to talk very frankly, as she does in her real life, because that was the easiest for her ("I was the same as always, 'a rose is a rose is a rose'"). For her, the meetings were not solely physical but involved genuine conversations as well, with most of the time devoted to activities beyond sex, such as talking, showering together, or enjoying a cup of coffee. Sivan found that for most men the personal attention was more important than the sexual aspect. Meetings were limited to two hours, and Sivan never saw more than one client per day in order not to feel too "prostitute-like": "It was important for me to keep my dignity and to listen to myself. I tried to act according to my personal rules and integrity. This was the only way for me to feel that I was in control of things and not a victim." Sivan established clear boundaries and had no difficulty stating which activities she would not partake in, such as BDSM or role-playing, and her clients respected those limits.

Sivan asserts that she did not experience shame, disgust, or embarrassment in her sex work. If she had, she claims she would have stopped. Occasionally, she rejected men she didn't like, but for the most part, she maintained an accepting attitude and didn't have specific expectations as she wasn't seeking a permanent relationship. Sivan describes that luckily she has never felt endangered or frightened in her work.

Sivan was astonished by the substantial amounts of money she earned in a short time. When her grandfather called to provide her the 800 shekels he used to give her monthly, which had been very helpful for her in the past, she inwardly laughed, thinking she could make that amount in half an hour.

After about ten months, Sivan retired from sex work after reaching her desired financial goal. Since then, she pursued other sources of income and has no intentions of returning to that line of work. Sivan has no regrets about that period in her life. She views her choices as conscious decisions made for her own benefit, using her resources to the fullest, and takes pride in that. She believes that societal norms often shape others' attitudes toward sex, yet she views things differently. Despite her psychologist's efforts to uncover feelings of regret, shame, or guilt within her, Sivan deems it unnecessary to dwell in those emotions. She even considers such probing as a form of gaslighting.

However, Sivan acknowledges that in her current state of mind she would not have chosen this work today:

> Presently, I am more connected to myself in a different way than before. In the past, I lacked the spiritual awareness that I possess today. I used to overlook my body's needs, living predominantly in my head. Nowadays, I am teaching myself to respect my body, perceiving it as a tool that serves my soul and deserves respect. I am redefining my relationship with the physical world, and part of this is to respect myself, my body, love, and sex, and to acknowledge the purity of my energies. As a result, I am more discerning about whom I choose to share my energies with.

MOTIVATIONS AND CHALLENGES IN AUTISTICS' WORK IN THE SEX INDUSTRY

Drawing from the narratives above, along with additional research and evidence, I will outline key aspects regarding autistics' involvement in the sex industry:

Autistics may gravitate toward working in the sex industry primarily out of financial necessity, as their autism-related challenges often make it more difficult for them to find and maintain jobs. The perceived ease of acceptance into the sex industry and the opportunity to earn quick money with flexible working hours might be particularly enticing for them.

Autistics who have worked in the sex industry describe how this kind of work suited them for several reasons:

First, although they often encounter challenges in navigating daily interpersonal situations, the structured nature of interactions within the sex industry offers predictability and repetition, enabling them to prepare by using scripted language or predetermined actions. They may create a specific "persona" tailored to specific types of sex work. For example, Parker describes how she learned BDSM laws and created a persona suited for this type of work (Parker, 2019).

Sex work may also suit autistics because it is focused on only one task at a time, as Piper describes: "I'd work with a structure, and that helped me. I got to focus on just one thing at a time, which I really enjoy. When you work in an office, you have to focus on eight different things" (Luterman, 2021).

Many autistics prefer to work independently, enabling them to control their working hours and create an environment that matches their sensory sensitivities. Parker, for example, describes that she chose to work in a relatively dark environment because she could not stand strong lights (Parker, 2019). She also describes that she forbade her clients to touch some of her body parts, such as her left ear or the area between her buttock and thighs, which were more sensitive (Parker, 2019).

Many autistics also feel more comfortable when not having to talk much, as Hayley describes: "If they don't talk, I break the tension with touch, because as a semi-verbal autistic I'm more comfortable without talking anyway" (Hayley, 2021).

Some autistics report that working in the sex industry helped them develop interpersonal skills that benefited them outside of work, too, such as navigating small talk or deciphering others' intentions. Autistics may also gravitate to the sex industry to find personal connections, facing challenges in establishing such connections elsewhere; there they may feel desired or loved as they may not feel in their regular lives. Hayley, for example, writes: "I found it incredible that men would pay hundreds of dollars an hour to spend time with me and that the more I was myself, the more they wanted to see me." Or: "I don't have to worry about knowing the right thing to say like I would on a civilian date. My clients already want to be there" (Hayley, 2021). Piper also accounts that in sex work she did not fear rejection as she used to in the company of others, and that for her it was "a safe way to open my heart and body to someone." She reports having deep emotional connections with some of her clients and missing them after she retired from that job (Piper, 2019). It seems that this kind of work may at times even provide autistics with sexual satisfaction. (Hayley, for instance, describes that this kind of work helped her connect with her body and get sexual satisfaction; Hayley, 2022.) It also appears that some autistics can tolerate or are even drawn to BDSM practices, partly due to their hyposensitivity to pain, though, of course, not all autistics have this inclination.

Contrary to the myth that autistics lack empathy, many of them exhibit excessive empathy, and they may find fulfillment in offering empathy, listening, and healing to their clients. They may be especially empathic toward people with disabilities, as they typically experienced unhappiness, anxieties, and loneliness themselves, as Hayley describes: "Disabled, chronically ill, and mentally ill people could relate to me—and I loved being able to work my own hours while giving others the affection they desired. I knew how it felt to feel lonely in your own skin." (Hayley, 2021). Autistics also tend to be very accepting or overlooking factors such as age, origin, status, gender, or disabilities.

It seems that autistics' tendency to detach sometimes from their emotions can help them in avoiding feelings of shame, embarrassment, or disgust, as evidenced in the accounts of Roux, Rona, and Sivan. They express no regret regarding those episodes in their lives, and it seems that they were able to leave them and go on with their lives with seemingly not much difficulty. However, one may wonder whether this work did leave unconscious negative effects that may have been repressed, rationalized, or dissociated.

Some autistics rationalize their sex work with ideological justifications, such as providing care, pleasure, or feminist arguments: Roux, for example, explained her attraction to this kind of work as stemming from to her will to give other people care and pleasure and justified it also as a feminist act allowing women to regain power from the patriarchy. Hayley writes, "I want to help my clients build unforgettable memories together, or at least find some relief in the tiny bubble which is our appointment . . . We're all going to die someday, and it would be a pity not to enjoy life as much as possible before we go" (Hayley, 2021). However, such justifications may overlook the emotional and physical challenges inherent in this kind of work, perhaps because of the autistics' tendency to be detached from their emotions or their tendency to regard things in "black and white." Nonetheless, these justifications may reflect an alternative value system, free from cultural conventions. In view of the complexity of things, I will leave these questions open.

It is important to acknowledge some of the numerous dangers and challenges that autistics may face in sex work:

Although the aforementioned stories presented voluntary involvement, most workers in this field are driven by emotional or economic distress, solicitation, or trafficking, often connected to a history of abuse (see Farley, 2003; Dalla et al., 2003). They also frequently are exposed to physical and emotional violence, anxieties, and pains.

Autistics may be more susceptible to dangers due to their challenges in identifying malicious intentions, advocating for their rights, expressing their emotions, and initiating changes. These difficulties place them at a higher risk of perilous situations and make it more challenging for them to extricate themselves from such circumstances. In addition, they may encounter more challenges in setting boundaries for their clients or for themselves, potentially leading to exploitation, burnout, and both physical and mental harm. Their heightened sensory sensitivities make them more sensitive to unpleasant sounds, lights, smells, and tastes. Emotionally, challenges with emotion regulation put them at risk of being overwhelmed by negative emotions, decreased self-esteem and anxiety, which may lead them to self-harm, suicidality, and the development of various psychological disorders, including post-traumatic stress disorder, eating disorders, dissociation, substance abuse, or psychosomatic problems.

CONCLUDING REMARKS

The involvement of autistics in the sex industry is a highly intriguing and underexplored phenomenon that deserves more public attention. It raises crucial issues concerning physical and psychological dangers, as well as questions of social justice.

Some questions around this phenomenon are related to broader issues surrounding sex work that have probably persisted since the inception of the world's oldest profession. The main concern is rooted in the fact that sex work most often arises from psychological distress and trauma, such as sexual abuse, neglect, violence, and economic hardship (Farley, 2003) and is connected to social problems such as inequality, deprivation, exploitation, and trafficking. Adding autism to the equation introduces additional complexities, as autistics may turn to sex work due to challenges in finding employment and feelings of loneliness, depression, and desperation. They may also lack integrative judgment in their job choice or have a black-and-white perception that skews their view of this type of work. Autistic sex workers may justify their choice with rational, ideological, or economic arguments, but it is essential to acknowledge the underlying psychological and emotional distress involved.

Health professionals working with this population may wonder to what extent this kind of work necessarily is traumatic, and in what ways. Must there necessarily be negative emotions present, such as sadness, worthlessness, shame, or anger? And if so, how can one help autistics connect to those feelings and work through them? Alternatively, should they view it as an "alternative psychology" and refrain from imposing social conventions on it? Similar questions for professionals in this field are discussed by Palermo and Bogaerts (2015) in a rare academic article that discusses the problems surrounding autistics' engagement in sex work. Palermo and Bogaerts present very similar questions regarding an 18-year-old autistic patient who earned a living by providing sexual services. They recount how he had voluntarily chosen this job, justifying it as an easy way to earn money and make new acquaintances, without feeling disgusted by his customers or perceiving himself as a victim. However, Palermo and Bogarts probe into the extent to which this choice was truly made of free will, taking into account his economic and emotional challenges and the extent to which factors such as his autism, social exclusion, and loneliness influenced this job choice. The authors refrain from providing definitive answers to these questions, and similarly I will abstain from doing so. However, it seems that, in general, there is a psychological concern when autistics engage in such work, as it is often rooted in economic, occupational, social, or emotional distress and involves significant psychological costs, of which they may not be fully aware due to their tendency to compartmentalize reason and emotion.

As a society, we must address the subject of autistics' involvement in the sex industry on multiple levels:

First and foremost, it is crucial to diagnose and offer appropriate professional support to help autistics integrate more effectively into the workforce and society, thereby mitigating the distress that might drive them toward the sex industry. Rehabilitation programs and psychotherapy should be accessible for autistics who have worked in the sex industry. On a broader scale, legislation and enforcement must combat the harmful practices of exploitation, trafficking, and sex slavery.

Further, it is crucial to conduct further research on autistics' involvement in sex work to gain a better understanding of its causes and to develop preventive measures and treatments for this population.

Last, it is crucial to emphasize that although some individuals mentioned in this chapter expressed a seemingly positive attitude toward their work in the sex industry, these cases are exceptional. In general, autistics are no less sensitive or vulnerable than anyone else, often even more so, and they may frequently experience mental crises, depression, and distress in response to their experiences in this field that may lead to self-injurious behaviors. It is imperative to respect their rights and ensure that they are not harmed.

Chapter 10

Autism and Dissociative Disorders—DID, Derealization, Depersonalization

> As an autistic, when not activating my filters, I may absorb hysterical amounts of information which activate me very intensively . . . Sometimes the way we calm ourselves down is by letting someone else take care of the trouble . . . If we weren't able to frame our experiences in a certain way, we might fall apart. (Casey, an autistic with DID, cited below)

Gitit (pseudonym), a 27-year-old woman, was referred to me from the mental health institute in which she was hospitalized due to her dissociative identity disorder (DID) for an additional diagnosis of autism. The captivating encounter with her ignited my curiosity, prompting me to explore the connection between autism and DID, previously known as "multiple personality disorder" (in the *DSM-3*). Over the ensuing years, I encountered several other individuals presenting with both conditions, suggesting that this co-occurrence is more prevalent than one may assume. Further exploration uncovered fascinating links between autism and DID, as fundamental characteristics of autism create a fertile ground for the development of dissociative disorders, as will be detailed below.

The connection between autism and DID has been almost unexplored thus far. Although the prevalence of each condition is significant—autism is estimated at about 2% (Maenner et al., 2020) and DID at about 0.4–3.1% (*DSM-5*, 300.14)—both are not sufficiently known to professionals. Similar to ASD, DID is usually not learned enough in training programs, and professionals typically have only superficial conceptions of it, which are either not well-founded or based on extreme media portrayals (e.g., *Sybil* or *Three Faces of Eve*). Until the 1980s, DID was considered very rare, and until recently its very existence was doubted. Some believed that it was nothing but an artifact of the media, clinicians' suggestibility, or some patients' impersonation. However, these ideas were not supported by empirical data, and they cannot explain certain research findings such as the physiological differences between different "personalities" or the fact that DID was found in populations with no prior knowledge of the subject, such as in China (see Manning & Manning, 2007; Sar et al., 2017). Numerous studies conducted in recent decades have offered significant clinical support for the existence of DID and contributed to an increasing acknowledgment of the disorder among professionals (Loewenstein, 2018; Loewenstein et al., 2017; Brand et al., 2006; Manning & Manning, 2007; McWilliams, 2011; Sar et al., 2017). McWilliams (2011) describes this as a paradigm shift in clinical research in recent years. However, unfortunately, it seems that clinicians still do not have enough well-established knowledge about DID (a survey among mental health experts in Israel found that only 37% of them were familiar with the disorder; Somer, 2000). The underdiagnosis of DID also stems from the fact that those who suffer from it often do not report their dissociative experiences and therefore often are misdiagnosed with schizophrenia, depression, borderline personality disorder, or bipolar disorder (Somer, 2014; Daie et al., 2020).

Further, the co-occurrence of autism and DID has been hardly diagnosed or researched. As far as I have found, no data exist regarding the prevalence of this co-occurrence. DID specialist Mike Lloyd noted that many of those who turn to him seeking help for DID also show signs of autism, though most of them have not received this diagnosis officially. Lloyd believes that if this were explored further, the high prevalence of this co-occurrence would surprise many (Lloyd, 2021a). Online platforms (such as QUORA, Reddit, Autism.Com, Wrongplanet, and others) feature increasing reports from individuals suggesting that they may fit this dual diagnosis.

The combination of autism and DID deserves higher acquaintance from professionals to provide those who suffer from it, who usually undergo dire experiences such as depression, self-harm behaviors, suicidal attempts, and hospitalizations, the proper understanding and treatment they deserve (Loewenstein, 2018).

The chapter will begin by presenting the different types of dissociative disorders. Then, it will focus mainly on DID and its intersection with autism: Three compelling personal stories of individuals with ASD and DID will be presented. Various factors explaining why autistics may be more susceptible to developing DID will be discussed, and the unique features of the combination of DID and ASD will be highlighted. The final part will explore the connection between autism and depersonalization-derealization disorder, another dissociative disorder, that appears to be very prevalent among autistics as well.

WHAT ARE DISSOCIATIVE DISORDERS?

According to the *DSM-5*, dissociative disorders involve disruptions or discontinuity in the normal integration of consciousness, memory, identity, emotion, perception, body representation, motor control, and behavior. The *DSM* refers to several types of dissociative disorders: dissociative identity disorder (DID), dissociative amnesia, depersonalization/derealization disorder, other specific dissociative disorder (OSDD), and unspecified dissociative disorder (UDD).

This chapter focuses primarily on dissociative identity disorders, which include both "dissociative identity disorder" (DID, code 300.14) and "other specific dissociative disorder" (OSDD-1; code 300.15). DID and OSDD are very similar, both featuring the presence of two or more distinct personality states. However, the key distinguishing factor is the presence of amnesia for these states in DID, whereas OSDD lacks such amnesia. In practice, the boundary between DID and OSDD is often blurred due to the presence of some degree of amnesia. This chapter primarily focuses on DID but acknowledges the potential overlap with OSDD, influenced by the extent of amnesia.

In DID, at least two distinct identities may emerge, each with different characteristics in terms of age, gender, body gestures, tone of speech, memories, traits, language, sexual preferences, and even physiological characteristics, such as blood pressure or EEG patterns. These identities may assume presence for varying durations, ranging from seconds to years. They can either take over consciousness or just convey messages to the host personality. Different identities may emerge in everyday situations, usually following certain triggers or threatening situations. The individual may have varying degrees of familiarity with these identities, and sometimes only in psychotherapy does he get to know them better.

Although different identities may sometimes interfere with daily functioning, they can also aid in functioning and in integrating socially (as may be seen in the cases described below). People with DID can achieve success in their studies, work, and family life, especially after successful therapy. Further, studies show that individuals with DID often possess high intellectual abilities, as well as creativity, humor, and hope (Loewenstein et al., 2017; Brand et al., 2006). When not affected by post-traumatic intrusions, they typically demonstrate a good reality check and a high capacity for self-observation (Loewenstein, 2018). These factors contribute to a positive outcome in insight-oriented psychotherapy (Loewenstein et al., 2017; Brand et al., 2006).

It is widely recognized that the main cause for developing DID is psychological trauma, particularly in early childhood. For instance, a meta-analysis of more than 1,500 studies found a strong empirical support for the post-traumatic basis for dissociative disorders (Dalenberg et al., 2012). Dissociation is a defensive response to physical or emotional pain in life-threatening situations, in which it is impossible or dangerous to fight or to run away. Developing alternate personalities that endure such experiences, helping to cut away feelings, perceptions, and memories of the trauma, allows the child to maintain a regular life and, at times, a distorted sense of a normal relationship with the abuser (Kohlenberg & Tsai, 1991). In the face of repeated attacks, dissociative defenses are employed whenever the individual feels threatened or anxious and may become linked to separate identities. These may become the distinct identities of the DID system that carry the traumatic history.

Studies show that the tendency to develop DID is more common among children with rich inner worlds, manifested in their tendency to create imaginary friends or engage in pretend play (see McWilliams, 2011, p. 338). Research has also associated the tendency to develop DID with a "disorganized" or "avoidant" attachment style, characterized by challenges in seeking assistance from caregivers and their difficulties in acknowledging and providing essential reassurance and support for the child's distress (Wieland, 2015; Watkins & Watkins, 1997; Kluft, 1984).

PERSONAL STORIES

I chose to share the narratives of three individuals diagnosed with both DID and ASD, whom I met for diagnostic or therapeutic purposes, and who generously agreed to recount their experiences in navigating the unique challenges that this combination poses. I extend my heartfelt gratitude to them for their openness in sharing their stories and providing invaluable insights. Notably, all three participants demonstrate a high level of self-observation, as well as an excellent level of intelligence, as evident in their psychodiagnostic test results. This suggests the likelihood that such qualities often may characterize this specific population, though broader sampling is necessary to validate this notion.

All three of them were diagnosed officially with dissociative identity disorder (DID), complex post-traumatic stress disorder (CPTSD), and autism (ASD). Their ASD diagnosis was based on meeting diagnostic characteristics, including challenges in navigating social situations, struggles in understanding implicit meanings, having intense specific areas of interest, difficulties in executive functions, rigidity and a strong adherence to routines, challenges in forming and maintaining relationships, overthinking, emotion regulation difficulties, struggles in expressing emotions, fluctuations between heightened emotional empathy (particularly toward animals) and emotional detachment, high levels of anxiety, repetitive movements, difficulties with eye contact, heightened sensory sensitivities, and more.

Gitit

Gitit, 27 years old, came to meet me wearing colorful clothes and multiple accessories. Her body language was very restrained, except for continuously playing with the multicolor necklace in her hands. Her facial expression was almost always sealed, yet it was later understood as concealing many underlying emotions and happenings. Gitit answered my questions with remarkable honesty, providing amazingly accurate and detailed responses on the very first try. I was profoundly impressed by her exceptional level of self-observation and insight, a quality that I later found to be commonly shared among others with both DID and ASD.

Gitit grew up in a religious family in Israel with parents who emigrated from Europe and worked in high-tech. They devoted most of their time to their work, were away from home for long hours, and paid little attention to their children's emotional needs, relying on changing nannies for their care. As a child, Gitit had a very rich inner world and imagination, spending many hours playing with Lego or Playmobil, painting, singing, watching cartoons, and observing animals, in which she had a keen interest. She used to gullibly believe what she saw in movies and books and was afraid of some of the creatures depicted, despite knowing that they were imaginary. She had lots of anxieties, such as fear of darkness, death, and strangers. She was also very afraid of her hot-tempered father, who strictly enforced religious laws and demanded obedience from his children. If they failed to comply, he would respond with verbal and physical violence, slamming Gitit to the floor or violently dragging her out of the house and locking her behind the door. She lived in constant fear of him and would often hide when he came home. Gitit took his words very seriously and felt frightened when he made statements such as "go find yourself a new home" or "I want to die," interpreting them literally and becoming even more compliant as a result.

When Gitit was about four years old, several boys from her kindergarten used to put her in a playhouse in the kindergarten yard, where they ordered her to take off her clothes and sexually touched her. Gitit doesn't remember exactly what happened there, but for her it was related to feelings of shame, confusion, and helplessness. She felt she could not resist because she used to be obedient. The children told her not to tell anyone about what had happened, and she obeyed that, too. In retrospect, Gitit thinks that her way to cope with the sexual assault as well as with her father's violence was by developing a mask of excessive joy, which became the stratum for one of her alters, as she probably began then to split herself into different parts.

In elementary school Gitit was considered very clever but had a hard time concentrating in lessons, used to doodle a lot in her notebooks, and never finished homework, like many other autistics. During breaks, she was often alone, in the school's animal corner, or writing stories and poems or watching other kids' behavior, which she always found very interesting. Often, she lied to her friends and perfected her lies extremely well, thereby giving expression to her wild imagination. At the same time, she was very gullible and tended to believe what she heard (e.g., when they learned about the Holocaust, she developed fears of showers and of gas).

At that period, a dark chapter in Gitit's life took place: She was exposed to porn movies on the internet and due to her intense curiosity became addicted to watching them and felt as if she was a part of them. Later, she used to force her younger siblings to apply what she had seen in those movies, up to physical sexual acts. She felt an inner compulsion to do this and felt that there was a split within her between the dark figure who did that and other parts, and therefore felt depressed and incomprehensible to herself. Gitit has throbbing flashbacks and guilt feelings about all this to this day.

During adolescence, Gitit often felt depressed and wanted to die but did not know how to seek help and resorted to self-harm, particularly through cutting. In high school, Gitit grappled with social challenges, vacillating between attempts to emulate other girls and a strong inclination to reject social norms and isolate herself entirely. Her difficulties manifested in frequent school absences, eventually leading her to complete her matriculation exams at an external school.

In the years that followed, Gitit tried to integrate into various study and work settings but dropped out of all of them. She suffered from persistent depression, self-harm behaviors, and suicide attempts. These led her to psychiatric hospitalizations, during which she was diagnosed with DID, and later with autism, too.

Gitit reports having various personalities within herself, each with its own unique character, perception, and habits. Among them there are a smiley gullible little girl; a schoolgirl with "tomboyish" demeanor who loves animals, grapples with academic challenges, and often experiences loneliness; a rock girl, with a history of sexual trauma, marked by self-harm, anxiety attacks, and suicidal attempts; a meditative and mature personality drawn to spirituality, writing, and teaching; a lesbian advocate for LGBT rights; a cat that enjoys caresses and snuggles; an empathetic and maternal personality, and more. In her ongoing psychotherapy, Gitit endeavors to acquaint herself with the diverse personalities, exploring the circumstances and reasons behind their emergence and confronting the traumatized aspects within her.

Gitit points out that the different personalities tend to surface primarily in response to triggers of trauma or in overwhelming interpersonal situations where she finds it challenging to navigate. Some of them provide her with comfort and calming (e.g., the cat figure) or with spirituality (e.g., the spiritual figure). In addition, they may assist her in communicating, in performing daily tasks such as cooking or cleaning, in expressing emotions, and in conforming to social norms. Gitit is reluctant to relinquish these personalities as she perceives them as helping her in crucial aspects of her life. She believes that her healing process should involve embracing all these personalities, considering a move toward uniformity only at a later stage in her journey.

Gitit highlights various intersections between the DID and ASD in her experience: First, each of her personalities embodies specific autistic characteristics—such as gullibility, gender dysphoria, a sense of loneliness, anxiety, truth-seeking, spirituality, sensual sensibilities, and more. Second, the personalities help Gitit in managing aspects that pose challenges for her due to her autism, such as navigating social situations, expressing emotions, or performing daily tasks. Alongside this, Gitit acknowledges that autism poses hurdles in her journey, such as making it challenging for her to get out of her cocoon and to identify and articulate her needs and desires, and it also makes her overthink and question various aspects that arise during her therapeutic process.

Another interesting interface between DID and ASD in Gitit's experience relates to issues of multiplicity and diversity. She describes that it has always been important for her to give space to diverse and multiple facets of herself, as evident in her preference for wearing multicolored clothes and socks of mismatched colors. Even as a child she always drew a figure with one eye shaped like the sun and the other like the moon. This inclination persists in her current experience with the different personalities within her, reflecting diversity in terms of age, gender, sexuality, and more, with no hierarchy among them. The inclination toward multiplicity and diversity aligns with the characteristic features of autism, evident in the challenges autistics face in prioritization and decision making. This aligns with the dominance of the right hemisphere and of primary processes in autism, where prioritization is notably absent (see chapter 13).

Casey

Casey, 36 years old, slender, tall, and long-haired, tends to pace back and forth incessantly, and his speech is notably very rapid. He effortlessly transitions between singular and plural, masculine and feminine. Casey may impress those around him with his high intelligence, extensive knowledge, linguistic richness, and associative thinking.

Growing up in Israel to parents who emigrated from the United States, Casey's mother was diagnosed as high-functioning autistic, and his father, although not officially diagnosed, also displayed autistic traits, such as an intense interest in specific subjects, difficulties in interpersonal situations and rigidity. His father often expressed anger and violence toward family members and animals at home.

From an early age, Casey stood out as sensitive and curious, displaying a keen interest in insects, numerical concepts, and existential questions. He grappled with many anxieties, ranging from a fear of the dark to discomfort around strangers and fictional characters from TV series. Highly sensitive in each of his senses, he frequently perceived the world as overwhelming, incomprehensible, or excessively confusing. This manifested in frequent emotional responses such as crying, shouting, and bursts of anger.

During his school years, Casey encountered significant social challenges. His long hair and unconventional interests, such as engaging with insects, and unconventional communication style contributed to his perception as peculiar. He experienced bullying and violence, which made him feel lonely and depressed. He had only a few friends, who shared his interests in fantasy, science fiction, and Dungeons and Dragons. Casey was granted an exemption from military service owing to his challenges, and in recent years engaged intermittently as a private tutor, deriving pride from his successes. Casey devotes his free time to playing computer games and delving into his wide array of special interests, which include politics, mental disorders, physics, computers, and mathematics. He also participates in role-playing with a group, where he perceives all members as sharing a kind of neurodiversity. Casey gravitates toward the company of individuals with similar neurodivergence, finding conversations with them more meaningful and logical compared to the typical discomfort he experiences with neurotypicals.

In recent years, Casey has faced bouts of depression and anxiety, notably triggered by conflicts with his father or engaging in compelling online arguments on political subjects, such as neo-Nazism. These challenges resulted in several hospitalizations, during which he was diagnosed with DID, complex post-traumatic stress disorder (CPTSD), and autism (ASD).

Casey reports experiencing different identities since childhood, even though his DID was officially diagnosed only about two years ago. Casey describes that he harbors dozens or even hundreds of identities, each distinct in age, gender, and even species, encompassing animals, plants, inanimate objects, and unspecified entities. Some of them are more present or dominant than others. Their communication abilities differ significantly: some of them invest substantial efforts in communicating with their surroundings, whereas others hardly express themselves due to their inability, fear of invalidation, or a long-standing habit of remaining concealed. The diverse identities may also fall along different points of a sensitivity spectrum. For instance, at one end, there is a man who displays characteristics akin to a psychopath, showing emotional detachment from people's suffering. At the opposite end, there is a woman who is so sensitive that, in the face of traumas, she felt compelled to undergo further fragmentation into distinct identities, as a form of DID within DID. Interestingly, these extremes align with the variations in sensitivity observed in individuals with autism.

Casey attributes the development of his DID to the challenging atmosphere in his parents' home, particularly his father's emotional and verbal violence, coupled with Casey's tendency to react strongly to adversities on personal, family, and national levels. Casey acknowledges: "as an autistic, when not activating my filters, I may absorb hysterical amounts of information which activate me very intensively." He also points out: "Sometimes the way we calm ourselves down is by letting someone else take care of the trouble" and "If we weren't able to frame our experiences in a certain way, we might fall apart."

Casey currently is undergoing therapy to address his CPTSD and explore his multiple identities. He adamantly expresses his unwillingness to relinquish them, as he cannot identify himself without them. He views the multiplicity as advantageous, affording him diverse perspectives, akin to "two eyes seeing things from different angles." Besides, various identities help him in distinct functions (e.g., some are adept at interpersonal communication, others at expanding his intellectual horizons, and others at meeting friends).

Casey underscores the collective operation of the identities within him, devoid of a designated leader, relying on internal communication, akin to a community meeting. In the same line, he prefers to call the different identities "headmates" (as is often used in the DID community), emphasizing his respect for all of them. His tendency to provide space for various identities stems from his commitment to justice as well as his heightened emotional empathy, characteristic of many autistics. Further, his decision-making style also reflects the typical autistic information processing style, marked by a "bottom-up" weighing of information.

As Casey becomes more aware of his diagnoses, he experiences increased self-acceptance and psychological well-being. He views having a set of identities as an evolutionary adaptation that allows him to approach situations from various angles, complemented by his autism, which fosters in him qualities such as incessant curiosity, depth, attention to detail, and what he terms "identisthesia" (identity + sthesia)—an ability to sense states of mind and transform them into distinct identities—similarly to the synesthesia often observed in autistics.

Casey holds hope for an enhanced understanding of DID among mental health professionals, advocating for a non-pathologizing and respectful approach that views DID as "a positive and functioning outcome of a complex human neurology," similarly to the ongoing transformations in the perceptions of autism, gender diversity, or homosexuality. He anticipates that such an approach will embolden individuals with DID to more openly share their experiences and foster more understanding and self-acceptance.

Dana

Dana, 23 years old, possesses a charming "girl next door" appearance, usually opting for comfortable, dark clothing to avoid standing out. In conversing with her, her high intelligence and quick perception are clearly evident, though she sometimes appears hesitant or disconnected and switches between female and male language.

Dana's father, an intelligent, introverted accountant, has several special interests, including public transportation, leading Dana to believe that he is autistic. Her mother, who experienced childhood traumas, grapples with persistent mood issues and challenges in emotional regulation, frequently lashing out at her children. Dana attributes many of her own emotional challenges to her mother's behavior. Demonstrating exceptional intelligence and curiosity, Dana learned to read by the age of three. Her trusting nature made her susceptible to believing everything she heard. Always trying to adapt to her surroundings to avoid anger, Dana feared her mother's outbursts. She faced intense anxieties, high sensory sensitivities, and likely experienced a sexual assault around the age of 6, as one of her identities is that of a 6-year-old girl who experiences flashbacks from that assault. Throughout her school years, Dana felt different from others due to her special interests in math, music, fantasy literature, and public transportation. Despite her social challenges, Dana excelled academically, completing her matriculation with minimal effort.

Upon commencing her university studies, Dana experienced a surge in anxieties and self-harming tendencies, leading to psychiatric admissions, where she received a diagnosis of complex post-traumatic stress disorder (CPTSD), dissociative identity disorder (DID), and later autism (ASD), too. She experimented with various medications without success, currently opting not to take any. Living alone with a cat and assisted by a caregiver, Dana dedicates much of her time to her varied interests, encompassing public transportation, Pokemon, psychological disorders, knitting, and music, with the rhythmic activities offering her a sense of relaxation.

Although Dana received a DID diagnosis at the age of 20, she believes that different identities have manifested since her childhood, evident in her diaries and therapy sessions through shifts in speech and behavior. In her ongoing therapy, Dana actively endeavors to deepen her understanding of the array of identities within her, encompassing boys and girls of different ages, Pokemon characters, and undefined entities such as shadows or clouds.

Dana believes that all her identities have autistic characteristics, such as experiencing challenges in comprehending contexts, navigating social situations, and deciphering implicit meanings. Moreover, most of them share a fervent interest in public transportation, music, or Pokemon, yet their unique expression is distinctive for each identity. For example, one identity, identified as a boy, harbors a deep passion for airplanes and delights in spending hours observing takeoffs at the national airport, whereas other identities focus on other facets of public transportation. Likewise, although many of them love music, each one maintains a distinct preference for a particular musical genre.

Dana contends that her various identities both assist and hinder her functioning, as for instance, the emergence of the identity of a seven-year-old girl during studies may be very challenging. She recognizes that, unlike some others with DID, such as Casey, who can recruit different identities according to what may be suitable in various situations, this is more difficult for her, especially under pressure. Dana surmises that this skill may require more psychological maturity than she currently possesses.

Dana posits that her DID evolved as a defense mechanism in response to a challenging environment, offering escape and relief through the creation of distinct identities. She believes that her autism made her susceptible to more challenges, including heightened sensory sensitivities (e.g., discomfort with school uniforms) and difficulties in adapting to changes (e.g., class cancellations). In addition, Dana attributes her autistic inclination to deeply identify with elements in her environment, such as literary characters like Harry Potter, as a catalyst that amplified her tendency to identify with various identities within her.

Dana sees her past traumas as the central challenge in her life, resulting in conditions such as depression, anxiety, self-harm, and flashbacks. She views her multiple identities as a defense mechanism against these traumas. Dana believes that individuals with CPTSD frequently turn to dissociative defenses to navigate difficult circumstances, with DID representing an extreme manifestation of such defenses.

Dana acknowledges that it is easier for people to accept her autism than her DID, leading her to be cautious about sharing the latter. However, she finds comfort in connecting with others who share this combination, both in real life and through social networks.

THEORETICAL CONNECTIONS BETWEEN AUTISM AND DISSOCIATIVE DISORDERS

The Heightened Susceptibility of Autistics to Developing DID

Autistics are more vulnerable to developing DID compared to neurotypicals for several reasons:

Psychological Traumas—As DID primarily arises from psychological traumas, especially in early childhood and/or through the accumulation of traumas, autistics are more susceptible to developing DID because they tend to experience a higher frequency of psychological traumas, including bullying and various forms of abuse (physical, emotional, verbal, and sexual) from peers or family members (Lloyd, 2021a, 2021b; Reuben et al., 2021). It was also found that autistics are more likely to perceive certain events as traumatic, such as social insults, degradation, sensory overstimulation, and abrupt changes in routines (see Haruvi-Lamdan, Horesh, & Golan, 2018).

"Autistic Traumas"—autistics typically undergo difficulties that they perceive as traumatic due to their tendency to experience the world as incomprehensible, unpredictable, overwhelming, threatening, or dangerous. Challenges in social situations, anxiety, sensory, and emotional dysregulation contribute to their vulnerability. Therefore, they find refuge and solace in escaping to dissociation. An autistic woman who calls herself on the internet Autistic Selves believes that her DID is different from the usual DID because it is caused by another type of trauma, which she calls "autistic trauma," created because of the difficulties that autistics experience in executive functions, flexibility, social and communication and sensory sensitivities (Autistic Selves, 2021). According to her, not being diagnosed as autistics also makes autistics feel misunderstood and traumatized: "The fact that we grew up without knowing that we were autistic caused us autistic trauma" (Autistic Selves, 2021).

Emotional Overwhelm and Anxieties—Studies indicate that individuals who are prone to dissociation often struggle with emotion regulation and frequently experience emotional overwhelm (Chefetz, 2000; McWilliams, 2011). Because autistics are particularly characterized by a tendency to experience strong emotions, having difficulties in regulating them, they are more susceptible to dissociation. Moreover, autistics often experience heightened anxiety due to challenges in integration and self-soothing. Given that dissociation is strongly related to anxiety, their susceptibility to dissociative experiences is increased.

Challenges in Seeking External Comfort—Dissociation is heightened in situations where the child's need for soothing is not recognized or fulfilled by caregivers (see McWilliams, 2011; Wieland, 2015; Watkins & Watkins, 1997). Autistics face an additional challenge in seeking help due to their difficulties in expressing their emotions and in breaking out of their "autistic cocoon" to ask for assistance. Further, as their parents are often more prone to be autistic due to genetic factors, they might face challenges in recognizing and addressing their children's needs for reassurance and support.

A Rich Imagination—Studies show that dissociation is more common in children who have rich inner lives and imagination, demonstrated by their inclination to create imaginary friends or engage in pretend play (McWilliams, 2011, p. 338). These characteristics are frequently found in many autistics, despite the misconception that autistics lack imagination; it is important to note that autistics exhibit extremes in their abilities to imagine, invent, and even lie. Further, autistics are more inclined to perceive their imaginary creations as tangible entities (e.g., many of them fear creatures from movies, books, and their own imagination as if they were real, even though their reality check is normal, and they understand that these constructs are not genuine). This tendency to cling to imaginative constructs might contribute to the development of DID.

Creativity—Many autistics are highly creative and associative due to the dominance of the right hemisphere and primary processes (see chapter 13). This enables them to effortlessly generate new images as well as fitting identities to cope with various threatening situations. Casey brilliantly termed this process "identisthesia," similar to synesthesia, which is also often found in autistics (where images from one sense are automatically translated in their mind into images of another sense).

Challenges in Integration—Dissociation is associated with difficulties in integrating different "self" experiences, especially in the context of trauma. These challenges may be augmented by obstacles in seeking help, caregivers' inability to facilitate integration, and structural impediments that hinder the process of integration. Several studies proposed models of lack of integration to explain dissociative disorders: Manning and Manning (2007) proposed the "Legion Theory," according to which all of us have different "selves" from the beginning of our lives, which perceive things from different angles, and there is a "collaborative self" that integrates these perceptions. However, in situations of extreme abuse or neglect, it may be difficult to integrate the different selves into the "cooperative self." As a result, some of the selves may be integrated and form the nuclear personality whereas other selves may become other personalities. Oppenheimer (2002) also suggests that DID involves the inability to associate self-relevant information, such as self-representations and social roles, and explains how in traumatic situations, integration is avoided to protect against further trauma. Integration problems are more prevalent in autistics because they suffer from disintegration between different parts of the brain, according to leading theories in the neurobiology of autism today (see Minshew & Williams, 2007; also see chapter 13).

Donna Williams, a prominent and influential autistic writer (Williams, 1992, 1994), diagnosed with both autism and DID around the age of 47, delves into the intricate interplay of these conditions in her writings. Williams offers compelling insights into the development of her DID (see Williams, 2012, 2015a–c):

First, she relates it to the traumas, loss, and neglect she has suffered, primarily from her mother. Second, she notes that growing up with different caregivers may have contributed to her lack of integration. Third, Williams believes that because she was autistic, she tended to dissociate more often and more deeply than other children. She contends that some people are biologically more prone to dissociation because they have deficits in the connections between various brain regions. In addition, she refers to Manning and Manning's Legion Theory (2007), proposing that everyone possesses different "selves" but those with DID have more problems in integrating the different parts into a cohesive self. Williams believes that her fetal alcohol syndrome, caused by her mother's alcoholism, and collagen deficiency might have further contributed to her brain dysconnectivity issues (Williams, 2015c).

In summary, autistics exhibit an increased susceptibility to developing DID owing to their vulnerability to psychological and "autistic" traumas, stemming from challenges in communication, social adaptation, inflexibility, executive function deficits, and sensory sensitivities. The heightened risk is compounded by difficulties in integrating diverse dimensions of experience, a proclivity to cling onto disintegrated experiences, and difficulties in seeking assistance. Consequently, autistics may develop DID not solely in the context of exceptionally adverse life experiences, such as severe physical, sexual, or emotional violence, which were traditionally linked to DID formation. Rather, their vulnerability extends to more prevalent situations, such as having a harsh, rigid, or dysregulated parent, as illustrated in the cases discussed. The inclination of autistics to perceive even seemingly less extreme situations as traumatic contributes to the heightened incidence of DID among them.

Characteristics of the Combination of ASD and DID

Considering the evidence presented above and additional information on the subject, several key characteristics emerge when examining the intersection of autism and DID:

Autistic Characteristics across Various Identities—It seems that in individuals with both DID and ASD, the various identities exhibit autistic traits. These may encompass gullibility, heightened anxieties, high sensory sensitivities, gender dysphoria, high emotional empathy versus lack of empathy, tendencies toward self-harming behaviors, among others, as in the evidences provided. For example, in those having DID and autism, various identities may share common special interests, yet each identity may engage with these interests in distinct ways. Dana's experiences illustrate this phenomenon, where different identities approach their shared interest in public transportation from diverse perspectives.

Further, the various identities may align with different poles commonly observed in autistics, as autistics often gravitate toward poles. For example, in terms of communication, some identities may demonstrate high efforts in communicating, embodying the tendency of some autistics to mask and imitate in an effort to better fit socially, whereas others may belong to the opposite pole, exhibiting a lack of motivation or an inability to communicate (in Casey's words: "They don't have the vocabulary or the patience to explain things, perhaps as a result of invalidation or of being used to being in the underground"). These communication difficulties are typical of the "primary processes," which are typical to autistics, in which there is no need to communicate, as in dreaming (see chapter 13). Similarly, concerning the ability to empathize, different identities may align with the poles observed in autistics, spanning from excessive empathy to apparent indifference.

Superpowers—As autistics generally tend to show extreme talents—which may be attributed to their hyper- or hypo-connectivity between different brain areas—their different identities may display remarkable abilities in various areas. I have met autistics with DID whose different identities exhibited extraordinary skills in painting, music, sports, high intelligence, or stamina. For instance, when a patient of mine had to move apartments, she brought forth a very physically strong identity who easily carried all the furniture, surpassing the efforts of all the men around her.

Navigating Autism-Related Challenges—The diverse identities often shoulder the responsibility of managing a range of hurdles associated with autism. These may encompass social, interpersonal, and communication challenges, such as engaging in small talk, as well as practical tasks, such as daily chores or emotional expression. Through their varied approaches, the identities may aid the individual in coping across different situations, as illustrated by the evidence above. However, at times, these identities may impede functioning, as they may emerge unexpectedly, often following trauma triggers, emotional and sensory overload, or anxieties, thereby disrupting regular functioning, as described above.

Overidentification—Given autistics' inclination to overidentify with objects in their surroundings, it seems that some of their identities incorporate objects they identify with, such as human figures, inanimate objects, nature elements (e.g., trees, clouds), animals (e.g., cats), fictional characters (e.g., Pokemons), and more. This aligns with the autistic tendency toward overidentification and their propensity to generate internal images and adhere to them ("monotropism")—akin to primary processes observed in dreaming.

Attraction to Multiplicity and Lack of Prioritization—The multiplicity of identities may be connected to the autistic inclination toward multiplicity and a lack of prioritization, which are characteristic of the "primary processes" dominant in autistics. This is apparent in their challenges with prioritizing and decision making in daily matters, as well as in broader considerations such as selecting educational, professional, and gender paths. This tendency is also reflected in the allowance for diverse identities, without imposing prioritization or designating a leader among them, as described in the evidence below.

High Abilities for Self-Observation and Insight—Individuals with ASD and DID frequently exhibit a heightened capacity for self-observation and insight. Research indicates that individuals with DID often demonstrate such a heightened ability (see Loewenstein et al., 2017; Brand et al., 2006). High self-observation is also frequently found in high-functioning autistics, attributed to their high intelligence, sensitivity to detail, truth-seeking, and interest in deep questions, with many of them having a special interest in the human psyche as a means to better understand themselves and the world around them, as demonstrated by the interviewees above.

Main Psychological Struggle—The central psychological struggle for individuals with DID and ASD frequently revolves around their complex post-trauma (CPTSD), encompassing elements such as depression, flashbacks, anxieties, and self-harm. Therefore, the therapeutic focus should primarily be on processing the traumas. Beyond this, one may strive to achieve more self-acceptance and even acknowledgment of the advantages stemming from this unique neurology. The ability to adopt such an attitude may be fostered by the freedom from adhering to societal conventions associated with ASD (as can be seen in the case of Casey).

Therapeutic Implications

From a therapeutic point of view, it is crucial to provide those suffering from DID and ASD with a treatment aimed at their ASD, DID, and their combination.

Regarding ASD therapy, it is important to get the appropriate diagnosis of autism, thereby raising the awareness of the strengths and challenges related to ASD and assisting in coping with them to reach more self-understanding and self-acceptance.

Regarding DID therapy, extensive literature has been published in recent years (see McWilliams, 2011; Kluft, 1991, 2000; Somer, 2014; Daie et al., 2020). This literature generally advocates for three main phases in the treatment of DID: the first phase aims to establish a therapeutic alliance, which may build trust and stabilize emotions by managing distress, calming and promoting emotional regulation. The second phase involves a gradual and patient process of familiarizing the patient with each identity's personal story and processing the traumatic memories associated with them, reducing guilt and shame, and processing grief and anger, with the goal of integrating the traumatic memories into a unified life story. Hypnosis or EMDR may also aid in this process (see McWilliams, 2011; Daie et al., 2020, pp. 185–186). The third phase focuses on identity integration and life restoration. Many patients with DID prefer not to relinquish their different identities, as they are part of their psychological makeup and often serve various coping functions. For them, the treatment's purpose is, rather, to achieve harmonious functioning among the different identities (see Somer, 2014).

Studies indicate that therapies aimed at integrating the different identities and processing the traumas linked to them lead to significant reductions in depression, post-traumatic and dissociative symptoms, as well as a marked decrease in hospitalizations, self-harm, and suicidal attempts. Further, these therapies promote increased psychological well-being and engagement in relationships, work, and studies (Brand et al., 2012; Loewenstein, 2018). From a medical perspective, because DID is not a biochemical disorder, no medications can "cure" it; however, these patients may benefit from antidepressant and anti-anxiety medications.

Several important aspects should be considered in the therapy of DID: First, it is often a lengthy process that may extend over several years and requires a great deal of patience. Second, therapists should create a space that welcomes all types of identities, whether they are kind, angry, or hurtful. McWilliams compares this therapeutic approach to family therapy within one person (McWilliams, 2011). In addition, McWilliams describes the typical transference and countertransference dynamics with these patients: initially, positive transference may occur, but more challenging aspects can arise later, such as mistrust and fears of abuse or exploitation stemming from past traumas. Patients may also try to involve the therapist in the role of a "savior," which can lead to boundary violations, such as extending therapy hours or making special requests. However, many individuals with DID develop a strong, hopeful attachment to therapy and are appreciative of helpful treatment.

Regarding the coexistence of ASD and DID in therapy, it should be acknowledged that autism adds complexity to the therapeutic process, given typical autistic challenges such as difficulties in expressing emotions, lack of focus, overthinking (which makes it difficult for them to calm themselves emotionally), or "black and white thinking." Therapists should help their patients recognize their autistic tendencies—such as thinking in "black and white," challenges in emotion regulation, and heightened anxieties—as factors that can exacerbate traumatic feelings and make it harder to let go of them. For instance, a patient of mine always strove to see things "in pink" and had to learn to see things in shades of gray to reconcile her traumatic experiences and get along with her life. Establishing a safe, respectful therapeutic framework with clear communication and adjusting to the patients' pace is crucial to foster a trusting alliance, as well as enabling them to express themselves through non-direct means such as drama, writing, or art.

On the positive side, autistics may bring advantages to the therapeutic process thanks to their high curiosity, loyalty, a search for truth and integration, and a significant capacity for self-observation. It would be interesting to explore in future studies whether the high capacity for self-observation is more characteristic of individuals with both DID and ASD than those without ASD. It is also essential to adopt a respectful, non-pathologizing approach when working with individuals who have both DID and ASD, recognizing this combination as a valid neurodiversity, encompassing both strengths and challenges.

From a health-care system perspective, the need is pressing to raise awareness among mental health professionals to these two conditions and their co-occurrence. Professionals should be guided how to identify them, using autism screening tools and tests (e.g., AQ, RITVO, or ADOS) and DID assessment questionnaires (e.g., DES) or structured interviews (e.g., DDIS or SCID-D). McWilliams emphasizes that patients with DID often do not give away having various identities, so professionals should know how to identify their condition based on signs such as a history of trauma, self-destructive behaviors, eye rolling, trance-like behaviors, and reports of internal voices; McWilliams regrets that in her training she was not instructed, for example, to ask patients who "hear voices" whether they perceive them as "inside" or "outside" (McWilliams, 2011, p. 352). The risk of refraining from exposing the multiple identities may be higher in autistics, given their frequent encounters with misunderstandings and invalidation, exacerbated by their general challenges in expressing difficulties.

Further, therapists are encouraged to receive specialized training to effectively treat patients with both DID and ASD, ensuring that they do not feel overwhelmed or unqualified in addressing either condition. An example illustrating this need is Jennifer, a patient with both ASD and DID, who shared her experience of a therapist discontinuing treatment after learning about her ASD, claiming a lack of understanding of it (Williams, 2012).

Further research is needed to deepen our understanding of these two conditions and their co-occurrence. Important questions remain unanswered regarding the prevalence, causes, characteristics, and treatment of this co-occurrence. For instance, it is intriguing to explore whether autistics are apt to engage in harmful behaviors during dissociative states, given their typically high ethical and moral standards. Such questions carry significant juridical implications, particularly concerning criminal responsibility, raising questions about the extent to which these behaviors are driven by lack of memory or control (Daie et al., 2020; Witztum & Margolin, 2009). Legal considerations should also incorporate factors such as the proclivity of autistics to gullibility, suggestibility, and challenges in emotion regulation, which can influence their criminal liability. It's essential for the legal system to thoroughly consider these factors when adjudicating cases involving autistics, acknowledging the unique aspects of their neurodiversity that may affect their actions and responses.

AUTISM AND DEPERSONALIZATION/ DEREALIZATION DISORDER

Another dissociative disorder in the *DSM-5* is Depersonalization/Derealization Disorder (*DSM-5*, 300.6). In the past, these two were separate diagnoses, but they are now combined into one disorder that encompasses both experiences.

Depersonalization refers to a person's experience of being detached from himself or observing his thoughts, feelings, body sensations, or actions from an external perspective. Derealization refers to a person's experience of being disconnected from one's environment, as if viewing it through a camera lens, a glass wall, fog, or a bubble, or perceiving reality as a show or a dream. These disorders may also manifest as sensations of floating in the air, acting like a robot, loss of pleasure in previously enjoyable activities, sensory distortions (e.g., visual or auditory changes), altered perceptions of time (e.g., feeling that things are happening in slow motion), existential questioning, and fears of going crazy. It is important to note that during derealization/depersonalization, reality testing is typically maintained, and the person can acknowledge that his feelings are not normal. According to the *DSM-5*, about half the population has experienced transient episodes of derealization or depersonalization, typically triggered by drug or alcohol use, traumatic events, anxiety, stress, or lack of sleep. However, when these episodes become frequent and persistent, Derealization/Depersonalization Disorder can be diagnosed.

Research indicates that anxiety plays a crucial role in the development of depersonalization and derealization (Holmes et al., 2005; Reuben, 2022), including social anxiety (Reuben, 2022; Scheweden et al., 2016) and panic attacks (Nestler et al., 2015). Due to their heightened vulnerability to anxieties, particularly in social situations, and to panic attacks, autistics are also more prone to experience depersonalization and derealization. For instance, a study by Storch et al. (2012) found that 18% of the autistic youth in their sample reported depersonalization and derealization alongside anxiety. I believe that autistics are more vulnerable to depersonalization and derealization due to their difficulties in integration—also referred to as "monotropism," "one-tracked-ness," or "tunnel vision" (i.e., sticking with one perception without being able to alleviate it by other perspectives).

Many autistics report experiences of depersonalization or derealization (e.g., on internet platforms such as Wrongplanet, Quora, Reddit) even if they do not label them as such. I have encountered numerous autistics who shared their experiences of perceiving the world as unreal, dream-like, unfamiliar, or devoid of meaning. Some express feeling as if there were a glass or a wall separating them from the world, or as though they were observing themselves from an external perspective. Some reported a sense of detachment from limbs and body or the perception of an entire world existing within their mind.

Many autistics report experiencing derealization and depersonalization particularly in situations of anxiety, panic attacks, meltdowns, burnout, and depression, or when confronted with sensory overload, such as heavy noises, annoying lights, or tactile sensitivity. For instance, a patient of mine described how he frequently turns to depersonalization because, due to his heightened sensory sensitivities, he often feels the need to disconnect from his body:

> I constantly feel sensory discomfort; for example, I sense every piece of clothing on me constantly and feel the need to get rid of it, though I try to suppress it because otherwise it would be intolerable. That is why I often disconnect from my body, and, for instance, I don't feel my body or only feel parts of it, such as my hands or legs, so you can call it depersonalization. I think that's why I constantly need to touch things or make repetitive movements—so as to feel the connection to my body again.

This description fascinatingly captures the link between sensory sensitivities, the need for repetitive movements, and depersonalization, all characteristic of autistics. It is plausible that many autistics experience such phenomena, even if it is not officially acknowledged as derealization or depersonalization.

Some autistics interviewed for this chapter describe DID as an extreme form of derealization and depersonalization. For instance, Gitit elucidates: "The personalities epitomize an extreme form of depersonalization and derealization. Initially, there is a dissociation from experiences too challenging to bear, and subsequently, it evolves into a more structured form in order to manage the overwhelming complexity."

CONCLUDING REMARKS

The chapter illuminated how autistics exhibit a heightened vulnerability to developing dissociative disorders, stemming from a combination of factors, including a higher incidence of traumas and a propensity to perceive various experiences as traumatic due to challenges in emotional regulation, expressing distress, and seeking help. Further, autistics experience unique "autistic traumas" arising from their struggles in comprehending and navigating social situations, executive function challenges, anxieties, emotional and sensory overwhelm, among other aspects inherent to autism. Their inclination to escape into imagination and latch onto imaginative creations, coupled with inherent difficulties in integration, can further contribute to dissociativity.

It should be emphasized that DID may manifest in autistics not exclusively in response to extreme physical abuse, as traditionally documented in professional literature, but also in less extreme situations that they may experience very intensely due to their emotional regulation challenges. This broadens the scope of DID within the autistic population, as well as in the general population.

In mental health care, precise identification of both conditions and their coexistence is crucial. An inaccurate diagnosis or inadequate treatment may result in adverse outcomes including depression, self-criticism, ineffective interventions, self-harm, hospitalizations, and suicidality. Conversely, accurate diagnosis and appropriate treatment offer the potential for significant benefits to the well-being of these individuals.

Chapter 11

Autistics Who Seem to Be "Stuck"

In contrast to the portrayal thus far in this book of autistics demonstrating high levels of curiosity, drive, imagination, creativity, awareness, and motivation, another group exhibits contrasting traits. These typically spend extended periods at home, engaging in activities such as playing computer games, watching TV, browsing the internet, or other passive pastimes. Their interests tend to revolve around narrow topics such as computers, fantasy, science fiction, or animals. They may encounter challenges in securing employment or maintaining low-paying jobs, and their interpersonal relationships are also limited, if they exist at all.

Although it's important to stress that this distinction is not absolute, as many autistics may fluctuate between these two poles, this chapter predominantly focuses on those who grapple with persistent challenges in achieving professional, social, and relational fulfillment. These challenges primarily arise from difficulties in executive functions, including goal setting, decision making, planning, and self-motivation, alongside challenges in understanding social situations and in behaving as expected in them, challenges in emotional and sensory regulation, sleep disturbances, anxieties, low self-esteem, and various health concerns, prompting them to refrain from coping and retreat to their secure environment. Consequently, many of them are inclined to remain financially and functionally dependent on their relatives for support.

Golan and colleagues (2016) describe the typical "dependence trap" observed among autistics and their parents, often persisting well beyond adolescence, as emerging from autistics' inherent challenges, compounded by parental tendencies to accommodate their needs in ways that inadvertently impede their growth. Such autistics often rely on their parents for even the most basic tasks such as meal preparation or logistical arrangements. Their parents often grapple with deep worries regarding their children's well-being and future, often experiencing guilt for either doing too much or not doing enough for them, as well as for the attention imbalance between their autistic child and their other children. Autistics may exhibit anger, demanding behaviors, a lack of care or interest, and feelings of jealousy or rivalry toward their siblings. These dynamics place a significant strain on family life, exacerbating familial tensions and conflicts.

Due to the current underdiagnosis of autism, many autistics in this category may not have received an official autism diagnosis. However, as awareness of this condition grows, some may seek a diagnosis, usually prompted by concerned family members feeling desperate or helpless in addressing their situation. In diagnosing this subgroup, certain characteristic features usually surface: Their body language often appears frozen or robotic, and their tone of voice tends to be monotonous, weak, unclear, too slow or too fast, giving the impression that they are "doing a favor" speaking. Their facial expressions are typically limited, and they rarely smile. They may present an unkempt appearance, including long hair and beards. They often have limited memories of their early lives, which can be attributed to their tendency to refrain from emotionally encoding experiences and perceiving daily life events as insignificant. It is also common for them to lack basic knowledge about their family members, such as where their parents grew up, their educational background, or employment history. They often provide general, superficial, or inaccurate responses when asked about such details, showing little effort to be precise. To gain a more comprehensive understanding, it is often necessary to ask their family members for additional information. During diagnostic tests, they frequently exhibit a lack of curiosity, imagination, and creativity. Their performance on IQ tests is often impacted by deficiencies in working memory, abstraction, accuracy, motivation, processing speed, distractibility, and concentration problems. They also typically display aloofness toward test results, making it challenging to leverage the new diagnosis to their advantage.

It is important to emphasize that autistics in this category may possess normal or high intelligence, yet their way of thinking is different. Drawing upon the concepts of Grandin (2020), they tend to lean more toward visual thinking (often associated with "low functioning") rather than verbal thinking (often associated with "high functioning"), which is more accepted in society, and therefore it is more difficult for them to adapt to societal expectations and norms.

Nevertheless, it is important to clarify that other autistics, too, including those with verbal thinking and a strong sense of curiosity, creativity, and self-observation, may encounter periods of frustration and challenges in fulfilling their talents due to factors related to autism. They, too, may drop out of educational or work environments, struggle to secure suitable employment, or invest their energies in pursuits that do not lead to personal growth, such as engaging in hobbies, games, or artistic endeavors such as writing a book, toward which many autistics gravitate. Such setbacks often lead to feelings of depression, despair, and a sense of failure, exacerbated by their characteristic difficulties in emotional integration and regulation. Given that many autistics experience periods of feeling stuck and frustrated, whether temporarily or permanently, regardless of their intelligence and other assets, a dichotomous classification into high functioning and low functioning is contested by many within the autistic community.

PERSONAL STORIES

Gonen

Gonen's parents sought a diagnostic assessment for him when he was 29 years old because they felt helpless and concerned, as he had been unemployed for several years, relied on them financially, and had no friends or future plans.

Gonen grew up in a small town in northern Israel as the eldest of three children. His father worked as an engineer and his mother as a secretary. As an infant, Gonen displayed a quiet, passive temperament, often spending long hours in his bassinet without much activity. He didn't start speaking until around the age of three after receiving speech therapy. His motor development was also delayed. In kindergarten, he preferred playing alone with Lego or organizing vehicles rather than interacting with other children. At home, he would watch cartoons repeatedly for extended periods. He had temper tantrums when unable to communicate his needs, and he was a picky eater, preferring only schnitzel and pasta. Gonen disliked physical touch and asked his parents to remove all clothing tags. He also experienced anxieties related to darkness and crowded environments, avoiding trips to the mall or family gatherings.

Throughout school, Gonen remained quiet and had no friends. He became a target of mockery and bullying, which he did not respond to, causing others to eventually ignore his presence. During breaks, he would walk in circles in the school yard. In the afternoons, he played computer games or watched TV. Although he excelled in math and sciences, he rarely did homework or studied for exams. He would play computer games late into the night and struggled to wake up for school in the mornings. Despite minimal studying, his natural intelligence allowed him to pass his matriculation tests.

During his military service, Gonen was assigned to a clerical role and avoided social interactions. He refused to eat in the common dining room, bringing instead a sandwich prepared by his mother. He used to commute home every afternoon via public transportation, enduring a 1 1/2-hour journey each way, as he refused to sleep anywhere except his own bed.

After completing his military service, Gonen faced uncertainty and often expressed anger toward his parents and siblings. Pressured by his parents, he enrolled in computer science studies at the university. Living in the student dormitories proved too challenging for him without his regular food and bed. In addition, his lack of organization caused him to miss several exams. As a result, he dropped out after one semester and returned to live with his parents.

In the years since then, Gonen has continued living with his parents. He lacks social relationships, has an inverted sleep schedule, and spends the majority of his time playing computer games or watching science fiction movies. He contributes very little to household chores, as his parents have ceased asking him for his assistance due to his negative reactions and failure to complete tasks when prompted. His parents handle all his arrangements, such as buying clothes (always the same items) or scheduling medical appointments, as Gonen hates making phone calls. Gonen barely communicates with his siblings, except for complaining about the noise they make. His parents are deeply concerned about his situation and worry about what will happen to him when they can no longer care for him.

Lena

Lena, a 42-year-old woman, grew up in Russia with a single mother who was an engineer. Raised primarily by her grandparents, Lena displayed exceptional verbal skills from an early age and exhibited a very rich vocabulary. She learned to read at the age of four and developed a fondness for fairy tales and stories about princesses. Throughout school, Lena rarely engaged in conversations with other children and would spend breaks either reading or resting her head on the table. Although she faced occasional bullying, she chose not to respond. In high school, Lena developed a strong interest in Judaism and immersed herself in learning about it. Following high school, she immigrated to Israel and attended an ultra-Orthodox seminary. She married an ultra-Orthodox man, and they had two children. After marriage, Lena's husband pressured her to find a job, but her confusion and awkwardness during job interviews resulted in repeated failures.

In recent years, Lena has been suffering from fibromyalgia (unfortunately common among autistics), which has prevented her from seeking employment. She has developed a deep interest in Kabbalah and spends numerous hours studying it. Lena actively avoids social interactions and, for instance, refrains from joining her husband and children on family visits. Neglecting her personal hygiene, she goes weeks without showering and struggles to attend to her children's needs. The only household task she takes on is laundry, but even that she does very slowly, wasting time sorting clothespins by color. The majority of household responsibilities and child care fall on her husband, causing him significant frustration.

Shay

Shay, a 32-year-old man, was born into a blue-collar family in central Israel. As an infant, he rarely cried, even when hungry. His motor development was delayed, and he began walking at the age of two. He developed a strong fascination with animals, spending hours observing insects or watching nature documentaries. In elementary school, Shay remained quiet, passive, and easily influenced by others. He belonged to a group of neighborhood children who frequently played with his toys and computer. Due to his concentration problems and learning disabilities, Shay was a mediocre student. In high school, he was diagnosed with ADHD and dyslexia, struggling particularly with humanistic studies and the interpretation of hidden meanings. Shay continued to associate with his old group of friends, who accepted him because of his calm, agreeable nature. During his military service, Shay consistently pleased others by agreeing to take their places when asked, showcasing his naïveté.

Over the past 10 years, Shay has worked in low-paying jobs, such as a gas station attendant, rarely engaging in conversations beyond the standard phrases used when refueling. He consented to sign as a guarantor for a colleague's apartment lease and now must pay off his debt for several years. In addition, he often incurs fines for failing to pay his own bills on time. Struggling to make a decent living, he feels stuck professionally. He expresses a desire to study computer science but consistently postpones the necessary steps to pursue it. A friend suggested that he might be autistic due to his unusual behaviors, such as consistently eating the same meals for extended periods, showing insensitivity to pain (even when he broke his leg, he felt almost no pain), difficulty recognizing faces, and an inability to identify when women are interested in him due to his good looks. That friend encouraged Shay to seek a diagnosis to better organize his life, which currently feels so stagnant.

WAYS OF COPING

Autistics who feel "stuck" often contend with frustration, depression, and despair, impacting those around them as well. Seeking a proper diagnosis is crucial to identify specific areas of difficulty and try to overcome them. Seeking professional help is recommended, focusing on enhancing social skills, executive functions, emotion regulation, and communication abilities.

It is also important to process past traumas in light of the autism diagnosis, alongside aiding individuals in setting goals and crafting concrete future plans. Autistics may need assistance in planning, prioritizing, and initiating actions. In the realm of employment, offering assistance with job selection, training, interview preparation, and workplace accommodations is essential. Similarly, given that many autistics desire relationships yet encounter challenges in initiating and maintaining them, targeted support in these areas is invaluable.

In addition to interventions tailored for the autistics themselves, it is important to address the needs of their family members, especially parents or partners who often need assistance in supporting them. Golan and colleagues (2016) propose an intervention for parents called "nonviolent resistance." This approach involves reducing parental assistance to encourage autistics to take on more tasks, training parents in deescalating conflicts by delaying their response, avoiding arguments, and demonstrating self-control. It also aims to enhance mentalization skills in both parents and children; encourage reliance on external support from family, friends, and professionals; and alleviate parents' feelings of helplessness and depression. Their study found this intervention to be significantly beneficial.

Partners can also benefit from strategies such as fostering clear communication, articulating mutual expectations, and acknowledging and showing consideration for each other's needs. These skills can be developed by practicing "nonviolent/compassionate communication" techniques.

Many autistics who successfully fulfill their potential are those who demonstrate awareness of their challenges and actively employ coping strategies. They may improve executive functions by using schedules, lists, or breaking down tasks to smaller ones; improve emotion regulation through cognitive strategies; and refine social skills through learning and practice. Some may benefit from medication to manage anxiety. Research indicates that struggling to overcome such obstacles can lead to increased feelings of success and competence, ultimately improving quality of life (see Webster & Garvis, 2017; Wylie, 2014). Autistics also document similar outcomes in their writings (e.g., Grandin, 2008, pp. 18–21; Robison, 2007, pp. 270–271).

However, it is crucial to warn against the danger of "ableism," which entails expecting autistics to adapt to social norms without adequate consideration of their challenges and rights. Each individual's autonomy must be respected, allowing them the freedom to decide whether to integrate into the labor market and existing social structures, and how to do so, without undue pressure to "normalize," out of respect and recognition of both their difficulties and their strengths.

In addition to self and family support, it is important for autistics to exercise their rights through health and welfare authorities and other organizations that offer assistance in areas such as employment, education, housing, and social life.

AUTISM AND HOMELESSNESS

An extreme outcome of autistics' being stuck is the risk of homelessness. Research on the connection between autism and homelessness is scarce, yet recent studies indicate a notable presence of autistics among the homeless population. For instance, Churchard and colleagues (2019) found that 12.3% of the 106 homeless individuals surveyed met the diagnostic criteria for autism. Similarly, Kargas and colleagues (2019) reported that 18.5% of the 65 homeless individuals they studied exhibited characteristics consistent with autism according to the AQ questionnaire.

Numerous factors contribute to the heightened risk of homelessness in autistics (see Churchard et al., 2019; Stone, 2019, 2022; Stone et al., 2022): Social and learning challenges at school frequently hinder the establishment of a foundation for employment, making it difficult to integrate into occupational, social, and familial contexts, ultimately leading to social and economic exclusion. Stone et al. (2022) found that many autistics become homeless following separation from spouses or relatives. Seeking assistance from authorities also poses challenges due to executive function deficits and difficulties initiating action. Some autistics may opt for homelessness due to ideological reasons, such as antimaterialistic ideologies or a desire to evade dependence on others. Nevertheless, even when seeking support, they may not be perceived as severely distressed, particularly without a formal autism diagnosis. In some cases, they may be offered solutions that are ill-suited for their needs: studies indicate that autistics often have problems in integrating into shared living settings such as hostels or shelters due to interpersonal and social challenges, as well as heightened sensitivities to sensory stimuli such as noise, lights, and smells (see Stone et al., 2022; Kargas et al., 2019).

Several strategies can mitigate the risk of autistics becoming homeless. First, it is crucial to increase awareness among professionals about autism so that they can better identify and provide appropriate assistance by developing tailored solutions that take into account their unique needs, difficulties, and sensitivities. Preventive measures are essential, including employment and psychological assistance, to prevent autistics from descending into homelessness. The health and welfare systems should prioritize and allocate resources to address these challenges effectively. In addition, further research is needed to identify the risk factors contributing to autism-related homelessness and to devise effective strategies to reduce such risks (see Stone et al., 2019, 2022; Kargas et al., 2019; Churchard et al., 2019).

Part III

BROADER THEORETICAL PERSPECTIVES

Chapter 12

Common Misdiagnoses and Key Differences Compared to Autism

Many autistics seek help from mental health professionals due to their significant psychological challenges. However, their autism diagnosis is often overlooked, resulting in frequent misdiagnosis with other conditions (Lever & Geurts, 2016; Fusar-Poli et al., 2020). Some of these misdiagnoses may be related to or co-occur with autism, including anxiety disorders, ADHD, and obsessive-compulsive disorders (Lai et al., 2019; Matson & Cervantes, 2014; Rinaldi et al., 2021). Nevertheless, autistics unfortunately often are misdiagnosed with mental disorders such as schizophrenia, mood disorders, or personality disorders, which do not entirely align with their overall clinical presentation (Tsuyoshi, 2015).

The misdiagnosis of autism can be attributed to various factors (see Au-Yeung et al., 2018; Luciano et al., 2014; Dossetor, 2007; Van Schalkwyk et al., 2015; Tsuyoshi, 2015):

The primary factor contributing to underdiagnosis is professionals' limited familiarity with autism diagnosis. Many professionals hold a superficial image of autistics as aloof, isolated, and emotionless, and are not aware of the diverse range of phenotypes within the autistic spectrum, as autistics can be either sensitive or insensitive, introverts or extroverts, curious or indifferent, and so on. The problem of underdiagnosis is more prevalent regarding women, who may exhibit several friendships, a deep interest in others, and high levels of empathy, supposedly challenging common stereotypes about autism. In addition, autistics often mask their autistic traits, for example, by struggling to make eye contact. Besides, many autistic characteristics overlap with those of other disorders.

Health-care professionals, often tasked with offering diagnoses for their patients to access services, may be inclined to provide diagnoses they are more familiar with and avoid in-depth assessments of their patients' psychological characteristics and early history. The challenges autistics face in communication can further complicate the articulation of their inner difficulties and life history, as well as their problems in understanding professionals' questions.

In this chapter, I will discuss common misdiagnoses that autistics may encounter, illustrating them with cases I have encountered. I will highlight the critical differences between these misdiagnoses and the diagnosis of autism. Recognizing these distinctions is paramount, as misdiagnosis can result in deep feelings of being misunderstood and depression among autistics, along with unnecessary treatments that can impose substantial mental and financial burdens on both patients and the health-care system.

AUTISTICS MISDIAGNOSED WITH SCHIZOPHRENIA

Natasha

Natasha contacted me at the age of 40 to explore the possibility of being autistic. At first glance, her low socioeconomic background was apparent, as she commuted by public transportation from a peripheral town in southern Israel, living in impoverished conditions as a single mother of two. Natasha was considerably overweight and spoke with a noticeable Russian accent, having immigrated to Israel from Russia with her parents when she was approximately 11 years old. Despite these external factors, attentive listening revealed her considerable intelligence. She sought my help after reading about autism and believing it to be a more fitting diagnosis than the schizophrenia diagnosis she had received nearly 20 years earlier.

As an infant, Natasha exhibited remarkable calmness, rarely cried, and consistently slept through the night. In her kindergarten in Russia, she displayed introverted tendencies, engaging in solitary play with sand or playing blocks, and was deeply attached to her dog. She was deeply naive and grappled with numerous anxieties, ranging from fear of the dark, doctors, and creatures seen on TV, to imaginary creatures such as a crocodile in the toilet. Natasha was also wary of talking to strangers and had various sensory sensitivities, including a reluctance to eat vegetables, a preference for specific foods (especially fried potatoes), a fear of loud noises, an aversion to certain fabric textures, and a heightened sense of smell.

Natasha attended a Russian school until she was around 11 years old, where she had no friends and spent breaks alone in the school's dining room, hoping for someone to approach her. After her family immigrated to Israel and settled in a low-income town, she had almost no communication with classmates. In middle school, she endured bullying, violence, and insults.

High school was similarly isolating and depressing, leading her to drop out and attend evening school instead.

Throughout her military service, Natasha excelled in her technical role but rarely spoke to others. Her naïveté often led her to agree to replace colleagues on shifts, leaving her feeling exploited, depressed, and lonely. Afterward, she worked as a chambermaid on weekends at a Dead Sea hotel. While she appreciated not having to interact with others, she felt deeply hurt when excluded from social activities with her coworkers. During weekdays Natasha developed a pattern of staying awake at night and sleeping during the day, a typical pattern observed in many autistics. Her parents frequently reprimanded her for seemingly doing nothing.

Accompanied by her mother, Natasha sought help at a mental health clinic, where she was diagnosed with a depressive episode and differential diagnoses of schizophrenia, schizoid personality disorder, or avoidant personality disorder. Prescribed antidepressants, she experienced weight gain, which further exacerbated her depression and irritability. During a follow-up appointment, Natasha expressed her belief that people were mocking her due to being overweight. The psychiatrist suspected ideas of reference and asked if she "heard voices," to which she answered affirmatively, interpreting the question literally, although she did not actually experience inner voices as individuals with schizophrenia do. Natasha agreed to be admitted to a psychiatric institution as a means of taking a break from her parents. In her discharge letter, it was noted that she did not exhibit any psychotic behaviors or symptoms but had thoughts related to her appearance that had a "psychotic vibe," leading to a diagnosis of schizophrenia. This diagnosis was approved by the National Health Insurance, and she began receiving a monthly allowance for schizophrenia. For many years, Natasha and her family believed she had schizophrenia, and she continued to take medications that caused her irritability and depression. A few years ago, she decided to stop taking these medications, which was approved by her psychiatrist, resulting in a significant improvement in her mental state. She lost weight and experienced no suicidal thoughts. In recent years, she has held various jobs and is raising her two children.

Natasha's literal understanding and difficulty expressing herself, coupled with executive dysfunction and social impairments related to autism, played a significant role in her misdiagnosis. In addition, because of her low socioeconomic status, she had no family or social lobby to object to her misdiagnosis. Neither Natasha nor her family had sufficient familiarity with autism, and the medical professionals she encountered did not recognize it either.

Replacing the schizophrenia diagnosis with that of autism, supported by a knowledgeable psychiatrist, brought an immense sense of relief and validation to Natasha. However, she also experienced anger toward the system for subjecting her to 20 years of misdiagnosis, preventing her from trying to fit in socially and occupationally. The misdiagnosis resulted in unnecessary and harmful medication and deprived her of the appropriate autism support that could have significantly improved her well-being much earlier.

Nir

Nir was brought to therapy around the age 40 by his discouraged mother. For several years, he had been spending most of his time at home, watching TV or surfing the internet, almost without work or friends, and lacking the motivation to change his situation. He is a tall, stout man with handsome features, but his face and body language appear expressionless. He speaks only when prompted, responding to questions in a monotone voice, and often keeps his gaze fixed on the floor.

Nir grew up in a wealthy family in central Israel. As a child, he was very stubborn and would bang his head against the wall when irritated. He exhibited heightened sensitivities in all his senses, avoided certain foods and tight or buttoned clothing, and was very sensitive to sounds, smells, and bright lights. He also had fears of the dark, injections, masks, and more. In elementary school, he had few friends and grappled with learning difficulties. The discomfort persisted in middle school, leading him eventually to leave. Under pressure from his parents, he completed the matriculation exams in an evening school. During his military service, he had a secretarial role, rarely speaking with anyone, and commuting more than two hours each day to sleep in his own bed.

Nir's parents urged him to pursue an academic degree, which he struggled to complete, with extensive help from his mother and testing accommodations, without connecting with any other students. Following graduation, he could not find appropriate employment due to his difficulties in interviews, often maintaining minimal speech and avoiding eye contact by staring at the floor. As a result, he worked in low-paying jobs for short periods of time. He was fired from his last job three years ago and has been unemployed since. He lives in his parents' house, rarely leaving it, and sometimes not even getting out of bed. He has reversed day and night, spending most waking hours at night watching historical series on television or playing chess on the computer. He rigidly adheres to routines and becomes angry if they are disrupted. He does not contribute to household tasks; his mother or sister make arrangements on his behalf.

Several years ago, Nir and his parents consulted a psychiatrist who, incorrectly, diagnosed him with a "latent schizophrenic process, with negative signs only"—a diagnosis that does not exist—due to his executive dysfunction, communication problems, and lack of motivation. Based on this diagnosis, he received a disability allowance and medications for schizophrenia, but his condition did not improve. He never experienced a psychotic episode or displayed positive signs of schizophrenia. Throughout our one-year therapy, I observed no problem in reality testing or thought disorders. However, he clearly met the criteria for autism, a diagnosis later confirmed by another psychiatrist. This allowed Nir to access suitable organizations for autistics and benefit from their services. He now feels more understood, blames himself less for his challenges, and receives increased understanding and empathy from his family.

Key Differences between Schizophrenia and Autism

Recent studies suggest that a significant portion of individuals previously diagnosed with schizophrenia may, in fact, be identified as autistic (see Perlman, 2000; Da Fonseca et al., 2008; Waris et al., 2013; Sheitmann et al., 2004; Barneveld et al., 2011; Van Schalkwyk et al., 2015; Dossetor, 2007; Attwood, 2007; Palucka et al., 2008; Raja & Azzoni, 2001). For instance, Tony Attwood, a prominent autism researcher, believes that in light of his current knowledge of autism, many patients he encountered during his training who had been diagnosed with atypical schizophrenia could have been diagnosed with Asperger's syndrome instead (Attwood, 2007, p. 343). Perlman, too, attests that he encountered several psychiatric patients who appeared to have negative signs of schizophrenia such as social withdrawal, apathy, lack of motivation, or communication challenges, yet did not have psychotic episodes or acute exacerbations—but, on the other hand, had many characteristics of autism—and should have been rediagnosed as autistic, based on his updated knowledge of autism (Perlman, 2000).

Several factors contribute to misdiagnosing autistics as schizophrenics (see Tsuyoshi, 2015; Perlman, 2000; Van Schalkwyk et al., 2015; Dossetor, 2007). In addition to professionals' lack of knowledge and failure to investigate autism characteristics adequately, an overlap in the clinical characteristics between autism and schizophrenia makes differentiation challenging (Waris et al., 2013; Sheitmann et al., 2004; Barneveld, 2011; Tsuyoshi, 2015; Fitzgerald, 2012; Van Schalkwyk et al., 2015; Dossetor, 2007):

First, there is an overlap between the characteristics of autism and the "negative symptoms" of schizophrenia, such as flat affect, lack of social interest, communication and attention problems, avolition (lack of energy, drive, and interest) and unconventional thinking and behavior.

Second, both autistics and schizophrenics may exhibit preoccupation with others criticizing, mocking, or persecuting them. However, whereas in schizophrenics this may stem from paranoid delusions, in autistics such thoughts may emanate from overthinking, compounded by challenges in grasping others' intentions and influenced by negative reactions they have encountered throughout their lives, making them more suspicious of others' intentions (Attwood, 2007; Craig et al., 2004; Blackshaw et al., 2001).

Moreover, both autistics and schizophrenics may display disorganized speech and thinking, with no prioritization or discernment between what is important and what is not. They may also encounter challenges in effectively communicating their experiences or desires and engage in unconventional behaviors. However, in autistics, these stem from problems in executive functions, such as organization or prioritization, whereas in schizophrenics they arise from thought disorders or psychosis. Further, autistics may engage in self-talk as a means of processing thoughts or experiences, behavior that might be misinterpreted as conversing with internal "voices" (Attwood, 2007). In addition, autistics are often preoccupied with their rich inner lives, a characteristic that could be misconstrued as delusions (LaSalle, 2003; Attwood, 2007), although their reality testing is typically intact.

The literature offers several instances of autistics being misdiagnosed with schizophrenia. For instance, Howlin (1997) recounts the case of a boy diagnosed with schizophrenia due to his claim of having a "shark inside him," later clarified by his mother as a literal interpretation from a childhood book; Lawson (1998) describes a woman misdiagnosed with schizophrenia because she responded "yes" when asked if she heard voices, as she interpreted the question literally; Palucka et al. (2008) describe a boy who was diagnosed as schizophrenic because he said he feared that the devil would think he was bad, but in light of his corrected autism diagnosis it was understood that his statements stemmed from his religious upbringing combined with his concrete attitude to things. These examples underscore how autistics may be erroneously diagnosed with schizophrenia due to their propensity for literal understanding, elevated anxiety levels, limited awareness of the impressions they make on others, and difficulties in conveying their perspectives to others. Although schizophrenia can sometimes co-occur with autism, studies indicate that the prevalence of schizophrenia among autistics is less than 1% (i.e., not higher than its rates in the general population) (Volkmar & Cohen, 1991; Tantam, 2000). Even Hans Asperger noted that only 1 of the 200 cases he dealt with developed clear signs of schizophrenia (Wolff, 1995). Nevertheless, research suggests that autistics may be more susceptible to psychotic episodes due to their increased exposure to bullying and abuse, thereby amplifying the risk of misdiagnosis (Tsuyoshi, 2015; Moulton et al., 2019; Van Schalkwyk et al., 2015).

Although the present discussion centers on adults, it should be noted that autistic children also frequently are misdiagnosed with "childhood schizophrenia," and therefore it is important to distinguish between psychotic hallucinations related to schizophrenia and the rich imagination and pseudo-hallucinations of autistics (Dossetor, 2007; Sullivan et al., 2013).

There are several ways to distinguish between schizophrenia and autism:

First, to diagnose schizophrenia one must prove the existence of at least two of the following three positive symptoms—delusions, hallucinations, and disorganized speech (criterion F for schizophrenia in the *DSM-5* explicitly states that if there is a history of a disorder on the autistic continuum, a diagnosis of schizophrenia will only be given if prominent delusions or hallucinations are present; see *DSM-5*, 295).

Second, to diagnose autism, one must confirm that specific challenges, such as in communication and social interactions, were present since early childhood, while in schizophrenia, difficulties may arise only in adolescence or young adulthood; Asperger wrote, "While the schizophrenic patient seems to show progressive loss of contact, the children we are discussing lack contact from the start" (Asperger, 1944 [1991], p. 39).

In addition, one must make sure to check the existence of a wide enough range of ASD characteristics, according to the *DSM* criteria, such as restricted interests and repetitive behaviors, heightened sensory sensitivities, intense special interests, and challenges in grasping implicit meanings. In addition, academic decline is associated with schizophrenia but not with autism, and autistics tend to respond better to anxiety-reducing interventions and less to antipsychotic treatment (Dossetor, 2007).

AUTISTICS MISDIAGNOSED WITH BIPOLAR DISORDER

Hagar

Hagar, a skilled dancer in her late thirties, is a woman of remarkable brilliance, effortlessly pouring profound insights with rapid and captivating eloquence. Although her facial expression usually remains composed, her emotions occasionally surface in bursts of laughter or tears that often well up in her eyes, as often can be observed in autistics, reflecting their challenges in regulating emotions.

Hagar was raised in an ultra-Orthodox background. As a child, she displayed heightened sensory sensitivities and anxieties and used to cry frequently. She had a strong inclination toward organizing things in rows and faced challenges in understanding social expectations. Her high intelligence was evident from an early age, and she developed a passion for reading. In school, the clear religious rules of conduct provided her with a framework for behavior, and she acquired social adjustment skills from a friend who mentored her in aspects such as proper dress, phone etiquette, and personal hygiene. Although Hagar felt different from other girls, she made efforts to behave like them. Being considered the smartest girl helped her, despite struggling with concentration issues. Shortly after high school Hagar got married and became a mother to multiple children, adhering to practices such as home birth and homeschooling.

After a decade of marriage, Hagar's husband filed for divorce, leaving her devastated. She decided to depart from religious life and, being inexperienced in the dating world, engaged in unconventional behaviors such as simultaneously dating multiple men, staying at their homes for extended periods, or spending nights on the beach. These actions were perceived as abnormal by her religious family, prompting them to request her hospitalization. Unfortunately, at the psychiatric department, Hagar's rapid speech, restlessness, bluntness, and open sexuality, which are often found in autistics, were misinterpreted as indications of manic symptoms. Due to her reported low mood following the divorce, she was wrongly diagnosed with bipolar disorder and underwent hospitalization for several weeks.

Several years later, Hagar learned about autism and pursued a diagnostic process, which unequivocally confirmed that she met the criteria for autism. Throughout all these years, Hagar has not experienced any manic or depressive episodes. She even completed an academic degree with excellent grades and now thrives in her career as a successful dance teacher. Hagar feels a deep anger toward the system that failed to accurately diagnose her, leading to traumatic hospitalizations and leaving her feeling unvalidated and misunderstood.

Nicole

Nicole, a 25-year-old woman, spent her early years in France with her mother and grandmother. Recognized as highly intelligent and eloquent from a young age, she harbored a deep passion for reading fantasy and science fiction books. In addition, she exhibited a profound fascination with insects, meticulously documenting details about them. She grappled with social interactions, often feeling isolated and misunderstood during her school years.

In her youth, Nicole developed a strong interest in Israeli culture and music, particularly fixating on a specific Israeli singer, a passion that endures to this day. At the age of 18, she immigrated to Israel and married a man twice her age (as autistics often overlook considerations of age, race, or status). Attempting to pursue higher education, Nicole faced challenges in time management and completing writing assignments due to executive dysfunctions. As her relationship with her husband became strained, she made threats of suicide. In response, her husband took her to a psychiatric emergency room, leading to her admission to a psychiatric hospital.

During her hospitalization, Nicole experienced difficulties falling asleep and exhibited repetitive behaviors such as singing, rocking, and excessive talk about her cats. This eventually resulted in a misdiagnosis of bipolar disorder. While in the hospital, she met an autistic patient who introduced her to the concept of autism, which strongly resonated with her experiences. With the support of a psychologist and psychiatrist, her diagnosis was later revised to autism, correcting the earlier misdiagnosis of bipolar disorder.

Key Differences between Autism and Bipolar Disorder

Quite a few autistics are misdiagnosed with bipolar disorder because professionals are more familiar with the latter, and the two disorders have overlapping characteristics (Lainhart & Folstein, 1994; Hellings & Witwer, 2014; Dell'Osso et al., 2021; Fusar-Poli et al., 2020; Lever & Geurts, 2016). Although some individuals may have both autism and bipolar disorder—for example, one study found that bipolar disorder appeared in 6–21% of the autistics tested compared to 2.4% in the normal population (Merikangas et al., 2011)—this section focuses on autistics who are mistakenly diagnosed with bipolar disorder, which does not accurately reflect their condition.

Autistics may be misdiagnosed with bipolar disorder due to the following overlapping characteristics:

Some autistic traits resemble the criteria for "manic" or "hypomanic" episodes, such as excessive talking, sleep difficulties, racing thoughts, distraction, hyperfocus, restlessness, and attraction to extreme or risky behaviors (which in autistics may result from a lack of planning; for instance, many autistic children are drawn to activities such as climbing, jumping, and swinging without fully considering the associated risks, due to their tendency to avoid future planning).

Hellings and Witwer (2014) found in their research that a significant number of autistic children exhibited symptoms that could be mistaken for bipolar disorder, including elevated mood, irritability, excessive talking, excessive activity, distractibility, and sleep disturbances.

Autistics may also display characteristics akin to those outlined in the criteria for depressive episodes, such as insomnia or oversleeping, reduced appetite, fatigue, loss of interests or activities, feelings of worthlessness, self-criticism, guilt, hesitancy, and suicidal thoughts or intentions.

Given that autistics often gravitate toward extremes or oscillate between them, their behaviors may resemble those observed in bipolar disorder. These extremes may include excessive versus minimal talking, being overly open versus socially withdrawn, sleeping excessively versus experiencing insomnia, and oscillating between feelings of superiority and inferiority. However, it's crucial to note that they often concurrently exhibit both so-called manic and depressive characteristics, such as insomnia and rapid speech alongside depression and social withdrawal. This simultaneous manifestation of features points toward a likelihood of autism rather than bipolar disorder.

Further, diagnosing bipolar disorder according to the *DSM-5* requires confirming that the symptoms represent a noticeable departure from the individual's typical behavior. Therefore, a comprehensive assessment of the person's developmental history is essential. Consistent features from an early age are more indicative of autism, whereas symptoms that arise suddenly are more suggestive of bipolar disorder. In addition, evaluating whether the person meets the specific criteria for autism is necessary.

Arriving at the correct diagnosis is crucial for appropriate psychological and pharmacological treatment. For example, lithium, a common treatment for bipolar disorder, can have side effects that may be more dangerous for autistics due to their difficulties in identifying bodily sensations as well as communicating them with caregivers (Hellings & Witwer, 2014).

Enhancing professionals' knowledge of the differences between autism and bipolar disorder is essential. Further research is needed to refine diagnostic tools and provide patients with the understanding and treatment they deserve.

AUTISTICS MISDIAGNOSED WITH DEPRESSION

Many autistics experience depressive disorders or episodes, which can co-occur with autism or arise from it. Depression is considered the most common psychiatric disorder in autistics, with rates ranging from 10.1 to 53% in various studies (Tsuyoshi et al., 2015; Ghaziuddin et al., 2002; Chandrasekhar & Sikich, 2015). The causes of depression in autistics can sometimes be a history of emotional, cognitive, and social difficulties, including bullying, rejection, difficulties in self-fulfillment, loneliness, low self-esteem, and emotion dysregulation (Chandrasekhar & Sikich, 2015; Tsuyoshi et al., 2015).

However, sometimes autistics are misdiagnosed with depression due to characteristics that are related to autism. These may include social withdrawal, sleep disorders, lack of motivation, lack of desire, picky eating, and self-neglect. For example, many autistics feel the need to withdraw from social activities not because of depression but due to difficulties with sensory, emotional, and social overload. They may lack motivation because of executive disfunctions. They may refrain from keeping personal hygiene (e.g., taking a bath, getting a haircut, or brushing their teeth) due to sensory sensitivities and difficulties with transitions. They may give up meals because of their sensory sensibilities or disregard of their body's needs. Therefore, one must examine carefully the reasons underlying such behaviors to determine whether they stem from depression or autism.

It is important to note that there is also a risk of *underdiagnosing* depression in autistics, because of their challenges in expressing their feelings and seeking help (Stewart et al., 2006; Chandrasekhar & Sikich, 2015; Lainhart & Folstein, 1994). To identify depression, it is crucial to assess for changes in comparison to previous behaviors. This involves examining alterations in emotions, interests, activity levels, sleep and appetite patterns, as well as the presence of self-harming behaviors and suicidal intentions or thoughts (Chandrasekhar & Sikich, 2015; Stewart et al., 2006; Lainhart & Folstein, 1994).

Identifying depression in autistics is crucial as it can lead to significant mental distress, self-harm, and suicidal intentions or actions. Studies have shown higher suicide rates among autistics compared to the general population: autistics are 7–9 times more likely to commit suicide. The suicide rate of autistics constitutes 11% of all suicides in the population. Suicide is the second most common cause of death in autistics. The average life expectancy of autistics is 54 (Doherty, 2020; Willgoss, 2021; Cassidy et al., 2021).

In conclusion, clinicians should be mindful of the risks of both overdiagnosis and underdiagnosis of depression in autistics. Further efforts should be directed toward developing tools for identifying depression in autistics to ensure that they can receive the necessary mental and medical support.

AUTISTICS MISDIAGNOSED WITH PERSONALITY DISORDERS

Many autistics who turn to professionals lacking sufficient familiarity with the autism profile are often misdiagnosed with a personality disorder, including any of the 10 outlined in the *DSM-5*: narcissistic, antisocial, schizoid, schizotypal, dependent, avoidant, obsessive-compulsive, histrionic, paranoid, and borderline personality disorders. The misdiagnosis typically stems from the overlapping characteristics between autism and each of the personality disorders, as further detailed later. Autistics most commonly are misdiagnosed with borderline, schizoid, schizotypal, avoidant, narcissistic, antisocial, or obsessive-compulsive personality disorders (Rinaldi et al., 2021).

To decide whether someone has autism or a personality disorder, one must thoroughly examine the psychological characteristics and the developmental history of the person. It is important to investigate early development, relying as much as possible on the reports of caregivers and/or professionals to determine the extent to which autistic characteristics were present from an early age, as autism is supposed to be present from birth, whereas personality disorders develop later. When evaluating whether an individual meets the criteria for autism, it's crucial to acknowledge that many autistics have developed the ability to mask their autistic characteristics by making efforts to establish eye contact or engage in small talk. Therefore, it is essential to explicitly inquire about their initial dispositions regarding such behaviors.

I will now outline some key differences between autism and each personality disorder to facilitate the arrival at an accurate diagnosis:

Borderline Personality Disorder (BPD)—Autistics are often misdiagnosed with BPD due to shared characteristics, such as identity problems, challenges in emotion regulation, split perceptions of self and others, a tendency to terminate jobs and relationships, and engagement in self-harm behaviors. Both disorders may also include a history of abuse and neglect. However, autism and BPD have some essential differences: Individuals with BPD often exhibit a heightened ability to perceive social cues and others' feelings (even though their perceptions may be colored by their subjective perceptions), and their social behavior can appear normative, making favorable first impressions, in, for example, job interviews. In contrast, autistics struggle with these aspects. In addition, those with BPD tend to display intense emotions in close relationships, being highly sensitive to rejection and abandonment—whether real or imagined—and resorting to dramatic and manipulative behaviors such as complaining, blaming, or threatening. In contrast, autistics tend to be more reserved and emotionally distant. Whereas those with BPD are often unstable in their close relationships, autistics tend to be stable and loyal, though their relationships may end due to their challenges in maintaining them properly. Self-injury in BPD is often triggered by relationship difficulties, aiming to provoke a reaction from others, whereas in autistics, self-injury can result from challenges in emotion regulation, feelings of being misunderstood or unvalidated, or from seeking sensory stimulation, frequently without even exposing these behaviors or seeking responses from others. Moreover, autism is essentially congenital, whereas BPD typically develops due to environmental factors such as neglect or abuse.

Schizoid Personality Disorder (SPD)—Autistics are often misdiagnosed with SPD due to shared characteristics such as withdrawal from social interactions, immersion in worlds of knowledge, limited emotional expression, and susceptibility to depression and anxiety. However, SPD and autism have significant differences: Autistics tend to withdraw from social situations due to challenges in comprehending social behaviors and knowing how to navigate them, whereas schizoids are capable of perceiving others' feelings and intentions but consciously prefer seclusion. Autistics often seek social relationships and can find satisfaction and pleasure in connections with people they feel comfortable with, whereas schizoids typically lack interest in social relationships, except for a few close ones. Autistics may exhibit intense and liberated sexuality, sometimes even hypersexuality, whereas schizoids often show minimal interest in sexuality. In terms of emotional expression, autistics may openly express simple emotions such as sadness, joy, or anger while struggling with more complex emotions. Conversely, schizoids typically refrain from displaying even simple emotions. Autistics also often display high emotional empathy and compassion toward others' distress, whereas schizoids tend to remain emotionally aloof or distant. Moreover, SPD develops in response to early caregivers who were perceived as intrusive or insufficiently soothing, coupled with an inherently sensitive temperament, whereas autism is a congenital syndrome.

Avoidant Personality Disorder (APD)—Autistics may be misdiagnosed with APD due to shared characteristics such as discomfort in social situations and avoidance of various life tasks. However, upon closer examination, these can be seen as almost opposite syndromes: individuals with APD are hypersensitive to others' reactions and are highly conscious of the impressions they may create, leading them to be overly cautious around others. In contrast, autistics, due to their challenges in reading others' emotions, often overlook the impressions they make and exhibit uninhibited or unconventional behaviors. For example, they may fearlessly approach figures of authority or show no apprehension in front of an audience. Nonetheless, many autistics do develop fears of rejection or criticism due to the numerous criticisms they encounter throughout their lives, leading to a heightened sensitivity to others' negative feelings toward them (Attwood, 2018). Consequently, they may exhibit avoidance symptoms. Therefore, the existence of other autistic characteristics must be considered in such cases. Moreover, autism is congenital, whereas APD typically develops due to a lack of sufficient empathy from early caretakers, resulting in an insecure attachment, excessive caution, and avoidance behaviors.

Paranoid Personality Disorder (PPD)—Autistics may be misdiagnosed with PPD due to common characteristics such as perceiving other people and situations as threatening, avoiding social interactions, struggling with expressing emotions, and experiencing high levels of anxiety and depression. However, fundamental differences exist between these two disorders: autistics may feel threatened by others due to innate challenges in deciphering social cues in addition to past experiences of hostility, bullying, or abuse. In contrast, individuals with PPD become suspicious because their early caretakers did not provide sufficient reassurance or even intensified their fears. Those with PPD tend to suspect almost everyone's intentions, whereas autistics often exhibit a tendency to be naive and often believe what they are told. Those with PPD tend to be suspicious even in close relationships, whereas autistics tend to be loyal and trusting in close relationships, sometimes to a fault, due to their tendency to think in black and white. Both autistics and those with PPD tend to have difficulties in expressing emotions, but in PPD these stem from fear, whereas in autistics these result from inherent difficulties in expressing emotions (alexithymia).

Schizotypal Personality Disorder (STPD)—Autistics may be misdiagnosed with STPD due to shared characteristics such as unconventional behaviors, withdrawal from social relationships, preference for solitary activities, difficulties in expressing emotions, and naïveté. However, these two disorders have fundamental differences. Autistics typically seek and find joy in specific relationships, especially those in which they share common interests and feel accepted, whereas schizotypals tend to be generally suspicious and uncomfortable in the company of others. Autistics typically exhibit fewer thought disorders and are less prone to magical thinking, ideas of reference, paranoid ideas, or experiences similar to psychosis, which are more common in schizotypals.

Narcissistic Personality Disorder (NPD)—Autistics may be misdiagnosed with NPD due to their tendency to be self-absorbed and sometimes disregard the feelings and needs of others. However, NPD and autism have fundamental differences. Narcissists have fantasies of power and success, constantly seeking admiration, whereas autistics typically do not pursue these goals per se. Narcissists often adeptly know how to impress others, whereas autistics often lack such knowledge. Autistics have difficulties in perceiving others' feelings, intentions, or needs, whereas narcissists may perceive them well but ignore them if they are not serving their own needs. Narcissists avoid relationships that do not serve their goals, whereas autistics are more inclined to be loyal. Narcissists have no qualms about hurting, exploiting, or humiliating others, whereas autistics often lack malicious intents. Narcissists tend to ignore others' distress, whereas autistics are often compassionate and act for the sake of others, frequently sacrificing their own interests. Beyond all these, narcissism arises from early-life circumstances characterized by emotional coldness and lack of empathy from early caregivers, whereas autism is considered a congenital syndrome.

Antisocial Personality Disorder (ASPD)—Autistics may be misdiagnosed with ASPD due to their tendency to be emotionally detached and distant, thereby creating an impression of lacking empathy. However, there are essential differences. Those with ASPD are highly manipulative, adept at perceiving others' intentions and feelings but using them for personal advantage. In contrast, autistics encounter difficulties in perceiving others' emotions and are not inclined to manipulate or exploit them for their own gain. Antisocial individuals may engage in malicious, exploitative, criminal, violent, and irresponsible behavior, whereas autistics often exhibit high emotional empathy. It is essential to distinguish between emotional empathy, which most autistics clearly have, and cognitive empathy—the ability to perceive the thoughts, feelings, and intentions of others—which they often lack due to difficulties in

Theory of Mind, whereas antisocial individuals lack emotional empathy but do have cognitive empathy, which they use to promote their own interests. Moreover, ASPD typically arises from environmental influences, such as emotional detachment, abuse, lack of reassurance, or overindulgence by early caregivers, whereas autism is a congenital syndrome.

Obsessive-Compulsive Personality Disorder (OCPD)—Autistics may be misdiagnosed with OCPD due to shared characteristics such as a proclivity for strict routines, repetitive behaviors, difficulties in expressing emotions, and rigidity in interpersonal relationships. However, distinct differences exist between the two. Those with OCPD typically uphold high standards for hard work, order, and cleanliness, whereas autistics typically struggle with these due to challenges in executive functions. However, some autistics compensate by adhering to the opposite extreme. Therefore, it's important to examine the underlying tendency in each case. OCPD individuals can usually read social cues and understand others' intentions, whereas autistics have innate difficulties in these areas. OCPD individuals tend to repress or isolate their feelings, whereas autistics grapple with expressing complex emotions due to alexithymia. Moreover, OCPD typically develops in response to a demanding, unempathetic early environment, whereas autism is a congenital syndrome.

Dependent Personality Disorder (DPD)—Autistics may be misdiagnosed with DPD due to overlapping traits, including challenges in decision making, a reliance on others for emotional and practical support, low self-esteem, a propensity to please others, and difficulties expressing emotions. However, those with DPD do not inherently possess the distinct characteristics of autism. In addition, the source of their problems lies in unsatisfied needs from early caregivers, contrasting with the congenital source of autism.

Histrionic Personality Disorder (HPD)—Autistics may be misdiagnosed with HPD due to shared characteristics such as low self-esteem, a strong need for confirmation and validation, dramatic behaviors, difficulties in emotion regulation, challenges in expressing complex emotions, somatization, a tendency to overlook others' emotions, anxiety, and depression. However, there are notable differences. Histrionics typically possess strong social skills, enabling them to make friends easily, and they are also prone to manipulative or seductive behaviors, whereas autistics typically have difficulties in forming friendships and tend to be more direct and honest. Histrionics strive for attention and find loneliness difficult to bear, whereas autistics often seek solitude. Histrionics may act dramatically for attention, whereas autistics' so-called dramatic behaviors often stem from feeling unvalidated or misunderstood. Autistics tend to be highly focused, seeking fundamental truths, and many of them constantly explore deeply their own psyches and their surroundings, whereas histrionics are more prone to superficiality and evading deep knowledge (Freud perceived "not knowing" as a central defense in hysteria), even though autistics may also sometimes be blocked to certain types of knowledge, mainly superficial knowledge. Moreover, autism is congenital, whereas the origins of HPD lie in insufficient attention or discrimination by early caregivers.

In conclusion, recognizing the nuanced differences between autism and each personality disorder is essential for accurate diagnosis and tailored interventions for individuals with either condition. However, it is important to note that despite these distinct differences, co-occurrence is a possibility. For example, Tanya Marshall describes the co-occurrence of autism and borderline personality disorder (BPD), characterized by communication difficulties, strained relationships, negative interpretations of others' intentions, intense emotional expressions, disregard for boundaries, "black-and-white" thinking, and suicidality (Marshall, 2019). Further research is needed to explore the potential coexistence of autism and personality disorders and to understand the nature of such co-occurrences.

CONCLUDING REMARKS

The chapter highlighted the common misdiagnoses among autistics, primarily due to the overlap between autism and other mental conditions, compounded by professionals' insufficient knowledge in this domain. Emphasis was placed on the imperative for professionals to enhance their understanding to enable a more accurate differentiation between diagnostic possibilities and facilitating improved understanding and treatment for patients.

Professionals are urged to conduct thorough investigations to ascertain whether an individual is autistic. Questionnaires such as the AQ or RITVO can be instrumental in this process. Given that autistics often mask certain characteristics, such as making eye contact or managing small talks, an in-depth examination of these aspects in their earlier lives is crucial. This investigation should incorporate self-reports, information from relatives if available, and assessments from previous reports.

Reaching the correct diagnosis has significant consequences for treatment. It can prevent unnecessary and potentially harmful medical treatments. For example, autistics typically do not require antipsychotic drugs but may benefit from medications that reduce anxiety, depression, or obsessive-compulsive behaviors (Fusar-Poli et al., 2020). It is also important not to medically suppress repetitive movements, as they may help regulate anxiety (Fusar-Poli et al., 2020). Providing appropriate treatment is essential for the patient's well-being and for the overall health-care system, potentially saving high costs of unnecessary treatments or hospitalizations.

In addition to providing the right psychological and medical treatment, it is also crucial to support autistics in exercising their rights in terms of employment, education, social, and leisure needs.

Last, further research is necessary to better understand the differences and relationships between autism and other mental conditions as well as to refine the existing diagnostic tools.

Chapter 13

The Disrupted Integration between Primary and Secondary Processes in Autistic Thinking

This chapter discusses the characteristics of autistic thinking in terms of the key psychoanalytic concepts of primary and secondary processes, formulated by Freud and his followers. Autistic thinking is described as characterized by the dominance of primary processes such as a tendency to associativity, subjective categorization, disregard of contexts, creativity, and more. Secondary processes may also come to the fore, mainly in the thinking of so-called high-functioning autistics—evidenced by logical, realistic, and organized thinking—yet with disrupted integration between these two kinds of processes. The extent of integration between the primary and secondary processes varies between autistic individuals and may improve by virtue of helpful psychotherapy.

Identifying the pathophysiological basis of autism is at the forefront of many contemporary studies. The leading theory in autism research is the "disrupted connectivity theory," proposing that autistics suffer from defective connections between certain brain areas, mainly between the right and left hemispheres (Paul et al., 2004; Vasa, Mostofsky, & Ewen, 2017). Thus, many studies indicate diminished connectivity between right-brain functions, such as holistic thinking, intuition, imagination, emotionality, associativity, visual thinking, and parallel processing; and left-brain functions, such as logical, analytical, and linear thinking, planning and organization, language use, and serial processing. Disrupted connectivity between the hemispheres was found in numerous studies to be related to many of the deficiencies found in autism, such as deficiencies in social functioning, understanding other peoples' emotional states, reasoning, problem solving, and decision making (see, e.g., Paul et al., 2004; Gepner & Feron, 2009; Vasa et al., 2017).

More specifically, research indicates that autistics typically exhibit a condition known as agenesis of the corpus callosum (ACC), where the bundle of nerves connecting the right and left hemispheres, called the corpus callosum, is either underdeveloped or absent (Paul et al., 2004). An illustrative case is Kim Peek, the man who served as the inspiration for the main character in the 1988 film *Rain Man*. Peek's brain revealed the absence of the corpus callosum, alongside pronounced autistic characteristics such as exceptional memory for visual and factual information, social challenges, and difficulties grasping metaphors or abstract concepts (Tammet, 2006).

I would like to refine the conceptualization of disrupted connectivity between the hemispheres by using the more specific psychoanalytic distinction between primary and secondary processes, involving the right versus the left hemisphere, respectively (see Bogen, 1969). Thus, I will describe the characteristics of autistic thinking in terms of a lack of integration between primary and secondary processes, and the dominance of primary processes therein. I will attempt to show how the detailed specification of the primary versus secondary processes, suggested by Freud and revised by Noy and others, sheds precious light on the main characteristics of autistic thinking.

To the best of my knowledge, no connection has been established between autistic thinking and primary processes versus secondary processes (interestingly, Bleuler, in his 1911 paper, introduced the concept "autistic thinking" to describe the mode of thinking divergent from logical, linear, and reality-oriented thinking while leaning on Freud's conceptualization of primary and secondary processes, but he referred to the thinking patterns of schizophrenics, not autistics). Further, psychoanalytical discussions of the subject have historically focused on a rather fixed list of manifestations of primary processes—including the thinking of schizophrenics and children, Freudian slips, dreams, art, fantasies, humor, neurotic symptoms, and free associations—overlooking autistic thinking, which now may be added to this list as a clear and significant manifestation of the primary processes.

The characteristics of autistic thinking will be described in this chapter based on the writings of autistic persons, numerous research studies, and my clinical experience with many autistics.

PRIMARY VERSUS SECONDARY PROCESSES

Historically, the distinction between primary and secondary processes as two basic cognitive processes was suggested by Sigmund Freud (1900, 1901, 1905, 1911). His biographer, Ernest Jones, even considered this distinction as Freud's "revolutionary contribution to psychology" (1953, p. 397). According to Freud, the primary processes appear in early infancy and are related to the pleasure principle and the immediate fulfillment of subjective needs; they are illogical and oblivious to external reality and the laws of time and space. Freud described how these processes are manifested throughout life in free associations, Freudian slips, the thinking of children and schizophrenics, fantasies, dreams, humor, art, neurotic symptoms, and primitive thinking. Secondary processes, on the other hand, are acquired during the second year of life and are related to the reality principle and the acquisition of language, communication, reality testing, the postponement of gratifications, and so forth.

Freud pointedly specified a number of primary processes: at first, he described condensation, displacement, and plastic representation, later adding other processes such as representation by the opposite, multi-determination, indirect representation, and more (see Freud, 1900, 1905). Freud ceased to define the primary processes at a rather early stage, and subsequent discussions also tended to avoid clearly defining them or compiling a formal list. However, psychoanalytic discussions generally refer to six main primary processes (as summarized by Noy, 1999, pp. 123–180)—displacement, condensation, multi-determination, concretization, representation by the opposite, and loosening of associations. All these processes will be elaborated on in greater detail below in relation to autistic thinking.

Freud's followers introduced revisions into the concepts of primary and secondary processes, mainly suggesting that in contrast to the Freudian conception of the primary processes as primitive and non-developing, they do develop throughout life and can be related to creativity, sophistication, and achievements in the arts and sciences (see, e.g., Noy, 1969, 1999; Suller, 1980). Noy, in his important revision, suggests that the main difference between primary and secondary processes lies in their different functions: whereas the function of the secondary processes is to cope with reality—that is, the objective perception of objects, their organization in accordance with the categories of space and time, understanding the social world, organizing and monitoring reactions, and proper communication with others, the function of the primary processes is the maintenance of the "self"—related to subjective experiences, emotions, sensations, and memories, with no need to adjust to realistic categories such as space, time, and object consistency. Thus, whereas the primary processes are *self*-centered, the secondary processes are *reality*-oriented (see Noy, 1999, pp. 120–121).

In neurotypical development, the integration of primary and secondary processes begins to occur naturally and automatically during the second year of life. This integration between these two kinds of processes, between the self and the world, the subjective and the objective, sustains many important psychological processes. In contrast, in autistics, the physiological disrupted connectivity between the hemispheres results in disrupted integration between primary and secondary processes, with primary processes gaining dominance, sometimes alternating with secondary processes, especially in so-called high-functioning autistics, as will be suggested below.

THE DOMINANCE OF THE PRIMARY PROCESSES IN AUTISTIC THINKING

I will illustrate how the dominance of primary processes manifests in autistic thinking in various aspects:

- first, through four major facets of thinking (outlined by Noy, 1999)—the train of associations, assignment of meanings, categorization, and consideration of contexts;
- second, through the six primary processes themselves: condensation, displacement, multi-determination, concretization, representation by the opposite, and the loosening of associations; and
- last, through other characteristics, such as intuition, creativity, and a tendency to disregard clear communication.

Primary Processes Unveiled in Key Aspects of Autistic Thinking

In his seminal book (1999), Pinhas Noy delineates the differences between primary and secondary processes across four major facets of human cognition: the train of associations, assignment of meaning, categorization, and contexts. I will illustrate how the dominance of the primary processes manifests in autistic thinking across each of these facets.

Train of Associations—In the secondary processes the train of associations follows a logical, linear path, prioritizing realism and effective communication. Conversely, the primary processes engage a broad network of subjective associations, encompassing diverse experiences, memories, emotions, sensations, and ideas. These associations emerge in parallel, often disregarding realistic limitations and the necessity for clear communication.

The autistic train of associations tends to follow the laws of the primary processes: many autistics testify that their thinking tends to wander associatively in various directions. Grandin, for example, writes: "My brain works like a search engine. If you ask me to think about a certain topic, my brain will generate a lot of hits. It can also easily make connections that will get off the original topic pretty fast and go pretty far" (Grandin, 2013b, p. 125). Tammet describes how, while listening to others, many different images occur to him automatically (Tammet, 2006). Similarly, a patient of mine attested how, for instance, whenever he would come in for a blood test, flashbacks from almost every blood test he had ever undergone would occur to his mind automatically. Bogdashina states that autistic memory tends to be associative, with one memory leading to another (2003, p. 107). In decision making, too, autistics tend to follow several lines of thought instead of adhering to one line—a phenomenon called "branched" thinking (see Baker & Shelly, 2015). Associativity is also revealed in autistics' communication, as they tend to shift associatively from one subject to the next, with no commitment to a clear, logical line of communication.

Assignment of Meanings—In the secondary processes, objects are assigned objective meanings by connecting them to elements in reality or to other objects. In contrast, in the primary processes, "subjective" meaning is attributed to objects through connections to "self-states," emotions, sensations, memories, fantasies, and similar subjective experiences.

Autistics tend to assign meanings according to the laws of primary processes: they tend to refrain from assigning objective meanings to objects, relating instead only to their immediate sensory or emotional attributes. Prince-Hughes, for example, writes, "So much stimulation streams in, rushing into one's body without ever being processed" (2004, p. 25). Many autistics assert that they only grasp a fraction of the information they encounter; some estimate understanding as little as half of the intended meanings (see Miller, 2015a, pp. 76, 117, 124, 174; Williams, 1994, p. 99).

The focus of autistics on concrete perceptions often causes them to miss abstract or implicit meanings, as reflected in their well-known struggles in perceiving implicit social rules, as well as in interpreting their own feelings, which are naturally ambiguous. Difficulties in assigning meanings also make it challenging for autistics to prioritize tasks, as evident in decision-making processes, discerning the important elements in communication, and focusing attention. Autistics tend to attribute similar importance to diverse stimuli, including peripheral ones, as described by Krumins: "I attend to everything the same way with no discrimination, so that the caw of the crow in the tree is as clear and important as the voice of the person I'm walking with" (Krumins, 2015, p. 88). Consequently, autistics are very easily distracted, as attending to a single stimulus in a multi-stimuli environment proves challenging for them.

Categorization—In the secondary processes, objects are categorized according to their objective qualities and placements in time and space, whereas in the primary processes they are categorized according to subjective qualities such as sensual perceptions, feelings, or wishes that are related to these objects.

The autistic manner of categorization tends to obey the laws of primary processes in many aspects: In language acquisition, neurotypical children learn to use one concept for different objects belonging to the same abstract category. Autistic children, by contrast, encounter difficulties in doing so, because for them each object stands for itself, as they are very sensitive to differences between objects. De Clercq, for example, observes that her autistic son had different names for each of the bicycles or glasses in their house (2003, p. 22). Grandin describes how, when she hears the word "church," she does not see a general prototype of a church, as neurotypicals typically do, but rather an array of specific churches she has encountered throughout her life (Grandin, 2008, p. 21).

When autistics do form categories, they tend to base them on subjective qualities, whether emotional or perceptual, such as on objects' smell, color, or texture. De Clercq, for example, recounts how her son included elephants, hippos, and rhinoceroses under the label "elephants" due to their color (De Clercq, 2003, p. 30). Similarly, Grandin recounts how in her childhood she considered dogs and cats to belong to the same category, grouping them together according to their size (i.e., in terms of a concrete visual perception; see Grandin, 2008, p. 30).

Beyond linguistic development, the autistic manner of categorization carries significant implications for their everyday lives, as they struggle with generalizing situational cues. For instance, De Clercq recounts her son's inability to generalize from a very early age: he would only nurse if she wore the same perfume, sweater, earrings, and so forth (De Clercq, 2003, p. 13) and he would wave at his grandfather only when the latter was driving his green car (De Clercq, 2003, p. 9). The difficulty in generalization persists into autistics' adulthood, as they experience every situation as a new one. Willey writes, "I approach each new obstacle we come to as if I have never met anything like it before" (1999, p. 107). Tucker (2015) notes, "Having Asperger's means relearning for every situation what I need to know. It means copying. It means acting sometimes."

Such challenges significantly impede autistics' lives, as they struggle to transfer behaviors from one context to another. Grandin writes, for example, that autistics children can be taught not to run out into the busy road in front of their house but often fail to generalize this knowledge to other roads (Grandin, 2008, p. 186). Miller intriguingly describes how, even after observing the sequence of actions performed in a car wash countless times, she cannot integrate the experience and strategize how to behave in this situation in recurring situations (Miller, 2015b). As a result of their struggles with generalization, autistics experience the world as bewildering, disordered, and inscrutable, contributing to their inclination to withdraw.

Autistics' difficulties in generalization can be also challenging for those around them, as they may often feel frustrated by the need to constantly repeat their statements. For example, a patient of mine whose husband is autistic was very frustrated by the fact that despite her repeated requests not to disturb her during naps, he continued to do so, each time for a different reason, as he could not ascribe these situations to the same category.

Nonetheless, abstaining from objective categorization also presents some positive aspects: it facilitates the exploration of unconventional viewpoints, fostering creativity and innovative insights in fields such as science, art, or humor. Moreover, it may prompt autistics to embrace progressive causes such as veganism, animal rights, alternative education, and other spiritual or political movements. Another usually positive aspect is their ability to accept people unconditionally, without categorizing them based on conventional criteria. This is often evident in their choice of partners, who frequently do not conform to conventional expectations regarding backgrounds, cultures, or age groups.

Consideration of Contexts—In the secondary processes, objective and realistic contexts are considered, including time, space, and causality. In contrast, the primary processes involve immediate sensual or subjective-emotional perceptions while disregarding realistic contexts.

Autistics typically refer to contexts according to the laws of primary processes, as manifested in various aspects: they often prioritize subjective ideas or feelings over broader and more realistic or objective settings; they may fixate on one emotion without integrating it with others; they tend to have a narrow attention span, a phenomenon sometimes referred to as "tunnel perception" (Bogdashina, 2003, p. 102) or "monotropism" (Murray et al., 2005); in conversations, they often concentrate on their own contributions while disregarding others' communications; likewise, they may demonstrate minimal interest in the lives of others. A patient of mine said that she was not interested in facts about her acquaintances' lives but could discern their general temperament and attitude toward her (i.e., that which was significant for her "self").

Autistics are also prone to ignore contexts of space, time, and causality. Alvarez writes, "An adequate sense of space, time or causality involves the notion of at least two points of reference"—which is challenging for autistics, who tend to adhere to one point. Thus, she writes of her patient, "He may . . . be unable to understand even quite simple interpretations of an explanatory type, for these involve holding two thoughts in the mind at once" (1992, p. 98).

An alternative way for conceptualizing autistics' difficulty in grasping contexts may be through the concept of a "one-track mind," which allows only "one thought to be thinkable at a time," as suggested by Alvarez (1992, p. 97). Many autistics and autism studies highlight their tendency toward "one-trackedness," wherein they process only one thought/feeling/stimulus at a time. Williams vividly illustrates this tendency with two metaphors: "My brain was like a department store where the people running different departments were working alternate shifts. When one came to work, the others went to sleep" (Williams, 1994, p. 96), and: "People who work in 'mono' are like the trains rather than the network. They are this train or that train or the other train but they generally aren't all the trains at once" (Williams, 1996, p. 96).

The phenomenon of "one-trackedness" is also revealed in the challenges autistics face in envisioning future events or outcomes. Alvarez observes, for example, "One of the things that perpetually astonished me about Robbie's mind was the complete absence in it of any concept of the future" (1992, p. 174). A similar difficulty also often is revealed in autistics' challenges in deciphering other people's thoughts and needs, as well as deciphering contextual cues in jokes, hints, or implicit social rules, contributing to their well-known naïveté.

Moreover, the disregard of contexts may also be linked to autistics' struggles with "executive functions"—a range of abilities including planning, prioritizing, mental flexibility, inhibition, regulation, rule acquisition, and information filtering—all of which necessitate consideration of context.

The Six Primary Processes as Expressed in Autistic Thinking

Psychoanalytic literature depicts six main primary processes: concretization, condensation, displacement, multi-determination, representation by the opposite, and the loosening of associations (see Noy, 1999, pp. 123–180). In the following discussion, I will illustrate how each of these primary processes manifests as characteristics of autistic thinking.

1. Concretization—This primary process involves presenting concepts, ideas, and thoughts in concrete forms, such as visual images or other sensory representations. In contrast, in the secondary processes, ideas and thoughts are presented abstractly.

Autistics exhibit a strong inclination toward concretization: they tend to gather information through their senses and recall it as sensory images of sight, sound, taste, or touch. Alvarez, for example, describes her autistic patient: "His main avenue of sensory investigation was his nose . . . he smelled literary everything" (1992, p. 22). Grandin observes that many autistics, including herself, perceive the world through visual images, often "translating" objects, including abstract ones, into concrete forms. For instance, while reading, concepts automatically transform in her mind into visual images; the word "elements" may evoke in her the image of the periodic table, whereas the word "peace" may evoke an image of a dove (Grandin, 2008, pp. 14–16). Grandin also reports her ability, shared by many autistics, to store complete images of the pages she reads due to a photographic (eidetic) memory (Grandin, 2008). Another manifestation of this inclination toward the concrete is evident in language acquisition, where autistic children find it much easier to comprehend the meanings of concrete objects than abstract concepts.

Under the umbrella term of concretization, one may also include autistics' prevalent inclination toward synesthesia—the translation of ideas, feelings, perceptions, and concepts into objects perceived by other senses. For instance, many autistics automatically "translate" words, numbers, days, people, and feelings into images or colors. Tammet (2006) describes how each number from 0 to 10,000 is transformed in his mind into a shape, a color, a texture, or a movement; Gerland (1996) describes how she spontaneously translates people, words, voices, or emotions into colors.

2. *Condensation*—The primary process of condensation involves merging various cognitive contents—words, ideas, images, and so forth—into a singular image or idea. In contrast, secondary processes assign each object or concept one meaning, for the sake of clear communication.

The autistic inclination toward condensation can be seen, for example, in their propensity to create neologisms. Alvarez, for instance, describes how her autistic patient would often combine words to form new ones, such as "prancelot" (probably combining "Lancelot" and "prancing") or "kisstone" (probably combining "kiss" and "stone"; see Alvarez, 1992, p. 33). Attwood attests that neologisms "are a feature of Asperger's syndrome," citing various studies to support this assertion (2007, p. 183).

3. *Displacement*—The primary process of displacement involves retrieving a psychic element—an idea, a thought, or a feeling—from its original context and assigning it to another context. In contrast, the secondary processes involve adherence to the original context logically and realistically.

The inclination toward displacement is evident in many autistics' affinity for creating new images through art forms such as painting, sculpting, or writing. In these endeavors, they often displace their feelings or ideas into different contexts, generating new images across various media through the primary process of displacement. Displacement is further evidenced by the autistic tendency to transcend the constraints of time and space, immersing themselves deeply in diverse eras or cultures such as ancient Greek, Japanese, or Korean cultures, as well as in the realms of science fiction or fantasy.

4. *Representation by the Opposite (Reversal)*—This primary process is characterized by a tendency to relate alternately either to objects or their opposites, with no intermediate increments. Freud postulated that in the primary processes there are "no negation, no doubt, no degrees of certainty" (Freud, 1915, p. 186). In contrast, the secondary processes typically involve various intermediate perceptions.

Indeed, autistics often exhibit a tendency toward "black and white thinking," readily shifting between opposites in their thought processes. This inclination can be observed in emotional oscillations between extremes or in their inclination to abruptly change professional, romantic, and other choices without entertaining intermediate doubts. Gerland aptly captures this phenomenon, remarking, "My system just had 'on' and 'off,' no intermediate setting" (1996, p. 185).

5. *Multi-Determination*—In this primary process, several meanings can be attached to one object. In contrast, in the secondary process, only one meaning is assigned to each object, for the sake of clear communication.

The process of multi-determination is evident in autistics' affinity for puns or jokes where words or expressions carry multiple meanings. Although autistics may face challenges in understanding jokes that rely on social contexts, they often grasp and produce puns or wordplays effortlessly.

6. Loosening of Associations—In this primary process, words are referenced through various perceptible qualities beyond their meanings, such as sound, rhythm, and shape. In contrast, in the secondary processes, words are solely considered in terms of their meanings.

Considerable evidence suggests that autistics often respond to the sensory aspects of words in addition to, or sometimes instead of, their meanings. Alvarez, for instance, describes how her autistic patient "tended to get hooked on the sound, shape, and I suspected . . . taste and color of a word . . . the meaning of words seemed irrelevant to him" (1992, p. 40). She further explains: "What meaning there was lay in the sensual qualities of the words themselves, not the stories . . . sounds were felt, quite literally, to touch him, caress him, tickle him, or, strangely, to provide visual thrills" (Alvarez, 1992, p. 52). Similarly, Willey expresses, "I loved the way most words played on my tongue . . . I would refuse words that looked ugly" (1999, p. 25). Gerland adds, "words . . . stuck, but only as words, interesting in their structure or flavor" (1996, p. 24). The phenomenon of echolalia, often observed in autistics, can also be interpreted as part of their tendency to focus on sound rather than content.

Other Features of Primary Processes Found in Autistic Thinking

Beyond the four key aspects of thinking and six specific primary processes described above, other prominent features of primary processes are revealed in autistic thinking.

Lack of Communication—The primary processes do not prioritize clear communication or realistic representations. This inclination is reflected in the tendency of autistics to reside within their own minds, often without a pressing need to communicate their rich inner world, brimming with emotions, images, and imagination. This inner world often remains mostly undisclosed, akin to dreams, which are also a product of primary processes.

Intuition—Autistics often possess remarkably strong and acute intuitions, enabling them to perceive things in a subliminal, sensory, and subjective manner, which aligns with primary processes. For example, they can be very adept in intuitively sensing other people's temperaments or attitudes toward them or rely on their intuition when choosing romantic partners.

Creativity—Autistics can be remarkably creative, due to characteristics associated with primary processes, such as access to unconscious knowledge, associativity, disregard for conventions, strong intuitions, and the ability to shift between contexts. Their heightened creativity may lead to groundbreaking discoveries across various domains, as evidenced by the works of numerous leading artists, scientists, and creators believed to have been autistic.

Resemblance to Animals—Although primary processes may manifest in high expressions such as creativity, intuition, and invention, they may also be related to a primary level of feeling and sensation reminiscent of animals. Grandin in her writings (1995, 2008, 2013b) highlights several points of resemblance between autistic thinking and animals' minds. These include perceiving the world through the senses (sight, smell, taste, hearing, and touch); exceptional sensory sensitivities; high sensitivity to details; and a tendency to focus on basic and simple emotions, such as happiness, fear, or sadness, with fear often being a dominant emotion (see Grandin, 2008, pp. 200–202). Intriguingly, autistics commonly report a sense of affinity, understanding, and emotional connection with animals—which can be attributed to the shared platform of primary processes.

ALTERNATIONS BETWEEN PRIMARY AND SECONDARY PROCESSES

Thus far, I have delineated the predominant role of primary processes in autistic thinking, as evidenced by the various aspects discussed above. However, it is crucial to stress that alongside these salient expressions of primary processes, autistics (particularly those considered high-functioning) undeniably exhibit manifestations of secondary processes as well. These secondary processes manifest in high language skills; episodes of linear, organized, and logical thinking; a pursuit of objective knowledge and objective categorization; and a consideration of time, space, and causality. These may be revealed, for example, through their special interests in areas such as science, history, computers, and research, and sometimes in meticulously organized and systematic lifestyles—adhering strictly to schedules and using preplanned lists and timetables. Their thought processes and actions often may adhere strictly to logic, with little consideration for their own or others' emotions, reminiscent of characters such as Mr. Spock from *Star Trek* or Sheldon Cooper from *The Big Bang Theory*. This lifestyle may appear stringent and even "robotic," with no emotional fulcrum to balance it. Further, when confronted with unexpected changes or intense emotional events they may experience anxiety and bewilderment, as though they have been thrust from the orderliness of secondary processes into the chaos of primary processes, with little integration between the two.

The extent to which the secondary processes manifest varies among individuals, and many autistics exhibit pronounced or even dominant expressions of secondary processes, alongside manifestations of primary processes, with deficient integration between them. (Similarly, autistics may demonstrate alternating dominance of each hemisphere, with some showing heightened functioning of the right hemisphere, characterized by visual thinking, imagination, intuition, creativity, unregulated emotions, and parallel processing, whereas others may display stronger functioning of the left hemisphere, evidenced by high language skills, linear and logical thinking, planning and organization, the pursuit of factual knowledge, and consideration of contexts. Autistics themselves attribute varying degrees of dominance to either the right or left hemisphere; see, e.g., Baker & Shelly, 2015).

The degree to which primary versus secondary processes manifest may correlate with the distinction between what is considered low and high levels of functioning in autism, respectively. Similarly, several studies have linked the low and high levels of functioning in autistics to the dominance of the right and left hemispheres, respectively (see, e.g., Duffy et al., 2013). Nonetheless, it should be stressed that even high-functioning autistics, who often exhibit secondary processes, may also show significant expressions of primary processes, manifested by the noticeable aspects I presented above, with a tendency to *alternations* between these two kinds of processes, due to the disrupted integration between them.

Acknowledging the oscillations between primary and secondary processes sheds light on numerous seeming contradictions in autistics. These include their baffling shifts between emotionality and aloofness, empathy and coldness, concretization and abstraction, imagination and a lack thereof, and more. Such fluctuations can be understood as stemming from the interplay between primary and secondary processes, with disrupted integration between them. The degree of integration between primary and secondary processes varies among autistics and may evolve over time. Enhanced integration may occur, for example, by virtue of a successful psychotherapy, as will be discussed below.

PROMOTING THE INTEGRATION BETWEEN PRIMARY AND SECONDARY PROCESSES THROUGH PSYCHOTHERAPY

Despite the basic inclination of autistics toward disrupted integration between primary and secondary processes, integration may improve with time. As Alvarez writes (based on the ideas of Bion, Klein, and others), autistics have an innate need for mental growth, unknowingly seeking better integration

(Alvarez, 1992, 2012). Grandin (2013b) also asserts that autistic brains are flexible and change over time.

One of the main paths toward integration is through psychotherapy, which can help autistics articulate their feelings, needs, and thoughts, thereby enhancing reflection and symbolization. Alvarez (1992, 2012) and Tustin (1986, 1992) highlight how psychotherapy may assist autistic children in assigning meanings. Through therapy, autistics can develop a more nuanced understanding of emotions and thoughts, countering their initial tendency toward "one-trackedness" and fostering emotional regulation and complexity. Williams (1994), for instance, describes how her therapy enabled her to experience complex emotions such as longing or belonging; such processes often occur in therapy with autistics. The enhanced inner integration fosters self-awareness, self-expression, self-acceptance, and self-fulfillment.

Successful psychotherapy may also help autistics gain a more realistic, objective, and nuanced understanding of the world around them. As a result, they may perceive the world as less threatening, improve their interpersonal relationships, and break through the confines of the "autistic shell." Williams movingly describes how, thanks to her psychotherapy, she could gradually leave the "prison of autism":

> My hearing with meaning began to improve more in a year [of psychotherapy] than it had since I was about ten years old. With it my security around people, my sense of empowerment, and my confidence soared . . . I began to experience "self" and "other" equally at the same time . . . I began to understand why people enjoyed conversing and saw a glimpse of what I had been missing. I was in love with my own aliveness and completeness. I was alive with the vision of light at the end of the tunnel of inner darkness and inner silence, a tunnel of meaning-deafness, meaning-blindness, and the inability to feel one's own experiences. All that mattered was to know I could see the end in sight, the birth of hope in the void of hopelessness . . . I had the keys to the door of "the world." (1994, p. 99)

Integration in therapy may be achieved by virtue of the therapist's containment, mirroring, validation, empowerment, and active assistance in assigning meanings. Alvarez (1992) emphasizes the importance of offering both "maternal" containment and "paternal" encouragement for learning and growth. Further, integration arises from inherent qualities within autistics themselves—such as sincerity, intuition, self-observation, and truth-seeking—which can lead them to a more comprehensive understanding of themselves and the world. I resonate deeply with Harris's profound insight that "autism contains within itself the seeds of its own liberation" (Harris, 2017, p. 23).

Chapter 14

A Proposed Matrix for the Categorization of Autistic People

Ever since I began delving into the subject of autism, I've contemplated how its diverse manifestations could be classified into subcategories. Over time, I've realized that these contrasting manifestations themselves might hold the key to categorization, as positioning them at the opposite ends of axes representing various traits enables the discernment of characteristic clusters, which then can be translated into distinct categories.

This chapter begins by presenting previous attempts at categorization proposed by Temple Grandin and Tony Attwood. Subsequently, I will introduce my proposal for positioning contrasting traits on major axes to identify distinctive clusters.

PREVIOUS CLASSIFICATIONS

Limited attempts have been made to classify the heterogeneous group of high-functioning autistics into different types. Here, I will highlight two proposals put forward by two prominent autism researchers, Temple Grandin and Tony Attwood:

Grandin (2020; Grandin & Barron, 2017) suggested dividing autistics into three types:

Visual thinkers process information through images. Sometimes they possess photographic memory. They are drawn to activities such as drawing, building, and composing. They may be drawn to careers in art, design, photography, engineering, and similar fields.

Pattern thinkers engage in abstract thinking and seek meaningful patterns, whether in music or mathematics. They may show early interest in music, math, or chess, and later pursue careers in fields such as computers, engineering, or music.

Verbal thinkers are drawn to language and may exhibit exceptional memory for verbal information and facts, as well as proficiency in learning new languages. They often pursue careers in fields such as history, geography, sports, transportation, linguistics, or sales, where communication skills are highly valued.

In her later work (Grandin, 2022), Grandin primarily differentiated between verbal thinkers and visual thinkers, dividing visual thinkers into "object visualizers," who rely on visual images; and "spatial thinkers," who seek patterns in areas such as music or mathematics. She underscores that although our culture tends to favor verbal thinking, visual thinkers make tremendous contributions to humanity in fields such as science, mathematics, music, art, and technology as well as in problem-solving, often by predicting potential dangers and addressing them.

Attwood (2021) highlights four potential adaptations to autism:

The *introvert* type tends to minimize or avoid social interactions, perceiving them as overly complex, overwhelming, and stressful. Introverts prefer solitude and uninterrupted accomplishment of tasks.

The *extrovert* type seeks social engagement despite challenges in reading social situations and in knowing how to navigate them. Extroverts are often perceived as overly intrusive or intense, sometimes leading to experiences of rejection, abandonment, misunderstanding, and despair.

The *camouflaging* type recognizes their challenges in understanding nonverbal communication and in forming and keeping friendships. Therefore, they observe social behaviors and try to learn social rules, using a "social mask" to navigate interactions. More common in women, camouflaging can result in negative consequences, including identity confusion, low self-esteem, depression, and self-harm.

The *compensating* type creates a lifestyle compensating for social difficulties by developing intense interests in areas such as science, computer games, writing, music, linguistics, fictional heroes, comics, or psychology. They form social connections based on these interests or belong to autistic communities for acceptance, connection, and authenticity. Those who belong to this category may maintain social connections, immerse themselves in these interests, and pursue work related to them, and may therefore remain below the threshold for a clinical diagnosis.

CLASSIFICATION ACCORDING TO CLUSTERS OF OPPOSITE TRAITS

Autistics often exhibit extremes in both their physiological and psychological traits, with some transitioning between these extremes whereas others maintain them constantly. I will now explore some of the primary axes of opposing traits observed in individuals with autism:

In terms of *skills*, autistics may belong to extremes and can showcase either very high or very low verbal, mathematical, musical, artistic, or motor abilities. They may also possess either exceptional or very poor memory abilities, including recall of facts, words, sights, or faces.

In terms of *physiology*, autistics can differ greatly in their motor skills; some are highly skilled and excel in sports, whereas others are clumsy and struggle with coordination. Fine motor skills may also vary, ranging from excellent to poor. Spatial orientation abilities may be exceptional or lacking. Sleeping patterns may range from insufficient to excessive sleep. Even from a very young age, they tend to exhibit such extremes, being either extremely calm or fussy, sleeping too much or too little, or displaying either very passive and withdrawn behavior or adventurous and activity-seeking tendencies.

Sensory-wise, autistics may exhibit hypersensitivity or hyposensitivity across all senses. This includes being sensitive or insensitive to smells, exhibiting selective eating habits or being open to various foods, having a strong aversion to physical contact or seeking it, preferring bright or dark environments, having exceptional or impaired hearing, and experiencing hypersensitivity or hyposensitivity to temperature and pain (often they are very sensitive to inner pains but less sensitive to external pains). Some autistics move between these poles, and may, for example, be very picky eaters in childhood and then not picky at all or be ansomic in their childhood and then hypersensitive to smell, and so on.

In terms of their *psychological characteristics*, autistics may also belong to extremes:

Curiosity versus Lack of Curiosity—Some autistics display very high curiosity, constantly seeking to unravel the workings of the physical and/or the human world and often maintaining interest in multiple fields, whereas others exhibit minimal curiosity, focusing narrowly on very few areas of interest.

Hypersensitivity versus Hyposensitivity—Many autistics exhibit heightened sensitivity, hyper-empathy, and compassion, whereas others may appear distant, aloof, and uncaring. This apparent aloofness often serves as a coping mechanism against overwhelming emotions. For example, Hillel (portrayed in chapter 2) described how he can absorb so much information about those around him that he often prefers to seclude himself completely to avoid overload. Likewise, many autistics avoid eye contact, finding it overwhelming due to the influx of information it entails.

Poor or Excellent Executive Functions—Most autistics typically display poor executive functions, characterized by their tendency to neglect, procrastinate, and refrain from planning, prioritizing, and initiating, whereas others gravitate toward the opposite pole and are meticulous planners, relying on strict schedules and lists, often as a compensation for their natural tendency to the first pole.

Preciseness versus Lack of Preciseness—Some autistics tend to communicate information in a partial, superficial, or imprecise manner, whereas others strive for precision in their expressions, as exemplified for instance in autistics' poetry or stand-up comedy.

Innocence versus Suspicion—Autistics may be either very trusting and naive or deeply suspicious of others' motives. Many of them become more suspicious after experiencing too much naïveté or keep fluctuating between these poles. This dynamic can surface in interpersonal relationships or in attitudes toward societal systems, as some autistics may unquestioningly conform to rules, whereas others may be highly critical of rules. They may demonstrate heightened sensitivity to injustice and emerge as advocates for various political or social causes.

Autistics also vary in their perceptions of others' attitudes toward them. Some may overlook criticism or ridicule against them, whereas others can be hypersensitive to negative feedback and frequently even misinterpret neutral or positive interactions as negative due to their challenges in deciphering others' emotions. Many autistics move between these poles throughout their lives.

Anxiety versus Lack of Anxiety—Most autistics have high levels of anxiety, often stemming from the lack of a calming perspective. However, some autistics experience low levels of anxiety on a regular basis or in specific situations. For example, many autistics demonstrate fearlessness and maintain composure in high-stress or emergency situations, such as on battlefields or in accidents, displaying rationality and control. Some exhibit adventurous tendencies, embracing risks without trepidation. Many autistics are fearful of watching news programs or movies containing depictions of violence or horror, whereas others may be drawn to morbid and scary contents such as disasters, wars, or dangerous animals. Further, although some autistics tend to experience severe anxiety when facing an audience, others completely filter out audience feedback, allowing them to feel little to no anxiety ("lowering the screen when raising the screen").

Self-Blame versus Blaming Others—Some autistics are inclined to blame themselves and engage frequently in self-criticism; others tend to blame others without even trying to consider their own contribution.

Hypo-Mentalization versus Hyper-Mentalization—Many autistics tend to either overthink or underthink, with some oscillating between these extremes or compensating for one with the other, such as making quick decisions to avoid overthinking. This inclination toward overthinking may stem from autistics' struggles with prioritization and their reliance solely on logic, which makes it challenging for them to integrate emotions that could otherwise assist in decision making.

Sticking to a Single Option versus Hesitating between Possibilities—Many autistics tend to hold multiple choices in their minds without being able to choose between them; others tend to adhere doggedly to one option, possibly as a defense against their initial difficulty in prioritizing. These contrasting tendencies manifest across various aspects: for instance, in managing emotions, autistics may experience a blend of emotions without prioritization, or focus intensely on a single emotion, struggling to recognize others. Likewise, in decision making, they may either oscillate among various options, struggling to decide, or demonstrate harsh decisiveness. Regarding gender identity, some autistics refuse to align with a singular gender, whereas others identify strongly with a specific gender, often the one diverging from their gender assigned at birth.

In general, autistics frequently demonstrate a strong affinity to multiplicity, reflecting the internal multiplicity within them, stemming from the lack of prioritization. It's unsurprising that the symbol chosen for autism is the colorful rainbow, that many autistics take pleasure in wearing multihued outfits, and that many autistic artists typically produce colorful art works. For example, a cursory search for "autistic art" on Google unveils a plethora of multicolor artworks that vividly capture the inner richness of autistics.

The artistry of the renowned Russian painter Vasily Kandinsky (1866–1944) provides a beautiful illustration of such abundance. Kandinsky, often presumed to have had many autistic characteristics, aimed to evoke deep emotional experiences through the inherent meanings of shapes, colors, and lines (Kandinsky, 1911, 1926), aligning with the autistic inclination toward seeking deep and abstract meanings. Another autistic trait that can be attributed to Kandinsky was his synesthesia, as he meticulously translated musical sounds into colors and vice versa, even crafting a systematic key for such translations (Kandinsky, 1911, 1926). Kandinsky also often incorporated contrasting shapes and colors in his works (such as yellow and blue, black and white, red and green) to represent opposing qualities, viewing the artist's role as aimed at creating harmony between contrasts based on his inner sensibility (Kandinsky, 1911, 1926). Kandinsky's multicolored paintings, characterized by bold contrasts, poignantly capture the multiplicity and inner dichotomies, as well as the intricate depths of the autistic soul.

As I sought to convey the richness and intricacy of the autistic spirit on the book cover, I chose a photograph of Antelope Canyon in Arizona. This image can serve as an emblem of the colorfulness, vibrance, and playfulness of the autistic soul, intertwined with a fascination for the wonders of nature that characterizes many autistics.

TYPICAL CLUSTERS

Autists can often be positioned at various points along the axes described above, and sometimes there are connections between these axes, leading to characteristic clusters. I would like to draw attention to two main clusters that I frequently encounter among those seeking an autism diagnosis, which can be labeled as the "open" versus the "closed" types. It's important to emphasize that this distinction does not encompass all autistics, and that many of them may oscillate between these two poles, yet a significant number I've encountered roughly fit into these categories.

"Open" autistics exhibit a high level of curiosity and a continuous desire to comprehend themselves, as well as the human and/or physical world around them. They constantly observe their surroundings to learn and refine their understanding. Autistics of this type often seek autism diagnosis, displaying a keen interest in the subject, and striving to deepen their self-awareness. They often try to perfect their understanding of others, too, and therefore may be drawn to professions involving interactions with others, such as therapy or teaching. Many of them display heightened curiosity, emotional empathy, and rich inner worlds, are also typically hypersensitive in all senses, and are sometimes inclined to synesthesia.

Autistics of this type invest significant efforts throughout their lives to adapt to society. They keenly observe and emulate others' behaviors, for example, by devising scripts for social situations. They may endeavor to conceal what are deemed socially unacceptable behaviors, such as repetitive movements, excessive talking about their special interests, or blunt speech. They may learn to decipher body language and facial expressions or to improve their executive functions by using strategies such as lists and reminders, as well as strict timetables. They may try to reshape their ways of thinking (e.g., by trying to refer to causality or to see things from different perspectives), their emotion management (e.g., by trying to achieve more emotion regulation or find ways to express their feelings) and physical characteristics (e.g., in trying to be more attentive to bodily sensations or postures). I sometimes refer to such autistics as "double agents," as they become well-versed in the rules of neurotypical society, yet deeply identify with autistic ways of thinking. Although such efforts may help them integrate into neurotypical society, they may also induce fatigue, burnout, or a sense of detachment from their innate tendencies, necessitating frequent respite. The autism diagnosis can be very liberating for this type, as it validates their natural tendencies.

In the terms of Grandin (2022), it seems that autistics of this type are more inclined toward verbal rather than visual thinking, as neurotypical thinking favors the former; Grandin also associates verbal versus visual thinkers with high versus low functioning, respectively (p. 100). In terms of primary versus secondary processes, it seems that autistics of this kind rely more than their counterparts on secondary processes to better adapt and communicate with their surroundings.

In contrast, the "closed" type are autistics who exhibit a more passive and disinterested demeanor, often showing limited engagement with a narrow range of topics, such as computer games, animals, or sports. They often display little interest in their human or physical environment. Self-understanding may not be a priority, and they may only pursue diagnosis at the behest of their relatives. Even after being diagnosed, they may not actively pursue increased awareness or personal changes. They may appear distant and passive in their interactions with others, displaying limited curiosity, empathy, and imagination. Sensory-wise, they may sometimes exhibit hyposensitivity, particularly in the senses of smell and touch. In Grandin's (2022) framework, they are more inclined toward visual thinking, and they rely less on "secondary processes" to adapt or to communicate with those around them.

It is important to note that the categorization into "open" and "closed" clusters is not a rigid dichotomy, as autistics may shift between these clusters throughout their lives.

It is worth mentioning that a similar division of opposing axes forming distinct clusters was proposed in the Myers-Briggs method, based on the teachings of Carl Jung. This method dichotomously places individuals along four axes—introversion-extraversion, sensing-intuition, thinking-feeling, and judging-perceiving—yielding 16 possible combinations. Personal characterization on these axes can be achieved by completing the MBTI questionnaire. The MBTI method captures well the dichotomies found in autistics, such as introversion versus extraversion, sensing versus intuition, thinking versus feeling, and judging versus perceiving, alongside other dichotomies observed in autistics. Some autistics I have encountered have expressed fascination with the MBTI method, possibly due to its ability to capture the oppositions and typical clusters they experience within themselves and in others.

Further research is warranted to explore the categorization of autistics into different groups and categories.

Endnote

Ways to Assist Autistic Adults

The book has presented some arenas in which autistics may find themselves in their adult lives in terms of both career and psychological struggles. In light of their tremendous abilities alongside their significant challenges, it is essential for us as a society to find ways to support autistics, both for their own well-being and for the benefit of society. I will sum up some of the implications for autistics, for mental health professionals, for government systems, and for future research in this field.

IMPLICATIONS FOR AUTISTICS

As repeatedly stressed through the book, obtaining an accurate diagnosis of autism is essential, as it can enhance self-understanding and self-acceptance and mitigate feelings of being misunderstood, criticized, or rejected, which often lead to depression, distress, self-injury, and suicidal ideation. Autistics are advised to develop awareness and coping strategies for their major challenges, including executive functions issues (which may be addressed through lists, reminders, or others' help in prioritizing); emotion regulation challenges (addressed by adopting a broader perspective); mental rigidity (addressed through fostering flexibility and exploring diverse viewpoints); social challenges (addressed through acquiring basic social understandings and skills), and more.

It is important to stress that autistics should not necessarily adapt to social norms; this is an "ableist" approach, which expects them to make excessive efforts at the cost of feeling exhaustion, anxiety, identity confusion, and depression. Instead, each person should strive to find the appropriate balance between adapting to society and embracing his authentic self. However, society must also make efforts to recognize their difficulties and demonstrate greater understanding and consideration toward them.

IMPLICATIONS FOR MENTAL HEALTH PROFESSIONALS

Mental health professionals play a pivotal role in alleviating autistics' mental distress by addressing their common challenges, which can include depression, anxiety, psychosomatic problems, eating disorders, self-harm, and suicidal tendencies.

Mental health professionals are encouraged to exercise some essential steps to improve their capacity to help autistics:

First and foremost, it is very important for mental health professionals to acquaint themselves with the characteristics of autism to accurately identify and help patients in understanding their psychological attributes. It is also very important for them to learn how to distinguish autism from other mental health conditions, such as mood disorders, schizophrenia, and personality disorders, to prevent the distress of being misunderstood and unnecessary treatments and hospitalizations. Nevertheless, vigilance against superficial misdiagnoses is essential, and in cases of uncertainty, seeking guidance from experts in the field is advised.

It may also be useful for mental health professionals to glean insights from autistic patients about their unique perceptions of the world and the specific ways to support them effectively.

Regarding therapy approaches, classical dynamic therapy may be less suitable for autistics due to their challenges in collaborating with some fundamental aspects of it, such as expressing complex emotions in the "here and now," analyzing transference nuances, or responding to open-ended questions. These challenges can lead to feelings of incompetence and frustration for both therapist and patient. Another issue is attributing many of their psychological difficulties to early caregiver relationships, whereas these often stem from inherent characteristics of autism. Although dynamic therapy can be beneficial in providing empathy, heightened awareness, trauma processing, and improved integration, therapists are advised to reconsider some of the traditional dynamic tools in favor of a more suitable toolbox for these patients. Classical cognitive-behavioral therapy (CBT) can partially benefit autistics by addressing behavioral aspects such as enhancing social communication skills, social understanding, executive functions, and emotional regulation, and cognitive aspects such as modifying negative thought patterns such as black-and-white thinking, catastrophizing, or negative self-perceptions. However, significant limitations of CBT for autistics include its focus on specific aspects rather than considering the holistic personality, and its tendency to prioritize "normalizing" autistics rather than acceptance, affirmation, and empowerment, as advocated by many in the autistic community today.

A more fitting toolbox for therapy with autistics would include elements such as psychoeducation about autism; processing past traumas through creating new narratives that take autism into account; prompting emotion expression and emotion regulation; helping in modifying cognitive distortions (such as "black-and-white" thinking, excessive self-criticism, blaming of others, or other forms of one-dimensional thinking) and promoting a more balanced, integrative thinking; assisting in prioritizing, planning, and executing plans; enhancing awareness of social norms and of other people's emotions and expectations. Throughout, it's crucial to maintain an empowering and affirmative approach toward autistics' strengths and challenges, thereby facilitating their personal growth and well-being. Professionals should be aware of the "double empathy problem," which highlights that just as autistics may miss neurotypicals' expectations, neurotypicals may also overlook autistics' perspectives and rights. It is important for professionals to validate autistics' experiences, as they too often feel misunderstood and invalidated. However, it is equally important to point out their blind spots, which they may not always be aware of.

Therapists are also advised to make efforts to accommodate the treatment environment to meet the needs of autistics. This entails maintaining clear and sincere communication with them and demonstrating consideration of their sensory sensitivities as much as possible.

Another crucial therapeutic need is in supporting family members and partners of autistics. They often experience exhaustion and frustration and can greatly benefit from professional assistance in understanding and improving their relationships with the autistics. Presently, the scarcity of specialization in this domain is noticeable, highlighting the urgent need for professionals capable of aiding both autistics and their relatives in fostering mutual understanding, communication, and consideration of each other's needs.

Given the increasing prevalence of autism and the tendency of many autistics to seek psychological help, even without an official autism diagnosis, I believe that treating autism should not be reserved for therapists specializing in this field but, rather, every therapist should be equipped with the necessary knowledge to identify and address autism, just as they should be skilled at identifying and treating other major psychological conditions.

Further, I contend that autism marks the onset of a new paradigm in psychology, relating to a substantial and ever-expanding segment of the population, characterized with a "different psychology" in terms of emotions, cognition, perceptions, and behavior. This calls for new ways of defining psychological causation, treatment objectives, and methodologies all while respecting each patient's individual psychological narrative. As professionals, it is imperative for us to be aware and embrace this new paradigm.

IMPLICATIONS FOR GOVERNMENT SYSTEMS

To ensure the well-being and rights of autistics, government policies must be tailored to address their needs across domains such as education, employment, health, law, and welfare. Adequate resources should be allocated to support the implementation of these policies. Moreover, representatives of autistics should be actively included in discussions regarding policies that directly impact them, aligning with the motto "nothing about us without us."

Below are suggested areas where new policies should be established to better accommodate the needs of autistic individuals:

In terms of welfare, it is crucial to provide essential assistance in education, employment, housing, and financial support for those who face difficulties in accessing them.

In terms of education, there is a need to rethink how to integrate autistic students into educational systems. It is recommended that schools offer study programs tailored for autistics. For example, Baron-Cohen recommends allowing autistic children to engage in their special interests at school (Baron-Cohen, 2020); Grandin recommends allowing those with visual thinking to study and express themselves through visual means rather than solely verbally (Grandin, 2022). Also, adequate adjustments and accommodations should be provided, such as time extensions, separate testing rooms, or soundproof classrooms. Educational institutions should establish specialized units and staff dedicated to addressing the needs of autistic students, ensuring that they receive appropriate support. This support should include the right to clear explanations from their teachers, practical guidance on their assignments, and both individual and group psychological support.

In terms of employment, it is essential to assist autistics in integrating into the workforce by offering employment counseling, training programs, assistance with job applications, and on-the-job accompaniment. It is advisable to enact laws related to autistic employment and provide guidance to employers on creating a more suitable work environment. This may involve maintaining clear communication, allowing breaks, minimizing frequent changes in the work environment, and adapting the environment to accommodate sensory sensitivities. In addition, having mediators who can facilitate communication between autistics and others in the workplace, clarify unwritten rules, and enhance social interactions is recommended.

In terms of legal matters, it is crucial to enhance the legal system's understanding of autistic characteristics, such as naïveté, suggestibility, and difficulties in emotional and sensory regulation, which can impact their criminal responsibility. Autistics should receive assistance in police and court investigations, including clear explanations of instructions, concepts, and situations. Efforts should be made to help them express themselves effectively and to ensure that they understand their legal rights. Autistics also often need support in mastering the executive functions required in legal procedures.

In general, the need is pressing to raise awareness among various systems and the public about the unique challenges autistics face, to foster greater consideration and understanding toward them.

IMPLICATIONS FOR RESEARCH

The study of autism and its various manifestations is still in its infancy, as evidenced by the limited number of studies on the crucial topics discussed in this book, such as the links between autism and gender diversity, eating disorders, dissociative disorders, the sex industry, and more. Further research is needed to deepen our understanding of the characteristics and needs of the autistic community.

It is particularly vital to explore topics carrying significant ramifications for the mental and physical well-being of autistics, such as the associations between autism and depression, suicide, physical ailments, criminal involvement, and various forms of exploitation.

In autism research, it is crucial to incorporate the perspectives of autistics to gain insights into what may be effective for them, as many of them possess high self-awareness and a quest for truth and accuracy. Autistics should be encouraged to engage in research and provided with opportunities to integrate into academia, potentially through affirmative action measures.

Moreover, the need is pressing to enhance the reliability and validity of the tools used for diagnosing autism, which would benefit various research endeavors.

In addition, further categorization of individuals with autism into different subtypes can contribute to a deeper understanding of autism and enable tailored interventions for distinct subgroups.

CONCLUSION

In conclusion, as a society it is imperative that we take substantial strides toward understanding autism not as a disease or a negative condition necessitating healing or "normalization" but, rather, as a condition warranting understanding, support, and opportunities to foster better integration into society. This pursuit should be driven not only by principles of social justice and considerations for the well-being of autistic people, but also by recognition of their immense contributions to society. Undoubtedly, our world would be far less advanced without the invaluable contributions of the autistics among us.

References

Alvarez, A. (1992). *Live company*. Routledge.

Alvarez, A. (2012). *The thinking heart*. Routledge.

Armstrong, T. (2012). *Neurodiversity in the classroom: Strength-based strategies to help students with special needs succeed in school and life*. Alexandria, VA: ASCD, 1–183.

Arnold, C. (2016). The invisible link between autism and anorexia. *Spectrum: Autism Research News*.

Asada, K., Tojo, Y., Hakarino, K., et al. (2018). Brief report: Body image in autism: Evidence from body size estimation. *Journal of Autism and Developmental Disorders, 48*, 611–618.

Asperger, H. (1991 [1944]). Autistic psychopathy in childhood. In U. Frith (Trans. and Ed.), *Autism and Asperger syndrome* (pp. 37–92). Cambridge: Cambridge University Press.

Asztély, K., Kopp, S., Gillberg, C., Waern, M., & Bergman, S. (2019). Chronic pain and health-related quality of life in women with autism and/or ADHD: A prospective longitudinal study. *Journal of Pain Research, 12*, 2925–2932.

Attwood, T. (2007). *The complete guide to Asperger's syndrome*. Jessica Kingsley.

Attwood, T. (2021). Exploring autism 1971–2021 [Web page].

Autistic selves. (2021). Autistic trauma and our dissociative identity disorder. YouTube, July 11, 2021.

Au-Yeung, S., Bradley, L., Robertson, A. E., & Shaw, R. (2018). Experience of mental health diagnosis and perceived misdiagnosis in autistic, possibly autistic and non-autistic adults. *Autism, 23*(6), 1508–1518.

Bachar, E. (2001). The fear of occupying space: Self-psychology in the treatment of anorexia and bulimia. Jerusalem: Magnes (in Hebrew).

Baird, A. (2020). Teaching while autistic: Constructions of disability, performativity and identity. *Ought: The Journal of Autistic Culture, 2*(1), 36–45.

Bakan, M. B. (2018). *Speaking for ourselves: Conversations on life, music, and autism*. Oxford University Press.

Baker, Ava. 2004. Invisible at the end of the spectrum: Shadows, residues, "BAP," and the female Asperger's' experience, *Ava Baker* [home page]. www.avaruthbaker.com/articles.html

Baker, A., & Shelly, S. (2015). Differences. In J. Kearns Miller (Ed.), *Women from another planet: Our lives in the universe of autism* (pp. 19–60). AuthorHouse.

Bargiela, Sarah, Steward, Robyn, & Mandy, William. (2016). The experiences of late-diagnosed women with autism spectrum conditions: An investigation of the female autism phenotype, *Journal of Autism and Developmental Disorders, 46*(10), 3281–3294.

Barneveld, P. S., Pieterse, J., De Sonneville, L., Van Rijn, S., Lahuis, B., et al. (2011). Overlap of autistic and schizotypal traits in adolescents with autism spectrum disorders. *Schizophrenia Research, 126*, 231–236.

Baron-Cohen, S. (2002). The extreme male brain theory of autism. *Trends in Cognitive Sciences, 6*, 248–254.

Baron-Cohen, S. (2017). Editorial perspective: Neurodiversity—a revolutionary concept for autism and psychiatry. *Journal of Child Psychology and Psychiatry, 58*(6), 744–747.

Baron-Cohen, S. (2020). *The pattern seekers: How autism drives human invention.* Basic Books.

Baron-Cohen, S., Ashwin, E., Ashwin, C., Tavassoli, T., & Chakrabarti, B. (2009). Talent in autism: Hyper-systemizing, hyper-attention to detail and sensory hypersensitivity. *Philosophical Transactions of the Royal Society B: Biological Sciences, 364*, 1377–1383.

Baron-Cohen, Simon, & Lai, Meng-Chuan. (2015). Identifying the lost generation of adults with autism spectrum conditions. *Lancet Psychiatry, 2*(11), 1013–1027.

Bhatara, A., Quintin, E. M., Fombonne, E., & Levitin, D. J. (2013). Early sensitivity to sound and musical preferences and enjoyment in adolescents with autism spectrum disorders. *Psychomusicology: Music, Mind, and Brain, 23*(2), 100–108.

Blackshaw, A. J., Kinderman, P., Hare, D. J., and Hatton, C. (2001). Theory of mind, causal attribution and paranoia in Asperger syndrome. *Autism, 5*, 147–163.

Bleuler, E. (1911). *Dementia praecox or the group of schizophrenias*. International Universities, 1950.

Blumrosen-Sela, S. (2021). *Asperger's lost generation: Adults with high-functioning autism: The characterstics, the problem of under-diagnosis, and a proposed psychotherapy*. Resling (in Hebrew).

Blumrosen-Sela, S. (2023). *Autistic people among us*. Resling.

Bogdashina, O. (2003). *Sensory perceptual issues in autism and Asperger syndrome.* Jessica Kingsley.

Bogen, J. E. (1969). The other side of the brain. *Bulletin of the Los Angeles Neurological Society, 34*(3), 135–162.

Boniel-Nissim, M., & Latzer, Y. (2011). The characteristics of pro-ana community. In D. Stein & Y. Latzer (Eds.), *Treatment and special issue of eating disorders* (pp. 73–84). Nova Science.

Bouvet, L., Donnadieu, S., Valdois, S., Caron, C., Dawson, M., & Mottron, L. (2014). Veridical mapping in savant abilities, absolute pitch, and synesthesia: An autism case study. *Frontiers in Psychology, 5*, 106.

Braiker, B. (2022). Roux is a multi-hyphenate sex worker. *Brooklyn Magazine*, January 3, 2022.

Brand, B. L., Armstrong, J. G., & Loewenstein, R. J. (2006). Psychological assessment of patients with dissociative identity disorder. *Psychiatric Clinics of North America, 29*(1), 145–168.

Brand, B. L., McNary, S. W., Myrick, A. C., et al. (2012). A longitudinal naturalistic study of patients with dissociative disorders treated by community clinicians. *Psychological Trauma, 5*(4), 301–308.

Brede, J., Babb, C., Jones, C., et al. (2020). "For me, the anorexia is just a symptom, and the cause is the autism": Investigating restrictive eating disorders in autistic women. *Journal of Autism and Developmental Disorders, 50*, 4280–4296.

Brown, L. (2016). Gendervague: At the intersection of autistic and trans experiences. *Autistichoya* [internet site], June 22, 2016.

Brown, W. A., Cammuso, K., Sachs, H., et al. (2003). Autism-related language, personality, and cognition in people with absolute pitch: Results of a preliminary study. *Journal of Autism and Developmental Disorders, 33*(2), 163–167.

Bruch, H. (1973). *Eating disorders: Obesity, anorexia nervosa, and the person within*. Basic Books.

Bruining, H., Swaab, H., Kas, M., & Van Engeland, H. (2009). Psychiatric characteristics in a self-selected sample of boys with Klinefelter syndrome. *Pediatrics, 123*(5), 865–870.

Bryar, L. (2015). *Young, gifted and autistic: How autism/Asperger syndrome affects young adult musicians' musical creativity* [BMus dissertation], University of East London.

Bury Simon, M., Flower, R. L., Zulla, R., et al. (2021). Workplace social challenges experienced by employees on the autism spectrum: An international exploratory study examining employee and supervisor perspectives. *Journal of Autism and Developmental Disorders, 51*(5), 1614–1627.

Caparrotta, L., & Ghaffari, K. (2006). A historical overview of the psychodynamic contributions to the understanding of eating disorders. *Psychoanalytic Psychotherapy, 20*(3), 75–196.

Casanova, E. (2014a). Is the female brain more resilient against harmful mutations? *Science over Cuppa* [internet site], March 2, 2014.

Casanova, E. (2014b). Klinefelter syndrome, autism, & the female protective effect? *Science over Cuppa* [internet site], November 30, 2014.

Cassidy, S., Cogger-Ward, H., Robertson, A. E., Goodwin, J., & Rodgers, J. (2021). Where do we go from here? Autism community priorities for future suicide research. MHAutism [internet].

Chandrasekhar, T., & Sikich, L. (2015). Challenges in the diagnosis and treatment of depression in autism spectrum disorders across the lifespan. *Dialogues in Clinical Neuroscience, 17*(2), 219–227.

Charlton, J. (1998). *Nothing about us without us: Disability oppression and empowerment*. University of California Press.

Chefetz, R. A. (2000). Affect dysregulation as a way of life. *Journal of the American Academy of Psychoanalysis, 28*, 289–303.

Chiang, Huey-Ling, Liu, Chia-Jen, Hu, Yu-Wen, et al., 2015. Risk of cancer in children, adolescents, and young adults with autistic disorder. *Journal of Pediatrics, 166*(2), 418–423.

Churchard, A., Ryder, M., Greenhill, A., & Mandy, W. (2019). The prevalence of autistic traits in a homeless population. *Autism, 23*(3), 665–676.

Coleman-Smith, R. S., Smith, R., Milne, E., & Thompson, A. R. (2020). "Conflict versus congruence": A qualitative study exploring the experience of gender dysphoria for adults with autism spectrum disorder. *Journal of Autism and Developmental Disorder, 50*, 2643–2657.

Cooper, K., Mandy, W., Butler, C., & Russell, A. (2022). The lived experience of gender dysphoria in autistic adults: An interpretative phenomenological analysis. *Autism, 26*(4), 963–974.

Cooper, K., Russell, A., Mandy, W., & Butler, C. (2020). The phenomenology of gender dysphoria in adults: A systematic review and meta-synthesis. *Clinical Psychology Review, 80*, 101875.

Craig, J., Hatton, C., Craig, F., & Bentall, R. (2004). Persecutory beliefs, attributions and theory of mind: Comparison of patients with paranoid delusions, Asperger's syndrome and healthy controls. *Schizophrenia Research, 69*, 29–33.

Da Fonseca, D., Viellard, M., & Fakra, E. (2008). Schizophrenia or Asperger syndrome? *La Presse Médicale, 37*(9), 1268–1273.

Daie, N., Daie-Gabai, A., & Witztum, E. (2020). *The enigma of dissociation*. Itay Bahur (in Hebrew).

Dalenberg, C. J., Brand, B. L., Gleaves, D. H., et al. (2012). Evaluation of the evidence for the trauma and fantasy models of dissociation. *Psychological Bulletin, 138*(3), 550–588.

Dalla, R. L., Xia, Y., & Kennedy, H. (2003). You just give them what they want and pray they don't kill you: Street-level sex workers' reports victimization, personal resources, and coping strategies. *Violence against Women, 9*, 1367–1394.

Damian, M. (2021). Ableist ivory towers: A narrative review informing about the lived experiences of neurodivergent staff in contemporary higher education. *Disability & Society*, 1–22.

Davidson, J., & Orsini, M. (2013). Introduction. In *Worlds of autism* (pp. 1–31). University of Minnesota Press.

De Clercq, H. (2003). *Mum, is that a human being or animal?* Sage.

Dell'Osso, L., Cremone, I. M., Amatori, G., et al. (2021). Investigating the relationship between autistic traits, ruminative thinking, and suicidality in a clinical sample of subjects with bipolar disorder and borderline personality disorder. *Brain Sciences, 11*(5), 621.

Di Ceglie, D., Skagerberg, E., Baron-Cohen, S., & Auyeung, B. (2014). Empathising and systemising in adolescents with gender dysphoria. *Opticon, 1826*. 10.5334/opt.bo.

Doherty, M. (2020). *Neurodiversity in practice: Autistic anaesthetists can be an asset.* Association of Anaesthetics.

Doherty, M., Johnson, M., & Bucley, C. (2021). Supporting autistic doctors in primary care: Challenging the myths and misconceptions. *British Journal of General Practice, 71*(708), 294–295.

Dohn, A., Garza-Villarreal, E. A., Heaton, P., & Vuust, P. (2012). Do musicians with perfect pitch have more autism traits than musicians without perfect pitch? An empirical study. *PLOS One, 7*(5), 7961.

Dossetor, D. (2007). All that glitters is not gold: Misdiagnosis of psychosis in pervasive developmental disorders—a case series. *Clinical Child Psychology and Psychiatry, 12*(4), 537–548.

DSM-5. (2013). *Diagnostic and Statistical Manual of Mental Disorders* (5th ed.). American Psychiatric Press.

Duffy, F. H., Shankardass, A., McAnulty, G. B., & Heidelise, A. (2013). The relationship of Asperger's syndrome to autism: A preliminary EEG coherence study. *BMC Medicine, 11*, 175.

Engelbrecht, N. (2020). Autistics make excellent therapists. *Embrace-autism* [internet site], December 18, 2020.

Farley, M. (2003). *Prostitution, trafficking, and traumatic stress.* Routledge.

Fitzgerald, M. (2005). The genesis of artistic creativity: Asperger's syndrome and the arts. Jessica Kingsley.

Fitzgerald, M. (2012). Schizophrenia and autism/Asperger's syndrome overlap and difference. *Clinical Neuropsychiatry, 9*(4), 171–176.

Freud, S. The interpretation of dreams (1900), Psychopathology of everyday life (1901), Jokes and their relation to the unconscious (1905), Formulations on the two principles of mental functioning (1911), The unconscious (1915), An outline of psycho-analysis in *The Standard Edition* [1953], Ed. and Trans. J. Strachey. Hogarth Press.

Fusar-Poli, L., Brondino, N., Politi, P., & Aguglia, E. (2020). Missed diagnoses and misdiagnoses of adults with autism spectrum disorder. *European Archives of Psychiatry and Clinical Neuroscience, 272*, 187–198.

Gabbard, G. (2000). *Psychodynamic psychiatry in clinical practice.* American Psychiatric Press.

Geist, R. A. (1989). Self psychological reflections on the origins of eating disorders. *Journal of the American Academy of Psychoanalysis, 17*, 5–27.

Gepner, B., & Feron, F. (2009). Autism: A world changing too fast for a mis-wired brain? *Neuroscience and Biobehavioral Reviews, 33*(8), 1227–1242.

Gerland, G. (1997 [1996]). *A real person* (J. Tate, Trans.). Souvenir Press.

Geschwind, D. H., Boone, K. B., Miller, B. L., & Swerdloff, R. S. (2000). Neurobehavioral phenotype of Klinefelter syndrome. *Mental Retardation and Developmental Disabilities Research Reviews, 6*, 107–116.

Geschwind, D., & Dykens, E. (2004). Neurobehavioral and psychosocial issues in Klinefelter syndrome. *Learning Disabilities Research & Practice, 19*(3), 166–173.

Ghaziuddin, M., Ghaziuddin, N., & Greden, J. (2002). Depression in persons with autism: Implications for research and clinical care. *Journal of Autism and Developmental Disorders, 32*, 299–306.

Glidden, D., Bouman, W. P., Jones, B. A., & Arcelus, J. (2016). Gender dysphoria and autism spectrum disorder: A systematic review of the literature. *Sexual Medicine Reviews, 4*, 3–14.

Golan, O., Shilo, H., & Omer, H. (2016). Non-violent resistance parent training for the parents of young adults with high functioning autism spectrum disorder. *Journal of Family Therapy, 40*(1), 4–24.

Gollwitzer, A., Martel, C., McPartland, J., & Bargh, J. A. (2019). Autism spectrum traits predict higher social psychological skill. *Psychological and Cognitive Sciences, 116*(39), 19245–19247.

Goodsitt, A. (1977). Narcissistic disturbances in anorexia nervosa. In S. C. Feinstein & P. Giovacchini (Eds.), *Adolescent psychiatry* (Vol. 5, pp. 304–312). Jason Aronson.

Grandin, T. (1995). How people with autism think. In E. Schopler & G. B. Mesibov (Eds.), *Learning and cognition in autism* (pp. 137–156). Plenum.

Grandin, T. (2008). *Thinking in pictures*. Vintage Books.

Grandin, T. (2013a). The world needs all kinds of minds. YouTube [TED]. February 10, 2013.

Grandin, T. (2013b). *The autistic brain: Helping different kinds of mind succeed.* Mariner.

Grandin, T. (2020). Different types of thinking in autism. In *The way I see it* (p. 55). Arlington, TX: Future Horizons.

Grandin, T. (2022). *Visual thinking*. Riverhead.

Grandin, T., & Barron, S. (2017). *Unwritten rules of social relationships: Decoding social mysteries through the unique perspectives of autism* (new ed.). Future Horizons.

Gratton, F. V. (2019). Working with families. In *Supporting transgender autistic youth and adults: A guide for professionals and families* (pp. 105–131). Jessica Kingsley.

Harris, R. L. (2017). *Contemplative therapy for clients on the autism spectrum.* Jessica Kingsley.

Harrison, A., Tchanturia, K., Kerr-Gaffney, J., & Halls, D. (2020). Exploring relationships between autism spectrum disorder symptoms and eating disorder symptoms in adults with anorexia nervosa: A network approach. *Frontiers in Psychiatry, 11*, 401.

Haruvi-Lamdan, N., Horesh, D., & Golan, O. (2018). PTSD and autism spectrum disorder: Co-morbidity, gaps in research and potential shared mechanisms, *Psychological Trauma Theory Research Practice and Policy, 10*(3), 290–299.

Hason Rozenstein, M., Latzer, Y., Stein, D., & Eviatar, Z. (2011). Perception of emotion and bilateral advantage in women with eating disorders, their healthy sisters, and nonrelated healthy controls. *Journal of Affective Disorders, 134*, 1–3.

Hayley, J. (2021). I'm an autistic sex worker, and here's why it works for me. *Huffpost Personal* [internet magazine], April 30, 2021.

Hayley, J. (2022). I'm a disabled escort living with chronic illness. *Unrevolution* [internet site].

Heaton, P. (2009). Assessing musical skills in autistic children who are not savants. *Philosophical Transactions of the Royal Society B: Biological Sciences, 364*, 1443–1447.

Hellings, J., & Witwer, A. (2014). Autism and bipolar disorder. *Autismspeaks* [internet site], May 22, 2014.

Hendrickx, S. (2015). *Women and girls with autism spectrum disorder*. Jessica Kingsley.

Hill, A. (2022). Clients say it feels like we've always known each other. *The Guardian* [internet site], March 2, 2022.

Holmes, E. A., Brown, R. J., et al. (2005). Are there two qualitatively distinct forms of dissociation? A review and some clinical implications. *Clinical Psychology Review, 25*, 1–23.

Howlin, P. (1997). Psychiatric disturbances in adulthood. In P. Howlin (Ed.), *Autism: Preparing for adulthood* (pp. 216–235). Routledge.

Jacobs, L. A., Rachlin, K., Erickson-Schroth, L., & Janssen, A. (2014). Gender dysphoria and co-occurring autism spectrum disorders: Review, case examples, and treatment considerations. *LGBT Health, 1*(4), 277–282.

Jacobs, P. A., Hassold, T. J., Whittington, E., et al. (1988). Klinefelter's syndrome: An analysis of the origin of the additional sex chromosome using molecular probes. *Annals of Human Genetics, 52*, 93–109.

Jha, P., Sheth, D., and Ghaziuddin, M. (2007). Autism spectrum disorder and Klinefelter syndrome. *European Child and Adolescent Psychiatry, 16*(5), 305–308.

Jones, E. (1953). *Sigmund Freud, life and work*. Basic Books.

Kandinsky, W. (1911). *Concerning the spiritual in art* (Michael T. H. Sadler, Trans., 2004). Kessinger Publishing.

Kandinsky, W. (1926). *Point and line to plane* (Howard Dearstyne and Hilla Rebay, Trans., 1979). Dover.

Kargas, N., Harley, K. M., Roberts, A., & Sharman, S. (2019). Prevalence of clinical autistic traits within a homeless population: Barriers to accessing homeless services. *Journal of Social Distress and the Homeless, 28*(2), 90–95.

Kerr-Gaffney, J., Hayward, H., Jones, E., et al. (2021). Autism symptoms in anorexia nervosa: A comparative study with females with autism spectrum disorder. *Molecular Autism, 12*, 47.

Kinnaird, E., Norton, C., Stewart, C., & Tchanturia, K. (2019). Same behaviours, different reasons: What do patients with co-occurring anorexia and autism want from treatment? *International Review of Psychiatry, 31*(4), 308–317.

Kinnaird, E., Norton, C., & Tchanturia, K. (2017). Clinicians' views on working with anorexia nervosa and autism spectrum disorder comorbidity: A qualitative study. *BMC Psychiatry, 17*, 292.

Kluft, R. P. (1984). Treatment of multiple personality disorder: A study of 33 cases. *Psychiatric Clinics of North America, 7*, 9–29.

Kluft, R. P. (1991). Multiple personality disorder. In A. Tasman & S. M. Goldfinger (Eds.), *American Psychiatric Press Review of Psychiatry* (Vol. 10, pp. 161–188). American Psychiatric Press.

Kluft, R. P. (2000). The psychoanalytic psychotherapy of DID in the context of trauma therapy. *Psychoanalytic Inquiry, 20*(2), 259–286.

Kohlenberg, R. J., & Tsai, M. (1991). Functional analytical psychotherapy: Creating intense and curative therapeutic relationships. Plenum.

Krumins, D. (2015). Coming alive in a world of texture. In J. K. Miller (Ed.), *Women from another planet: Our lives in the universe of autism* (pp. 85–91). AuthorHouse.

Lai, M. C., Kassee, C., Besney, R., et al. (2019) Prevalence of co-occurring mental health diagnoses in the autism population: A systematic review and meta-analysis. *Lancet Psychiatry, 6*, 819–829.

Lainhart, J. E., & Folstein, S. E. (1994). Affective disorders in people with autism: A review of published cases. *Journal of Autism and Developmental Disorders, 24*, 587–601.

LaSalle, B. (2003). Finding Ben: A mother's journey through the maze of Asperger's. Contemporary Books.

Lawrence, C. (2019). "I can be a role model for autistic pupils": Investigating the voice of the autistic teacher. *Teacher Education Advancement Network Journal, 11*(2), 50–58.

Lawrence, M. (2001). Body, mother, mind: anorexia, femininity and the intrusive object. *International Journal of Psychoanalysis, 83*, 837–850.

Lawson, W. (1998). *Life behind glass: A personal account of autism spectrum disorder.* Jessica Kingsley.

Lever, A. G., & Geurts, H. M. (2016). Psychiatric co-occurring symptoms and disorders in young, middle-aged, and older adults with autism spectrum disorder. *Journal of Autism and Developmental Disorders, 46*, 1916–1930.

Levy, G. (2018). Music is a powerful tool for people with autism. *Political Reporter*, June 8.

Levy-Shiff, R., & Rothschild-Yakar, L. (2013). Mentalization, attachment, pathology and therapy. *Sihot, 27*(2), 148–157 (in Hebrew).

Lloyd, M. (2021a). Autism and dissociation: Part one. YouTube, August 16, 2021.

Lloyd, M. (2021b). In conversation . . . about autism, trauma and dissociation. YouTube, September 16, 2021.

Loewenstein, R. J. (2018). Dissociation debates: Everything you know is wrong. *Dialogues in Clinical Neuroscience, 20*(3), 229–242.

Loewenstein, R. J., Frewen, P. A., & Lewis-Fernández, R. (2017). Dissociative disorders. In B. J. Sadock & V. A. Ruiz (Eds.), *Kaplan & Sadock's Comprehensive Textbook of Psychiatry*, 10th ed. (Vol. 1, pp. 1866–1952). Wolters Kluwer/Lippincott Williams & Wilkens.

Luciano, C. C., Keller, R., Politi, P., Aguglia, E., Magnano, F., et al. (2014). Misdiagnosis of high function autism spectrum disorders in adults: An Italian case series. *Autism, 4*, 131.

Luterman, S. (2021). How autistic sex workers make the world's most social job work for them. *MEL* [internet magazine].

Lyons, V., & Fitzgerald, M. (2012). Critical evaluation of the concept of autistic creativity. *Recent Advances in Autism Spectrum Disorders, IntechOpen*, Vol. 1, 215–232.

Maenner, M. J., Shaw, K. A., Baio, J., et al. (2020). Prevalence of autism spectrum disorder among children aged 8 years—Autism and developmental disabilities monitoring network. *Surveillance Summaries, 69*(4), 1–12.

Manning, M. L., & Manning, R. L. (2007). Legion theory: A meta-psychology. *Theory & Psychology, 17*(6), 839–862.

Marshall, T. (2015). *I am aspienwoman: The unique characteristics, traits, and gifts of adult females on the autism spectrum*. Aspiengirl.

Marshall, T. (2019). Moving towards a profile of borderline personality disorder and autism. *Tania Marshall's home page*, July 27, 2019.

Martin, N. (2020). Perspectives on UK university employment from autistic researchers and lecturers. *Disability & Society, 36*(9), 1510–1531.

Masataka, N. (2017). Neurodiversity, giftedness, and aesthetic perceptual judgment of music in children with autism. *Frontiers in Psychology, 22*(8), 1595.

Masterson, J. (1978). The borderline adolescent: An object relations view. In S. C. Feinstein & P. Giovacchini (Eds.), *Adolescent Psychiatry* (Vol. 6, pp. 344–359). University of Chicago Press.

Matson, J. L., & Cervantes, P. E. (2014). Commonly studied comorbid psychopathologies among persons with autism spectrum disorder. *Research in Developmental Disabilities, 35*(5), 952–962.

McDougall, J. (1989). *Theaters of the body*. Free Association Books.

McWilliams, N. (2011). Dissociative psychologies. In *Psychoanalytic Diagnosis* (pp. 332–358). Guilford.

Merikangas, K. R., Jin, R., He, J. P., Kessler, R. C., Lee, S., et al. (2011). Prevalence and correlates of bipolar spectrum disorder in the world mental health survey initiative. *Archives of General Psychiatry, 68*, 241–251.

Miller, J. K. (Ed.). (2015a). *Women from another planet: Our lives in the universe of autism*. AuthorHouse.

Miller, J. K. (Ed.). (2015b). Scenes from a car wash. In *Women from another planet: Our lives in the universe of autism* (pp. 229–232). AuthorHouse.

Minshew, N., & Williams, D. (2007). The new neurobiology of autism. *Archives of Neurology, 64*(7), 945–950.

Minuchin, S., Rosman, B., & Baker, L. (1978). *Psychosomatic families: Anorexia nervosa in context*. Harvard University Press.

Molnar-Szakacs, I., & Heaton, P. (2012). Music: A unique window into the world of autism. *Annals of the New York Academy of Sciences, 1252*, 318–324.

Monk, R., Whitehouse, A. J. O., & Waddington, H. (2022). The use of language in autism research. *Trends in Neurosciences, 45*(11), 791–793.

Moseley, R., & Renshaw-Vuillier, L. (2020). Link between autism and eating disorders may be due to an inability to identify emotions—new research. *The Conversation* [internet site].

Mottron, L., Dawson, M., Soulières, I., Hubert, B., & Burack, J. J. (2006). Enhanced perceptual functioning in autism: An update, and eight principles of autistic perception. *Journal of Autism and Developmental Disorders, 36*(1), 27–43.

Moulton, A., Ford, M., & Elkady, R. (2019). An autistic adolescent exhibits psychotic symptoms: Is this schizophrenia or part of his autism? *Psychiatric Annals, 49*(11), 501–505.

Murphy, J., Prentice, F., Walsh, R., Catmur, C., & Bird, G. (2020). Autism and transgender identity: Implications for depression and anxiety. *Research in Autism Spectrum Disorders, 69*, 1–11.

Murray, D., Lesser, M., & Lawson, W. (2005). Attention, monotropism and the diagnostic criteria for autism. *Autism, 9*(2), 139–156.

Ne'eman, A. (2012). The future (and the past) of autism advocacy, or why the ASA's magazine, *The Advocate*, wouldn't publish this piece. In Julia Bascom (Ed.), *Loud Hands: Autistic People, Speaking* (pp. 88–97). Autistic Press.

Nestler, S., Jay, E. L., Sierra, M., & David, A. S. (2015). Symptom profiles in depersonalization and anxiety disorders: An analysis of the Beck Anxiety Inventory. *Psychopathology, 48*, 84–90.

Nobili, A., Glazebrook, C., & Arcelus, J. (2018). Quality of life of treatment-seeking transgender adults: A systematic review and meta-analysis. *Reviews in Endocrine and Metabolic Disorders, 19*(3), 199–220.

Notbohm, E., & Zysk, V. (2010). *Great ideas for teaching and raising children with autism or Asperger's*. Future Horizons.

Noy, P. (1969). A revision of the psychoanalytic theory of the primary process. *International Journal of Psychoanalysis, 50*, 155–178.

Noy, P. (1999). *Psychoanalysis of art and creativity*. Modan (in Hebrew).

Opitz, J. M., Smith, J. F., & Santoro, L. (2008). The FG syndromes: Perspective in 2008. *Advances in Pediatrics, 55*(1), 123–170.

Oppenheimer, L. (2002). Self or selves? Dissociative identity disorder and complexity of the self-system. *Theory & Psychology, 12*, 97–128.

Palermo, M. T., & Bogaerts, S. (2015). Sex selling and autism spectrum disorder: Impaired capacity, free enterprise, or sexual victimization? *Journal of Forensic Psychology Practice, 15*(4), 363–382.

Palucka, A. M., Bradley, E., & Lunsky, Y. (2008). A case of unrecognized intellectual disability and autism misdiagnosed as schizophrenia: Are there lessons to be learned? *Mental Health Aspects of Developmental Disabilities, 11*(2), 55–60.

Parker, A. (2019). Closing my eyes when we kiss: A piece about autism and sex work. *Subbed In* [internet magazine], July 4, 2019.

Paul, L. K., Corsello, C., Kennedy, D. P., & Ralph, A. (2004). Agenesis of the Corpus Callosum and autism: A comprehensive comparison. *Brain, 137*(6), 1813–1829.

Perlman, L. (2000). Adults with Asperger disorder misdiagnosed as schizophrenic. *Professional Psychology: Research and Practice, 31*, 221–225.

Petterson, R. (2004). Nameless desire: Alexithymia and the anorexic patient. *American Journal of Psychoanalysis, 64*(1), 77–90.

Piper, R. (2018a). New US laws targeting sex workers will harm autistic people. *Metro* [internet magazine], April 17, 2018.

Piper, R. (2018b). Secret life of an autistic stripper. *Narratively* [internet magazine].

Piper, R. (2019). Autism, sex work and empathy. *Queer Majority* [internet magazine].

Porter, R. (2020). Autism, masking, & trans identity. *Medium.com* [internet site].

Pretorius, H. (2020). Reflections on being an autistic psychologist. *Mullumroad* [internet site].

Prince-Hughes, D. (2004). *Songs of the gorilla nation*. Random House.

Raja, M., & Azzoni, A. (2001). Asperger's disorder in the emergency psychiatric setting. *General Hospital Psychiatry, 23*, 285–293.

Reuben, K. (2022). Dissociation in autism spectrum disorders: An under-recognized symptom. In E. Christensen (Ed.), *Perspectives of Dissociative Identity Response* (pp. 151–186). HWC Press.

Reuben, K. E., Stanzione, C. M., & Singleton, J. L. (2021). Interpersonal trauma and posttraumatic stress in autistic adults. *Autism in Adulthood, 3*(3), 247–256.

Rinaldi, C., Attanasio, M., Valenti, M., Mazza, M., & Keller, R. (2021). Autism spectrum disorder and personality disorders: Comorbidity and differential diagnosis. *World Journal of Psychiatry, 11*(12), 1366–1386.

Robison, J. E. (2007). *Look me in the eye: My life with Asperger's*. Crown.

Ross, C. (2009). Psychodynamics of eating disorder behavior in sexual abuse survivors. *American Journal of Psychotherapy, 63*(3), 211–226.

Roux, L. (2018). Congress attacked sex workers. Now we need you to stand with us. *Vice* [internet magazine], June 1, 2018.

Roux, L. (2021). *Whore of New York: A confession*. Repeater.

Sage, J. (2020). Stripping helped autistic woman notice the dichotomy between her club persona and autistic self. *Pittsburgh city paper* [internet site], June 8, 2020.

Samango-Sprouse, C. A., Stapleton, E., Sadeghin, T., & Gropman, A. L. (2013). Is it all the X: Familial learning dysfunction and the impact of behavioral aspects of the phenotypic presentation of XXY? *American Journal of Medical Genetics, 163*(1), 27–34.

Şar, V., Dorahy, M. J., & Krueger, C. (2017). Revisiting the etiological aspects of dissociative identity disorder: A biopsychosocial perspective. *Psychology Research and Behavior Management, 10*, 137–146.

Schillace, B. (2021). Coming out autistic. *Scientific American*, May 11, 2021.

Schweden, T. L. K., Pittig, A., Brauer, D., et al. (2016). Reduction of depersonalization during social stress through cognitive therapy for Social Anxiety Disorder: A randomized controlled trial. *Journal of Anxiety Disorders, 43*, 99–105.

Selvini-Palazzoli, M. (1974 [1963]). *Self-starvation*. Chaucer Publishing.

Sheitmann, B. B., Kraus, J. E., Bodsh, J. W., & Carmel, H. (2004). Are the negative syndromes of schizophrenia consistent with an autistic spectrum illness? *Schizophrenia Research, 69*, 119–120.

Shumer, D. E., Reisner, S. L., Edwards-Leeper, L., & Tishelman, A. (2016). Evaluation of Asperger syndrome in youth presenting to a gender dysphoria clinic. *LGBT Health, 88*(5), 81–3.

Silberman, S. (2015). *Neurotribes: The legacy of autism and the future of neurodiversity*. Avery.

Silva, C. C., Morais, S., Areias, G., Meneses, M. S., Madeira, N. G., & Ramos, C. R. C. (2022). Autism spectrum disorder associated with 48, XXYY: Case report of a rare clinical syndrome. *Journal of Autism and Developmental Disorders, 52*(8), 3755–3757.

Skuse, D. H. (2006). Sexual dimorphism in cognition and behaviour: The role of X-linked genes. *European Journal of Endocrinology, 1*(155), S99–S106.

Smith, A. (2009). The empathy imbalance hypothesis of autism: A theoretical approach to cognitive and emotional empathy in autistic development. *Psychological Record, 59*, 489–510.

Somer, E. (2000). Israeli mental health professionals' attitudes towards dissociative disorders, differential diagnosis considered, and reported incidence. *Journal of Trauma and Dissociation, 1*(1), 21–44.

Somer, E. (2014). Dissociative identity disorder: Diagnostical and therapeutic principles. *Hebrew Psychology, 3191* (in Hebrew). Specter, E. (2021). Liara Roux's debut is a vivid, defiant meditation on sex, labor, and power. *Vogue* [internet site].

Sreedhar, A., Feden, D., Perilli, G., Nair, R., & Magaji, V. (2015). 48, XXYY genotype: Case report of a rare clinical syndrome. *Journal of Endocrinology and Diabetes, 3*(1), 1–3.

Stanutz, S., Wapnick, J., & Burack, J. A. (2014). Pitch discrimination and melodic memory in children with autism spectrum disorders. *Autism, 18*(2), 137–147.

Stewart, M. E., Barnard, L., Pearson, J., Hasan, R., & O'Brien, G. (2006). Presentation of depression in autism and Asperger syndrome: A review. *Autism, 10*(1), 103–116.

Stone, B. (2019). "The domino effect": Pathways in and out of homelessness for autistic adults. *Disability & Society, 34*(1), 169–174.

Stone, B. (2022). Homelessness as a product of social exclusion: Reinterpreting autistic adults' narratives through the lens of critical disability studies. *Scandinavian Journal of Disability Research, 24*(1), 181–195.

Stone, B., Cameron, A., & Dowling, S. (2022). The autistic experience of homelessness: Implications from a narrative enquiry. *Autism*. 13623613221105091.

Storch, E. A., Larson, M. J., Ehrenreich-May, J., et al. (2012). Peer victimization in youth with autism spectrum disorders and co-occurring anxiety: Relations with psychopathology and loneliness. *Journal of Developmental and Physical Disabilities, 24*, 575–590.

Strang, J. F., Kenworthy, L., Dominska, A., et al. (2014). Increased gender variance in autism spectrum disorders and attention deficit hyperactivity disorder. *Archives of Sexual Behavior, 43*(8), 1525–1533.

Strang, J. F., Klomp, S. E., Caplan, R., et al. (2020). Community-based participatory design for research that impacts the lives of transgender and/or gender-diverse autistic and/or neurodiverse people. *Clinical Practice in Pediatric Psychology, 7*(4), 396–404.

Strang, J. F., Knauss, M., Van der Miesen, A. I. R., et al. (2020). A clinical program for transgender and gender-diverse autistic/neurodiverse adolescents developed through community-based participatory design. *Journal of Clinical Child and Adolescent Psychology, 6*, 1–16.

Strang, J. F., Meagher, H., Kenworthy, L., et al. (2018). Initial clinical guidelines for co-occurring autism spectrum disorder and gender dysphoria or incongruence in adolescents. *Journal of Clinical Child & Adolescent Psychology, 47*(1), 105–115.

Strang, J. F., Powers, M., Knauss, M., & Sibarium, E. (2018). "They thought it was an obsession": Trajectories and perspectives of autistic transgender and gender-diverse adolescents. *Journal of Autism and Developmental Disorders, 48*(12), 4039–4055.

Sullivan, S., Rai, D., Golding, J., Zammit, S., & Steer, C. (2013). The association between autism spectrum disorder and psychotic experiences in the Avon longitudinal study of parents and children (ALSPAC) birth cohort. *Journal of the American Academy of Child and Adolescent Psychiatry, 52*(8), 806–814.

Suller, J. R. (1980). Primary process thinking and creativity. *Psychological Bulletin, 1*, 144–165.

Tammet, D. (2006). *Born on a blue day*. Hodder & Stoughton.

Tantam, D. (2000). Adolescence and adulthood of individuals with Asperger syndrome. In A. Klin, F. Volkmar, & S. Sparrow (Eds.), *Asperger syndrome* (pp. 367–399). Guilford.

Tartaglia, N. R., Miller, R., Rafalko, J., et al. (2017). Autism spectrum disorder in males with sex chromosome aneuploidy: XXY/Klinefelter syndrome, XYY, and XXYY. *Journal of Developmental and Behavioral Pediatrics, 38*(3), 197–207.

Taylor, J. L., & Corbett, B. A. (2014). A review of rhythm and responsiveness of cortisol in individuals with autism spectrum disorders. *Psychoneuroendocrinology, 49*, 207–228.

Tsuyoshi, K. (2015). How and why is autism spectrum disorder misdiagnosed in adult patients?—From diagnostic problem to management for adjustment. *Mental Health in Family Medicine, 11*(2), 73–88.

Tucker, K. (2015). 'Cause its Friday. In J. K. Miller (Ed.), *Women from another planet: Our lives in the universe of autism* (pp. 219–227). AuthorHouse.

Tustin, F. (1986). *Autistic barriers in neurotic patients*. Routledge.

Tustin, F. (1992). *Autistic states in children* (2nd ed.). Routledge.

Van der Laan, D. P., Postema, L., Wood, H., et al. (2015). Do children with gender dysphoria have intense/obsessional interests? *Journal of Sex Research, 52*, 213–219.

Van Der Miesen, A. I., Hurley, H., & De Vries, A. L. (2016). Gender dysphoria and autism spectrum disorder: A narrative review. *International Review of Psychiatry, 28*(1), 70–80.

Van Rijn, S., Swaab, H., Aleman, A., & Kahn, R. S. (2006). X chromosomal effects on social cognitive processing and emotion regulation: A study with Klinefelter men (47, XXY). *Schizophrenia Research, 84*(2–3), 194–203.

Van Rijn, S., Swaab, H., Aleman, A., & Kahn, R. S. (2008). Social behavior and autism traits in a sex chromosomal disorder: Klinefelter (47XXY) syndrome. *Journal of Autism and Developmental Disorders, 38*(9), 1634–1641.

Van Schalkwyk, G. I., Peluso, F., Qayyum, Z., et al. (2015). Varieties of misdiagnosis in ASD: An illustrative case series. *Journal of Autism and Developmental Disorders, 45*, 911–918.

Vasa, R. A., Mostofsky, S. H., & Ewen, J. B. (2017). The disrupted connectivity hypothesis of autism spectrum disorders: Time for the next phase in research. *Biological Psychiatry Cognitive Neuroscience Neuroimaging, 1*(3), 245–252.

Veale, J., Byrne, J., Tan, K., et al. (2019). Counting ourselves: The health and wellbeing of trans and non-binary people in Aotearoa New Zealand. Transgender Health Research Lab. University of Waikato: Hamilton, NZ.

Volkert, V. M., & Petula, C. M. (2010). Recent studies on feeding problems in children with autism. *Journal of Applied Behavior Analysis, 43*(1), 155–159.

Volkmar, F., & Cohen, D. (1991). Comorbid association of autism and schizophrenia. *American Journal of Psychiatry, 148*(12), 1705–1707.

Vries, A. L., Noens, I. L., Cohen-Kettenis, P. T., van Berckelaer-Onnes, I. A., & Doreleijers, T. A. (2010). Autism spectrum disorders in gender dysphoric children and adolescents. *Journal of Autism and Developmental Disorders, 40*(8), 930–936.

Vuillier, L., Carter, Z., Teixeira, A. R., & Moseley, R. L. (2020). Alexithymia may explain the relationship between autistic traits and eating disorder psychopathology. *Molecular Autism, 11*, 63.

Waris, P., Lindberg, N., Kettunen, K., & Tani, P. (2013). The relationship between Asperger's syndrome and schizophrenia in adolescence. *European Child and Adolescent Psychiatry, 22*, 217–223.

Warrier, V., Greenberg, D. M., Weir, E., et al. (2020). Elevated rates of autism, other neurodevelopmental and psychiatric diagnoses, and autistic traits in transgender and gender-diverse individuals. *Nature Communications, 11*(1), 3959.

Watkins, J. G., & Watkins, H. H. (1997). *Ego states: Theory and therapy*. Norton.

Webster, A., & Garvis, S. (2017). The importance of critical life moments: An explorative study of successful women with autism spectrum disorder. *Autism, 21*(6), 670–677.

Wenhart, T., Bethlehem, R. A. I., Baron-Cohen, S., & Altenmueller, E. (2019). Autistic traits, resting-state connectivity, and absolute pitch in professional musicians: Shared and distinct neural features. *Molecular Autism, 10*, 20.

White, B. (2016). The link between autism and trans identity, *The Atlantic* [internet journal].

Wieland, S. (Ed.). (2015). *Dissociation in traumatized children and adolescents: Theory and clinical interventions* (2nd ed.). Routledge.

Wikiart. Wassily Kandinsky. https://www.wikiart.org/en/wassily-kandinsky/composition-vi-1913

Willey, H. (1999). *Pretending to be normal: Living with Asperger's syndrome*. Jessica Kingsley.

Willgoss, S. (2021). Suicide and autism, a national crisis. In RCPSYCH [internet page].

Williams, D. (1992). *Nobody nowhere*. Doubleday.

Williams, D. (1994). *Somebody somewhere*. Jessica Kingsley.

Williams, D. (1996). *Autism: An inside-out approach*. Jessica Kingsley.

Williams, D. (2012). Dissociative identity disorder, autism and a conversation. *Polly's pages* [internet blog], June 7, 2012.

Williams, D. (2015a). Dissociative identity disorder (DID) and integration. *YouTube*, March 26, 2015.

Williams, D. (2015b). What causes dissociative identity disorder? *Donnawilliams* [internet blog], April 14, 2015.

Williams, D. (2015c). We're all multiple—Legion theory and my DID team. *Donnawilliams* [internet blog], April 22, 2015.Wing, L. (1981). Asperger's syndrome: A clinical account. *Psychological Medicine, 11*(1), 115–129.

Witztum, E., & Margolin, J. (2009). Dissociative disorders and criminal responsibility. In A. Grinshpoon, J. Margolin, & E. Witztum (Eds.), *Forensic Psychiatry—Israeli Aspects* (pp. 145–160). Aryeh Nir (in Hebrew).

Wolff, S. (1995). *Loners: The life path of unusual children*. Routledge.

Wood, R., & Happé, F. (2021). What are the views and experiences of autistic teachers? Findings from an online survey in the UK, *Disability & Society*.

Wylie, P. (2014). *Very late diagnosis of Asperger syndrome*. Jessica Kingsley.

Yurkievicz, Ilana. (2009). Overlooked and under-diagnosed: Distinct expression of Asperger's syndrome in females. *Yale Review of Undergraduate Research in Psychology, 1*(1), 78–88.

Zupanič, S., Kruljac, I., Šoštarič Zvonar, M., & Drobnič Radobuljac, M. (2021). Case report: Adolescent with autism and gender dysphoria. *Frontiers in Psychiatry, 12*, 671448.

Index

About the Author

Sagit Blumrosen-Sela is an Israeli clinical psychologist who also holds a PhD in comparative literature. Her recent focus on autism has led to the authorship of three books and numerous articles on the subject, all of which have received significant attention.

www.ingramcontent.com/pod-product-compliance
Ingram Content Group UK Ltd.
Pitfield, Milton Keynes, MK11 3LW, UK
UKHW021904150926
475560UK00004B/332

9 781538 197165